SHIRDI SAI

A lot has been written about Shri Shirdi Sai Baba, the Master of the Age. Here is a book that explains His teachings and lessons in a rational and sagacious manner. Spiritual philosophies are explained logically and in a simple language. The author also introduces the concept of *Sai-ism* in the book.

This book contains thoughts and messages from the author which have been published in magazines like *The Heritage of Shri Shirdi Sai* and others. These articles, in quintessence, are based on the spiritual precepts of Baba, which are further elucidated from a devotee's perspective. Some of the articles relate to different concepts of religion and spiritualism for proper appreciation of the divine role of Sadguru Shri Sai Baba. Each concept is explained in a elucidative and lucid style for the easy understanding of the readers. The excellent clarity and presentation of the thoughts indicate the author's immense popularity as a guru, guide, speaker and a leader of the global Sai movement.

A must-read for all those who want to understand Shirdi Sai Baba.

By the same author

SHIRDI SAI BABA and Other Perfect Masters
English and translated into Slovenian and eight Indian languages

BABA MAY I ANSWER
English and translated into eight Indian languages

Shri Guru Bhagavat in 5 volumes
Odia and translated into English, Hindi and other Indian languages

Gopyaru Agopya: A treatise on the Cosmology and Cosmogeny of Hinduism
Odia and translated in Sanskrit under the title of
'Srushti Tattwanuchintanam'

THE AGE OF
SHIRDI SAI

Dr. C.B. Satpathy

STERLING PAPERBACKS
An imprint of
Sterling Publishers (P) Ltd.
A-59, Okhla Industrial Area, Phase-II,
New Delhi-110020.
Tel: 26387070, 26386209; Fax: 91-11-26383788
E-mail: mail@sterlingpublishers.com
www.sterlingpublishers.com

The Age of Shirdi Sai
© 2014, Dr. C.B. Satpathy
ISBN 978 81 207 8700 1

Printed in India

Printed and Published by Sterling Publishers Pvt. Ltd.,
New Delhi-110020.

Contents

Contents   vii

Prologue

All men's souls are immortal,
but the souls of the righteous are immortal and divine.

Socrates

Howsoever I desist from introducing Shirdi Sai Baba, the Spiritual Master, in a language full of oriental hyperbole, it taxes my vocabulary when I attempt to write on Him. It is easy to overstate His miracles, as has generally been the practice, but difficult to relate His magnificence and hyper-kinetic influence on people over the past few decades.

By the fifteenth of October 1918, when Shri Sai completed His earthly sojourn, Shirdi had turned from an insignificant village of Maharashtra into a spiritual haven, teeming with devotees, spiritual seekers, mendicants of different religions, celebrities like Bal Gangadhar Tilak, curious onlookers, government officials, psalm and hymn singers, rural acrobats, British government officials and spies, traders and even beggars. Shri Sai Baba the Sadguru to the Hindus and a Fakir (dervish) to the Muslims, was the axis (the word *axis* is like the word *Qutab* in Sufi parlance and usually refers to Sufi saints) around which the life of His devotees revolved. Many people, who have recorded their first encounter with Shirdi Sai Baba in books and personal diaries, are unequivocal in their opinion—they were captivated by His divine charm and overcome by His compassion. He was the divine protector of all those who visited Him, having accepted Him as their spiritual guide. To Sai Baba, differentiation in fate and pedigree of the devotees made no difference. Visitors were at a loss to decide if His divine personality, full of miracles or His humaneness, full of compassion, was the more imposing, as He simultaneously displayed a surfeit of both.

As a result of His multi-dimensional activities—both temporal and spiritual—for the amelioration of his protégés, music, literature, folklore, drama and even some amount of gossip filled the social environment of the village. It is said that 'not a leaf moves without His desire'. This is what used to happen at Shirdi. Be it the construction of a temple or a house, the sickness of an individual, the spread of cholera in the village, the education or rearing of children, the celebration of any religious or social festival, or the settlement of conflict, the Master's decision was the final word of wisdom and judgement. He stood between His devotees and suffering. Most of the villagers and the visiting populace willingly followed this way of living with Baba. Those who failed to do so experienced that any deviation from such practices and procedures — even if not obligatory — became a risky adventure. They misunderstood the actual as plausible.

Shirdi Sai Baba was the soul of the village, which had a population of a few hundred at the time of His first appearance and expanded to a few thousand by 1918. After His departure, the splendour and ongoing festive environment of Shirdi vanished. No more was there the hustle and bustle of religious activities, the palanquin procession on Thursdays from *Dwarakamai* to *Chavadi*, the compassionate and stately demeanour of Baba and the mirthful singing of devotional songs reverberating in the courtyard of Dwarakamai, the dilapidated mosque which Baba used to regard as a 'home to Him and to His devotees'.

After His departure, intense yearning for Baba by the devotees translated into a multitude of symbols. A great void had been created in their lives, which they painfully sought to fill up. Like the resurrection of Christ, they used to pray to Him to revisit them. They used to console themselves by remembering the promise that Baba had made to His devotees — the bones of His body would listen to their prayers and woes and help them even after He went into a Samadhi.

For about 3 years, Shirdi village had a lifeless existence, with minimal activities covering the daily puja at His Samadhi. Since 1920, after the formation of Shri Sai Baba Sansthan Trust, Shirdi, worship of the Samadhi was followed through the creation and enforcement of certain rules, regulations and practices. This was followed by the publication of the first issue of the magazine *Sai Leela*, in Marathi in the year 1923, which has, since, become the official publication of the Sansthan. Later, the magazine started being published in three languages—English, Hindi and Marathi—for the propagation of the philosophy, divine activities and the name of Shri Sai beyond the village of Shirdi and the state of Maharashtra. In the year 1954, a marble statue of Baba was installed inside Butiwada at Shirdi, about which Baba had given prior indication. The installation of Baba's statue and the regular running of this temple gave a fillip to the Sai movement and the number of visitors to Shirdi increased manifold.

During my visits to Shirdi, I take the opportunity to discuss, with a number of devotees and trustees, about the ever-increasing number of Sai devotees to Shirdi from all over the globe and the feelings and ideas they express about Shri Shirdi Sai Baba. My first visit to Shirdi, in the last quarter of 1989, was not pre-planned. I was at Mumbai on official duty and, on request, visited Shirdi with a friend on a Thursday. Baba's tomb, His marble statue in Butiwada and other important places connected with Him, and the entire ambience of Shirdi gave me a feeling of belonging, protection and euphoria, which I had not experienced in any other holy place. From that time till now, the same feeling endures in me and inspires me to work towards the propagation of His thoughts and values. Even when passing through the most difficult phases of life, the feelings of the first day do not get diluted.

My personal experience of about twenty five years, and being privy to similar experiences of thousands of other devotees coming from different backgrounds and cultural groups, has convinced me that a mighty divine stream of consciousness is attracting these human souls and propelling them to undertake certain noble activities with a definite purpose. I have also experienced that during the last quarter of a century, millions of people, not only in India but also in other countries have, consciously or unconsciously, played their role as tiny actors in this divine drama brought about by Shri Shirdi Sai Baba, the Divine Incarnation of the age.

During this period, I have observed with awe and surprise the evolution and exponential growth of this Sai phenomena all over the world. This can be seen in many different facts. First, the manifold growth in the number of Sai devotees and their visits to Shirdi, which has reportedly increased from an average of about five thousand visitors a day in 1990 to about sixty thousand as on today. This includes a large number of international travellers and dignitaries. Secondly, the creation of a huge number of registered and unregistered, charitable and non-charitable, trusts or other organizations in India and abroad. Thirdly, the construction of a large number of temples in India and abroad. Thousands of temples have come up, even in the remotest areas of Assam and Sikkim in India. Besides, in many existing temples in India and abroad, dedicated to the worship of other deities of the Hindu pantheon, Baba's statues have been installed. As per available information, more than a thousand temples are under construction in India and a few in other countries. Sai Baba temples have come up in different cities of US, Canada, UK, Australia, Africa, Europe, Singapore, Thailand and many more places. Being associated with this international Sai movement, I have the information of temples coming up in countries like New Zealand, Sri Lanka, Mauritius, Fiji and elsewhere. These temples are neither financed nor controlled by Sai Baba Sansthan, Shirdi. They are built by self-motivated devotees who, individually and in groups, are trying to propagate the name and teachings of Baba, wherever they live.

Besides the temples and trusts which are devoted to the cause of Shirdi Sai Baba, devotees have created a number of social service groups to help the poor in distress on a regular basis and also ,during natural disasters. Some NGOs, named after Him, are busy providing healthcare and creating excellent educational institutions.

Hundreds of books on Baba and His teachings, in most of the Indian languages and a few foreign languages, are available. A large number of magazines and journals are published in different Indian languages. The audio-video market is full of devotional music on Sai Baba, with songs sung by the best singers of India. Finally, the love towards Shri Sai Baba has so filled the devotees that a large number of them have named their homes, businesses, products and even children after Sai Baba. These are all too numerous to be mentioned — information is readily available on the internet.

Why do the devotees do so much for the cause of Shri Sai, so intensely? Why do they accept Him as an essential part of their existence? The devotees, born after the Samadhi of Baba, have only read about Him, visited Shirdi, prayed at His tomb and some other places related to Him. Yet, to them Baba truly exists and helps them in many ways. They get from Him a lot of solace, courage and help, at times unexpectedly, almost bordering on miracle.

The word for *God* in Sanskrit language is *Bramha*. Etymologically, the word *Bramha* means 'that which expands automatically'. Any place or any person who is imbued with divine power will automatically attract devotees and visitors from near and far. Anyone meeting such a person will be automatically drawn towards Him, remain attached with Him till his end and would attribute divinity to Him. This is the reflection of the divinity in Shri Sai Baba of Shirdi. Such a powerful spiritual personality rarely advents on earth and, as some believe, only once in a seven hundred year cycle of time does such a power incarnate on earth and becomes the Master of the Age, as ordained by God. During that age or period, He is responsible for the spiritual evolution of all human beings on earth. Since He acts as the agent of God during that period of time, His spiritual personality looms large. As the present century advances, the whole world and humanity will experience the influence of this old Fakir.

One day at Shirdi, Baba, in a state of spiritual ecstasy, had revealed, '*Main guli guli mein rahene wala hun,*' He uttered it in rustic Marathi language, which means 'I shall be there in every lane.' Today, if one visits even Delhi, the capital of India, one will be surprised to see Baba's statues not only in temples, but under trees and every nook and corner. This is the Sai Age, which has made its advent with full glory.

Generally, myth surrounds divine personalities. However, the history of Shri Sai Baba has been recorded, during the period of His physical embodiment, by persons who had long association with Him. Any researcher can find a treasure of primary data if He wishes to delve into the depths of this compassionate and divine being. It is interesting to note that words like 'Sai-ism' can be used to define the spiritual path shown by Baba to His devotees.

This book is a compilation of articles, written by me and published in magazines like *The Heritage of Shri Shirdi Sai* and others. The articles could have been arranged chronologically, but have been deliberately arranged topic-wise for convenience of the readers. These articles, in quintessence, are based on the spiritual precepts of Baba, which has been further elucidated from a devotee's perspective. Some of the articles relate to different concepts of religion and spiritualism that are required to be understood in order to properly value the divine role of the Sadguru Shri Sai Baba.

I thank Ms Shipra Shukla for helping me in the preparatory work in arrangement of the manuscript. A word of appreciation for my son Arunabh, who collated and edited the articles with due diligence. I thank Mr Surinder Kumar Ghai, the Managing Director of Sterling Publishers, who has done yeoman service in publishing and popularising Sai literature, for publishing this book.

My reward for this work lies in the fact that the book goes into the hands of the devotees of Shri Shirdi Sai Baba.

1

Role of Sadguru in God Realization

Sadguru Is Your Diety

The path towards finding and associating with the Sadguru is the real path, more so, in this age of conflicts, contradictions and acute materialism. As Swami Vivekananda, in his famous Chicago speech, said—like all rivers that lead to the sea, all the paths that men take lead to Him, the God Eternal. The paths that are mostly adopted by the seekers are *Rajayoga, Karmayoga, Bhaktiyoga, Hathayoga, Layayoga, Nivriti Marg, Pravriti Marg,* and so on. There are *avadhoots, kapaliks, aghoris* and many other types of spiritual practitioners. Different religions have different approaches. In the path of God realization, there has to be something common and universal that all these different groups accept. In short, there must be a common spiritual denominator among the groups.

Sitting in Shirdi Masjid, Baba had said that there are many paths that lead to God, and one of the paths leads to God through Dwarakamai. An analysis of how Baba led thousands and thousands of people towards God realization at Shirdi brings certain cardinal principles of ethics to the fore, as explained below:

(a) A Perfect or Divine Being, known variously as a Perfect Master, a Sadguru or a Qutab (as called by the Sufis) exists in physical form. A Qutab simply means an axis or a pivot around which the living and non-living aspects of the world revolve. The Perfect Master, having gone through different stages of spiritual evolution, reaches the state of God. However, those among these Perfect Beings, who out of infinite compassion, make the greatest sacrifice of not enjoying the blissful state of God, but choose to incarnate in a human body on earth to serve the suffering humanity, are called Sadgurus or Perfect Masters. It is believed that at any point of time, there are five Perfect Masters on the earth in embodied form.

(b)   When in human body, these Perfect Masters act both as human beings and as God. As God, they have infinite power, infinite knowledge, infinite happiness and infinite existence. Like God, they are Omnipotent, Omnipresent and Omniscient, enjoying the powers of the Almighty. They share their power, knowledge and divine bliss with millions of persons by methods unperceivable by human beings. These methods are generally understood as *leelas* or divine sports. Most of the miracles are nothing but manipulation of some of the laws of nature, the methods of which are known only to a very small number of people. Only a few can manipulate these with the use of their mental powers and by adopting certain procedures. The systems of *Tantra* and *Hathayoga* also describe such procedures. All the elemental forces of nature like fire *(Agni Deva)*, water *(Varuna Deva)*, air *(Vayu Deva)*, etc., are defined as deities by the Hindus and worshipped. Miracles sometimes take place around Sadgurus, as is reported to have happened around Christ, Shirdi Sai Baba, Sant Gyaneshwar, Tukaram, and so on. As Gods, they see everything in themselves and themselves in everything. So they serve everyone without any differentiation, as if they are serving themselves. They see God in everyone, even though others may not be able to see God in them.

They give infinite love to others and take infinite pain from them. Once any human being or any species is linked with them in any manner, they ensure that these creatures are evolved, life after life, till they merge with God—from where they came in the first place. This ultimate stage of evolution is ordinarily known as *mukti* or *moksha*.

(c) These Perfect Masters alone are capable of leading human beings to God realization. They follow what is common and universal in all religions, that is, humanism, based on love. Out of love, they not only take care of the spiritual evolution of the devotees, but also their temporal requirements. Once a person has surrendered to them, they look after all needs of the devotee as a mother would look after a child. They can go to any extent, even to sacrifice their human body, to protect their children. This is what Baba did for many devotees, as can be read in *Shri Sai Satcharita*, and as experienced by many. To develop closer and closer link with Him, one has to develop faith in Him, patiently, even under the most trying circumstances. Also, one has to develop the qualities of humility, sacrifice, tolerance and steadfastness in devotion and perform all actions desired by the Sadguru. One will evolve earlier than others who may be worshipping too many deities, if one follows this path of the Sadguru.

Baba used to give visions to many people in the form of their deities, like Hanuman, Ganesh, etc., which convinced them that there is no difference between Baba and any other deity or even God. One can, therefore, at the first stage try to see all deities in Baba and worship Him in the method in which these deities are usually worshipped. In short, one should try to see and seek everything in and from Baba. This path may be difficult at the initial stage, but can certainly be achieved with steadfastness and faith in Baba. So let us try.

— *Ram Navami, 2000*

Search for God

The spontaneous human instinct is to have an amicable relationship with other individuals, groups or situations considered more powerful. Before the evolution of the cerebral potentialities, the earliest human beings considered the forces of nature like fire, clouds and even some other species to be more powerful than themselves and thus started the earliest systems of worship. In this concept, at the level of consciousness of the earliest human beings, God was interpreted as being the more powerful forces of nature around and was based only on fear.

With the expansion of the thinking capabilities, the human race started understanding the all pervading and subtle forces of nature, which they called God. Gradually, they realized that behind the manifested forms of sun and fire, there existed a subtle consciousness. They further knew that this subtle consciousness was the primordial causative force creating the visible and non-visible aspects of the universe. The developed intellect and expanded consciousness of the spiritual minds of India delved deep into these subtle, causative forces of the universe and realized the existence of an Eternal Entity which they defined as God and the Ultimate Truth. This Primordial Entity, known in the *Vedas* as *Param Purusha*, is not bound by time, space or mutability, although It creates time, space and mutability.

The different incarnations of God and the Perfect Masters came on this earth to reveal this Ultimate Truth to the human beings through their conduct and precepts. The instances of their exemplary actions, at times bordering on miracles, created a conviction about the superior powers that they possessed, in the minds of the devotees. Initially, it is these wonderful and unexplainable miracles that started drawing devotees towards these highly powerful entities of nature. Would one like to logically understand the causes of such acts of miracles, at the end of the search, one will find that one's limited intelligence and intellect are poor instruments to properly appreciate such phenomena. Even if the human race has gone beyond the earth and landed on the moon, yet the question that naturally comes to mind is: What exactly has been achieved by the homo sapiens in the context of the yet unconquered universes, having billions and billions of solar systems? Human beings seem like an ant moving from one pebble to another pebble on the cosmic sea shore.

As the Spiritual Masters have revealed from time to time, beyond the boundaries of the perceptible and imperceptible universes, there lies the vastness of an infinite void or *Mahashunya*. Only after crossing the chains of universes, can one enter that void. In the path of spiritual journey, the first step is to cross this void and have an experience of the Eternal Being or Primordial Being or the *Adi Purusha* or *Ananta Purusha*.

Given this unimagined and unimaginable vastness of the creation of God, is it possible to comprehend or cross this vastness with only the help of our very limited intellect and by the endeavours of a lifetime? A positive answer to this question will indicate that the person has not entered the path leading to the spiritual world as yet. A negative answer will indicate that he is yet to understand the potentiality of a human soul which is part of the Over Soul. If the person reacts to this question neither in affirmation nor negation, then he is in a neutral state of mind, which can simply be called a state of 'be as it may'. This is a better state of mind than others, in order to evolve in the path.

If a person is in such a state of mind, then who will give him a correct answer and who can possibly lead him to the path? In the *Satyayug*, the answers to such questions were revealed through meditation *(samadhi)*, in *Tretayug* through Yoga, in *Dwaparayug* though *yagna* and today in the *Kali Yuga* it is being revealed through science. However, the answer given by science is due to a natural process of expansion of the cerebral capacities of human beings, as ordained by nature. But if a person would like to shorten the process of his evolution and grow at a faster pace, he has to go through a certain special experimentation on himself. He has to bring into focus his entire physical and mental potentialities and combine them with his will power by increasing the will power enormously. In short, he has to put his entire energy, time, will and aspirations into a single focus of action. Experience with the laws of human motivation has shown that love and not fear can create the highest motivation in a human being. If the approach to this path emanates out of devotion and love rather than fear, then the path becomes easier and takes less time.

The laws of nature are well defined and exact and they are applicable universally. To understand these natural laws, one should have commensurate thought vibration and insight. All the saints on this earth had a simple, innocent and guileless personality. It is difficult, rather impossible, to evolve in the path of spiritualism purely with an intellectual and logical approach. Kabir, Nanak, Tukaram, Meera, Ravidas, Buddha, Christ, Shri Sainath of Shirdi, all went through this path and made people understand that only this path is the correct one.

Shri Sainath, in spite of being in the state of total divinity, lived with illiterate and semi-literate rural folks of Shirdi for more than sixty years. He established a tradition with these people, which is today attracting millions of others from within the country and abroad. Millions of intellectuals have surrendered at His feet, after getting attracted by this simplicity and truthfulness. This is so, because the soul is always in search of simplicity, peace and love. Wherever these qualities appear, they become centres of attraction. This is not the attraction of intellect, but the attraction of the soul. This is not based on fear, but on devotion and love.

Let us pray at the holy feet of Shri Sainath, who is always there to help His devotees in their spiritual evolution through the easy path He has shown.

– New Year, 2003

2

Sadguru as the Confluence of All Devotees

On a Divine Plane

Sadguru Shri Sainath Maharaj is in the highest divine state of God, with the divine attributes of unlimited power, knowledge, happiness and existence. This is why He is addressed, verily, as Param Bramha and Satchidananda. Since the entire creation emanates from God the Almighty and ends in Him, He is the only permanent and universal reality. The Primordial Consciousness evolves out of Him, rather, He is the Primordial Consciousness.

This Consciousness manifests in millions and millions of forms, both living and non-living. Whether it is a stone, a plant, an ant, a tiger or a human being — all have come out of this Primordial Consciousness. They, again, merge in Him just as all the rivers merge into the sea. The sea is the confluence of all rivers, just as God is the confluence of the entire consciousness of the universe, including human souls. Similarly, the Sadguru is the confluence of all his devotees.

The Hindus call the confluence place of Ganga, Yamuna and Saraswati at Allahabad as *sangam*. In the path of Spiritual Science, the confluence of the three powers, that is, Bramha, Vishnu and Mahesh — the *Tri-deva* — together form the confluence or *sangam* of the divine creative energy. Similarly, the combination of Knowledge *(Gyan)*, Devotion (Bhakti) and Duty (Karma) is also a *sangam*. The Yogis concentrate at a point on the forehead between the eyebrows, known as Trikuta, Triputa or Triveni, where the three important *nadis* (nerves) called *Ida, Pingala* and *Sushmna* join. Once a man has realized God, his power of will *(Ichcha Shakti)*, power of knowledge *(Gyan Shakti)* and power of action *(Kriya Shakti)* are focussed. Thus the word *sangam* has many connotations in the spiritual world of the Hindus.

During our times, in the form of Shri Shirdi Sai Baba, had taken place the biggest confluence of all spiritual paths, all religious groups, all cultures and devotees, notwithstanding their wide-ranging variations. The Hindus, Parsees, Muslims and followers of other religions used to come to Him, both for temporal as well as spiritual benefit. The high and low, the young and old, men and women, beggars and rulers, all took shelter in Him. He was the kind Father to all — the great equalizer of His time.

He was a spiritual revolutionary and the greatest social reformer. At Shirdi, He ushered in an epoch of universality and mutual tolerance by meting out equal treatment to all who came — no matter to what religion, social or economic status they belonged. There was no differentiation between male and female devotees before Shri Sai. Thus, Bayaji Maa, Radhakrishnamayi and Laxmi Bai — all became important characters during the time of Shri Sai Baba. The richest man of Nagpur, named Buti, was there side-by-side with a devotee like Mhalsapati, who could hardly eke out his living. Das Ganu, the police constable was treated at par with Nanasaheb Chandorkar, who was a Magistrate. Megha, the cook of Raibahadur Sathe, was as important as his master. Kaka Saheb Dixit, one of the greatest solicitors of Maharashtra, used to beg on behalf of Baba at Shirdi, when Baba was sick. Abdul, the Muslim, used to look after Baba's personal needs, as much as Shama, the high caste Brahmin. Saints and Fakirs used to meet Him for spiritual guidance, as also the lesser mortals. Even the birds and animals had a place in Him. In Shirdi, one can see the tomb of a horse and a tiger, as also the tombs of saints like Nanavali, Kumbhar, Bhaw, etc. Ram Navami and Shri Krishna Janma were celebrated by Baba, as well as Idulfitr.

Baba introduced group dinners, group celebrations and even group smoking from *chillum*. Under the divine umbrella of Shri Sai, all devotees forgot their pettiness of caste, religion and creed and lived together happily. Important people like Bal Gangadhar Tilak, Kaka Saheb Dixit, Buti and many high level government officials used to visit Him. Magistrates, judges, businessmen, merchants, teachers, police personnel as well as beggars, destitutes and the poorest of the poor used to visit Him for solace and support.

This was certainly no easy task to perform in a society ridden by religious, social and caste differentiation in the late nineteenth and early twentieth century. Shri Sai, the son of God, not only achieved this with ease, but set a standard for the emancipation of human souls out of their bondages, where human souls meet, purely on a divine plane. For the devotees of Baba, Shirdi was the heaven on earth, a place which they ran to whenever the call came from the Master, just as they do today.

In this month of *Makara Sankranti*, when the Kumbha Mela is taking place at Sangam, we pray to Shri Sainath to bring about a creative and loving confluence among His devotees and all the living beings on earth.

– New Year, 2001

3

Sadguru's Role in War and Conflict

War—A Divine Drama

While at Shirdi, Baba used to mutter something occasionally, a sort of loud-thinking, which only He understood. At times, He would say astounding things, either completely out of context for the listeners or out of reach of their comprehension. On one such occasion, He was heard telling a devotee that in future big buildings would come up in Shirdi, big people would visit the place and also that people would make a beeline for visiting there. The meaning of His divine utterances was not understood then. Today, a crowd of about sixty thousand people, on average, is visiting Shirdi every day. People from all parts of India and abroad, both the richest and the poorest, are visiting Shirdi. As numerous devotees have experienced, Baba had complete knowledge of the past, present and future of all who visited Him. He also knew about the events happening at a distant place.

Incarnations like Baba play a role, both at micro and macro levels, in the world in which they operate. At the micro level, they take care of the individual souls, not only of human beings but also of other species, who are drawn to them by their mighty will, like a bird who is pulled by the chain tied to its leg, as Baba used to say. As mentioned in *Shri Sai Satcharita*, Baba used to recall His past lives' relationships with many of them, and in one case, stretching to seventy-two lives earlier. He also spoke about the past lives of other species. There is a story in *Shri Sai Satcharita* about past lives of two goats, whose earlier lives were known to Baba.

At a macro level, Baba is reported to have said that between 1856 and 1858 (during the Sepoy Mutiny), He was busy with Rani Laxmibai of Jhansi, thereby indicating His role in a critical transitional phase of Indian history. Baba has reportedly spoken about one of His earlier life in which He was born as a Spiritual Practitioner by the name of Mukund, when Emperor Humayun had met Him and Akbar was born due to His blessings.

Limited human intelligence can only perceive of the micro level activities of the Perfect Masters; it can never perceive their role at the macro level. History is, therefore, a limited projection of human activities at micro level. No historian has been able to understand the unseen activities of the Perfect Masters in influencing the temporal powers or rulers on this earth.

Baba's activities, visible and non-visible, were extremely intense during the First World War period between 1914 and 1918. He left His body on 15th October 1918, when the war had almost ended, completing His mission. He is reported to have saved an Indian Captain and his ship from drowning in the Pacific. When Bal Gangadhar Tilak met Him at Shirdi in 1917, He asked him to take rest, as the person to liberate India was coming. Bal Gangadhar Tilak left his body shortly; thereafter Mahatma Gandhi appeared on the scene.

Today, the world is in a transitional phase. Old order is bound to change, giving place to new. The human society needs a new meaning to life and a new system. Incarnations like Ram and Krishna had brought about such transitions through wars. War is the culmination of a divine drama where the heroes of truthfulness are ultimately victorious. This macro role of the spiritual powers is going to be enacted in a more perceptible manner in the days to come. All of us understand the meaning of a war. Let us then pray to Him to have mercy. Let us pray to Him to bring about a better order, where human beings and other species can live happily together.

– Ram Navami, 1998

4

Birth- Death Cycles and Moksha

The Righteous Path

Birth and death are the two terminal points of human life. To be born is to die. In the cosmic period of time, human existence is like a bubble of moments. All embodied souls, be it human beings or any other species, will have to go through this short journey of a lifetime. Such embodied souls are known as *jiva* or life forms. There are millions of such life forms, both visible and invisible, on this earth. Many of these forms are known to human beings due to research and others are yet to be discovered. Their body forms, capabilities, intelligence level and period of existence between birth and death are different and too numerous to be codified. However, the main principle of these manifested life forms is that once they are born, they must die, after carrying out certain activities in accordance with their inborn capacities.

Once they die, that is, when the life force holding the body elements together departs from the body or stops functioning in the form of a pulsating heartbeat, the body elements separate from one another. The earth goes to earth, water goes to water and air goes to air. Hindu philosophy holds that *panch bhuta* (five elements) of nature merge with their primordial elements, once the life force departs from a living organism.

Then comes the next question as to what happens to the *jiva* without the body? What happens to the life force that holds the body together? Do the *jiva* and the life force (prana) have any existence and significance after separating from the body? Some spiritual thinkers define the life force (prana) as the manifested dynamics of the soul (atman). According to some religions and philosophies, the *jiva*, after death, is reborn again and again. According to others, there is no rebirth or reincarnation of human souls.

The series of rebirths continues till the *jiva* reaches the stage of *moksha*, as Hinduism believes, or *nirvana* as Buddhism states. Therefore every Hindu, from his very childhood, is taught to perform good deeds and avoid evil ones. Like Newton's law of motion of matter, which states that every action will have an equal and opposite reaction, Hindus believe that every good or evil act committed by a human being shall have an equal and opposite reaction. The only difference is that, in the case of human beings committing such acts — good or evil — the reaction may not manifest in a single lifetime. It may stretch to the next life or lives. Therefore, Hinduism prescribes each human being to be prepared to enjoy or suffer the results of his good or evil deeds in future lives. This is known as the famous Karma theory, as propounded so meticulously in *Srimad Bhagavad Gita* and other Hindu scriptures.

One often hears of Hindu teachers and pupils speaking in terms of *moksha* as a panacea to the unending series of painful births and deaths. Such people give donations to temples, feed the poor, perform numerous *pooja*, visit places of religious significance (called *tirtha*) with the aim of achieving *moksha* or, at least, to go to heaven (*swarg*), a place of unhindered and absolute enjoyment, and receive benefits for the so-called good deeds performed during their life time. Many such activities are programmed like a modern corporate system — investment and profit; doing noble jobs like feeding the poor and rendering services to the needy people to earn *punya*. The problem is that such an approach contradicts the other basic principle of Hinduism, which says that such acts should not be performed with any desire, as desire leads to a series of births necessary to fulfil these desires. *Shrimad Bhagavad Gita* advises desireless (*nishkama*) activities rather than activities performed with the aim of fulfilling a certain desire.

Shri Sai Satcharita and other literature on Shri Shirdi Sai Baba indicate that Shri Sai believed in rebirth of human beings. He, in fact, revealed to some of His devotees about their past lives and about His relationship with them during these past lives. He always advised His devotees to follow the righteous path of sacrifice, tolerance and faith in God, with patience. He never spoke anything about Heaven. His devotees were asked to cleanse their minds of evil or negative thoughts and fill them with pure and divine qualities and serve others without the desire to get returns.

In the backdrop of what has been said earlier, it is for each devotee to examine whether his approach towards the extant religious activities he is performing is in accordance with the dictates of the Master. If confused, they should read *Shri Sai Satcharita* and pray to Baba for an answer.

I believe that answers are there if the questions are genuine.

May Shri Sai bless us all.

— New Year, 2010

5

Complete Surrender to Sadguru

Complete Surrender

Devotees of Shri Shirdi Sai Baba often ask a question, 'Why is it that even if I have surrendered to Baba, my financial, physical, social and official situations do not improve?' Or, that 'I prayed to Baba for the last one week for the cure of my son; but why is he not getting cured?' Some of them even promise that they would visit Shirdi or a temple of Baba if their wishes were fulfilled.

The main problem lies in the conviction of people about their faith or surrender to Baba. The noble qualities, sacrifices and the period of time required to establish closer contact with a Sadguru are found to be lacking in them. In a social relationship, the approach of people is limited and their mutual benefit is pre-calculated. Any deviation from or non-achievement of the anticipated result from the other side easily spoils such a relationship. Today, even in families, relationships are, to a large extent, built on considerations of mutual benefit. Such norms of social relationships vary from society to society and from time to time. But when these norms are applied in relation to the Spiritual World or in relation to a Sadguru, the relationship becomes a non-starter from the beginning.

Bhakti Marg, at its highest point, leads to surrender. Surrender means sacrificing everything – our mind, body and soul — to God or the Sadguru we worship. Once surrendered, the devotee has to believe that his body, mind, will and soul belong to God or the Sadguru and not to him. Also, he has to utilize them for the cause of the Sadguru. Since everything belongs to the Sadguru, the devotee has nothing to be happy about, nothing to be sad about, nothing to complain against and nothing to desire for himself — materially, mentally or even spiritually.

Such a state of total surrender can be achieved only by a few from among the millions of spiritual aspirants who have received the kindness and support of a Sadguru.

How many devotees who claim to have surrendered to Baba have truly surrendered? Once Baba told His devotees that His Guru, in order to take His test, hung Him upside down from a wall with a rope tied around Him, for a few hours and went away. When the Guru, on return, asked as to how He felt, Baba replied that He was in an ecstatic mood. He had nothing at all to complain and was happy about what the Guru had done to Him. Having said this, Baba asked the devotees sitting around Him in Dwarakamai Masjid as to how many of them can have the same level of faith. No one had the courage to give a positive answer.

Therefore, simply to say, feel or show that one has surrendered is not correct, because a surrendered person will have no desires or will of his own and, therefore, no complaints. He would only follow the two prescriptions given by Baba, that is, *shraddha* (faith) and *saburi* (patience).

The word *shraddha* means:

1. Genuine devotional faith in the Master, that is, Baba for the Sai devotees.
2. An intrinsic faith that Baba is in a divine state of existence and is his Protector.
3. That their past, present and future are known to Baba and controlled by Him, from near and far.

4. To tolerate all vicissitudes of life with patience and equanimity.
5. To realize that Baba is always with the devotees and ever watchful for their welfare.
6. To follow the dictates of the Master in letter and spirit, without being concerned or worried about the consequences.
7. To hold on to Baba and not to run to different deities and temples for different purposes.

The word *saburi* means:

1. Tolerance and patience, both physical and mental, under all circumstances, while having faith in Baba.
2. In the spiritual sense, it has a wider and subtler connotation of natural acceptance of all problems of life with equanimity, not mere tolerance of something because one is forced to do so.

How many people can really maintain such an attitude of mind? Each devotee should examine his thought process to find out where exactly he stands. Then only would he be able to understand whether he has surrendered in the real sense of the term or not.

If anyone wants to establish a perfect association with a Perfect Master, then he should, at first, become a perfect devotee. Baba used to say that a devotee would experience Him according to his *bhava*. An imperfect mind will reflect an imperfect image of the Sadguru and the person will get imperfect results.

It is not so easy to completely surrender the mind without understanding its full implications. A better path would be to gradually develop the qualities prescribed by the Sadguru while living daily life like an ordinary person, enjoying and suffering happiness and unhappiness respectively while keeping the Guru in one's heart.

– Ram Navami, 1999

Shraddha and Saburi

For His devotees, Baba has set two cardinal principles for the path of devotion. The first is *shraddha,* which means devotional faith and the other is *saburi,* which means tolerance with patience. In almost all the literature on Sai, these two words find pre-eminent mention.

People understand the meaning of these two words according to their mental abilities and inner perceptions based on their experiences related to Baba. Some people believe that their *shraddha* in Baba is complete; others, even while having only a little faith, are too sure. Some have faith in Baba and simultaneously in many other deities of the Hindu pantheon. Thus, the word *shraddha* is the most confused and difficult concept to understand, and still more difficult to explain or experience.

Unflinching devotional faith (or *shraddha*) is the most difficult state of mind to achieve. If a devotee has absolute faith in his Guru, then sooner or later he will even start looking similar to the Guru, with all His attributes. However, the seed of faith takes a lot of time to germinate and grow. It may take years or even a few lives to reach there. One cannot have full faith in Baba merely by wishing for it. Further, externality of devotion may not necessarily be indicative of the internality of devotion.

At times, some devotees hold Baba responsible for generating or not generating *bhakti* in them, even if it is towards Baba Himself. Ultimately, it is true that the Sadguru generates *bhakti* in a devotee's heart to lead him along the spiritual path. However, the Perfect Masters sow the seed of devotion on fertile soil and not barren land. If one prays to

Baba for *bhakti* and yet conducts himself in a manner contrary to what Baba has advised, then how can *bhakti* awaken in the heart? Some people argue that even bad thoughts and conduct are created due to the will of God and without God's desire these can't be controlled. Such ignorant devotees place the burden of their self-created negativities on God, without taking any responsibility for their own conduct.

Realising his own limitations, if a person prays to Baba to help him, Baba can control his conduct. Baba does so in subtle ways, provided the person surrenders himself and leaves everything in Baba's hands. Faith or surrender means leaving everything on Baba — body, mind and soul.

Partial surrender will lead to partial *bhakti* and produce partial results only. In these circumstances, the devotee should neither work nor seek anything himself, and leave everything to Baba in totality. Thereafter, if he is prepared to bear the consequences of this state of utter inaction, then Baba will certainly control his conduct and evoke *shraddha* in him.

There are numerous examples of devotees who, during the lifetime of Baba, had left everything, including all their material and spiritual needs, on Shri Sai and He had satisfied all their genuine needs. If a devotee cannot evolve to this level of surrender, then he should be responsible for bearing the consequences of all his *karmas* without blaming God or the Master for it. Due to the kindness of the Master, he will surely progress, but progress will be slow. In comparison to all the other species on earth, God has given enough intelligence to human beings to discriminate between good and evil and to choose or avoid a particular path.

Rapid evolution takes place when, under all circumstances, the devotee patiently waits for the mercy of Baba. *Saburi* is, therefore, an essential factor for the creation, sustenance and growth of devotion. The qualities of faith and patience are complementary to each other. Faith without patience is a contradiction in terms and patience without faith is an exercise in futility. They are like two sides of a balance beam — if one comes down, the other goes up.

Again, faith means trying to do what is prescribed and resist from doing what has been forbidden by Baba. While doing so, even if one fails a few times, it does not matter. The main issue is whether or not the person is trying his best and stretching himself to his limits. When the devotee uses his physical and mental faculties, time and energy for spiritual evolution, then he has to cut down on his time from many other activities. Therefore, the person who wants closeness with Baba should always try to reduce the non-productive, capricious and non-essential activities like avoidable socialization, arguments and fruitless show-offs, addictions of any kind, unbridled thought, speech or actions, etc. Such endeavour will not only gradually control the mind, but will give the devotee a lot of time to study religious scriptures, to practice meditation and to render help to the poor and the needy.

The devotee should try continuously to fortify his qualities of patience, faith, tolerance, egolessness, and humility gradually. However, the two qualities which are fundamental are *shraddha* and *saburi*.

— *Maha Samadhi, 1999*

6

Conceptualizing God

The Master Source

Scientific research tells us that in the last thousands of years, many species have become extinct on this earth. Some of these species, like the dinosaurs, were much more powerful physically than most of the other species of that time. But because they could not adapt themselves to the onslaughts of the changing environmental conditions of the time, they became extinct. Various theories have been propounded, explaining the cause of such environmental changes. These physically gigantic and powerful species did not have the required level of intelligence to fight against these natural catastrophes, as their cerebral capacity was not well developed. On the other hand, the human race survived such dire situations due to its superior intelligence. From the stage of the Cave Man and the Iron Man, to the stage of the Modern Man, the human race, at every stage of evolution, proved the Darwinian principle of the survival of the fittest.

During the early stages of evolution, the human race did not have the concept of God as we understand today. It was afraid of natural forces like fire, thunder, rains and even dangerous animals like snakes, tigers and others. In order to escape from these forces of nature, the early man started a process of their appeasement. These acts were based on fear and not love. Later, the human mind imagined and created concepts like the Gods of war, of agriculture, of medicine and so on, with the hope to make life more comfortable with their help. As the intelligence and consciousness of human beings started evolving to higher levels, their concepts about God also evolved further. They began entertaining the idea of a mighty divine power and gave it different names such as God, Nature, Spirit, and so on.

Through the experience of ages, human beings realized the existence of their own consciousness. Through the search of their own consciousness, they conceived the idea of an all-pervading Super Conscious entity, which they termed as God. Gradually, they linked their own origin to this Super Conscious Being. Further, they realized that everything on Earth and the Universe emanated from this Super Conscious Being. Having realized this, they started worshipping this all pervading and creative Consciousness of Nature as God.

The initial systems of worship were, thus, based on the human ideas to receive help and the least possible amount of trouble from the different forces of nature and to receive the maximum possible help from the highest Supreme Conscious Being called God. Some human beings carried out experiments on their own consciousness, through the process of concentration and meditation. Some of them experienced the intrinsic link between their consciousness and the Super Consciousness. They realized that their consciousness was a part of this Supreme Consciousness and that, after departing from the human body, their consciousness would merge with It.

It is because of such superior intelligence that the human race became superior to all other species on the Earth. Some of the most advanced researchers, besides realising the existence of God in them, also learnt the process of drawing extra powers and capabilities from the Master Source—the Primordial Source of all living and non-living powers. Through the use of such powers they started helping other human beings and species. These people are known as Saints or the Masters, whom the human being apotheosizes and worships. Let us pray to them.

May Shri Sai bless us all.

— Maha Samadhi, 2010

7

Conduct in a Sai Temple

Unison of Minds

Often, during my visit to the temples of Shirdi Sai Baba and and when attending functions relating to Shri Sai Baba of Shirdi, I observe certain types of conduct of devotees and the general visitors to the temples, which to my mind do not seem appropriate for the place or the occasion. Not to speak of higher spiritual senses and sensibilities, even the common sense of an ordinary man would say that different dress and behavioural codes are required to be followed in different situations.

Let us take a few such situations, for example, a marriage party, an official conference, a funeral procession and a golf tournament. Can anyone think of attending a marriage party in an attire meant for playing golf, or attending an official function in the attire befitting a funeral procession? The dress codes prescribed for each of these occasions are different. Such dress specifications have evolved gradually over a long period of time in human civilization, because they are appropriate to the occasion. The idea is to maintain an environment comfortable for all and also to take into consideration the sensitivities of other human beings around. Since to be civilized means to compromise and accommodate the sentiments of others, it is essential that, while in a place meant for group activities, particularly in a temple, one must be dressed appropriately.

Now let us examine the way the devotees of some religions dress or conduct themselves while in a religious congregation. While in a church, the Christians are always properly and appropriately dressed. So also is the case of Sikhs, Muslims, and Buddhists.

When inside a place of worship, the devotees are supposed to concentrate all their faculties on a definite purpose and in a certain manner, that is, eyes (through which they concentrate and meditate on the image of the deity), mouth (through which they recite mantras or *aartis* and *bhajans* in praise of the deity), ears (through which they listen to mantras, *aartis*, discourses, and so on), nose (through which they smell the sweet smell of flowers and incense offered to the deity) and skin (through which they touch the feet of the deity). One can imagine the serene atmosphere of a temple, which gives a feeling of expansion of mental horizons and upliftment of the soul to an ecstatic mood.

The most desirable atmosphere in a temple is a situation where one can listen to the prolonged elevated notes of the Vedic mantras; there is no hustle bustle and no high pitched or cacophonic noise. The temple or the place of worship should also not project a picture of depression and melancholy, with sulking devotees vitiating the whole atmosphere with their never ending demands from the Lord. Such devotees, creating scenes in the temple due to non-fulfilment of their purely material desires, spoil the pleasant and peaceful atmosphere of the a temple.

The place of worship needs to be a place of unison of minds and souls of devotees when focusing on a deity, or when chanting mantras and also during group singing of *aarti*. When the purpose, the thoughts, the sentiments and the activities of the devotees are merged while invoking the deity or the Master, the love of the deity or the Master flows down to the devotees. This is the purpose of going to a temple or a place of religious congregation.

When such a pristine atmosphere is meant to raise the souls of the devotees to a state of sublime ecstasy, any sort of impropriety in dress and conduct, such as talking or laughing loudly, knowingly or unknowingly, is likely to disturb other devotees and vitiate the whole atmosphere. The focus of the devotee gets shifted from the deity, and in our case, it shifts from the holy image of Shri Sainath Maharaj of Shirdi, towards such individuals enacting undesirable scenes in the temple.

Shri Sai Baba of Shirdi was never in favour of His devotees and workers wearing any sort of gaudy dress when taking part in religious ceremonies. Once Das Ganu Maharaj, who sang ballads about Baba and other saints, came to Baba, on his way to a religious function where he was supposed to give a rendition of songs on Baba. He was donned in dazzling and colourful attire, which *kirtankars* and *kathavachaks* usually wear in Maharashtra and elsewhere in India. Baba asked him not to decorate himself in such lavish style and attend the function in the simplest possible dress. This incident finds mention in Chapter 15 of *Shri Sai Satcharita*. Following the dictates of the Master, thereafter, Das Ganu always conducted the *kirtans* wearing a simple dhoti.

In the light of what has been explained above, it is desirable for the Shirdi Sai devotees to worship Baba in the temple, or to participate in a congregation of devotees, in modest and simple attire. Baba's teachings show that lavish display of material aspects of life, including dazzling dresses, were not conducive to a spiritual life. Shri Sai Baba, the Fakir with the torn and tattered clothes, perhaps finds it more comfortable to be with His simply dressed, but truthful people.

In this context, I have also observed many devotees trying to copy the dressing style and manner of the Master, wearing *kafnis* (long flowing cloth covering the entire body) and *patka* (headgear). Some of them carry a *satka*, additionally, in their hand. The famous *Guru Gita* asks the devotees not to copy the look or the behaviour of the Guru. This is an accepted rule of law in the master-disciple relationship in the spiritual world. Even the famous Shri Vivekananda never imitated the attire of his Guru, Shri Ramakrishna Paramhansa. Although some Sai devotees tend to dress like Baba out of ignorance and simply as a feel-good factor, there are quacks who try to impress gullible devotees in order to extract money and other advantages. Some of these characters, having copied the Master's dress style, go a further step. They try to copy the sitting postures of the Master (right leg over the left leg), and start speaking and blessing other devotees, assuming to themselves the role of the Master Himself. Some of them also prefix or suffix the word 'Sai' to their names and bask in the glory of the name of Shri Sai. We should be aware of such charlatans.

The temple pandits carrying on the daily worship usually have a common dress code. However, the devotees need not wear such dresses. They can wear any clothes which they usually wear when they are moving about in a civilized society outside their homes. It is the duty of the temple management to surely but politely impress upon all visitors to the temple to be properly attired and behave properly when they are in the temple premises.

On the day of Maha Samadhi of Baba, I invoke Shri Sai Baba's blessing for the devotees and readers in helping them to evolve in the spiritual path.

— *Maha Samadhi, 2007*

8

Dawning of the Sai Age

The Incarnation of the Age

Whatever the form and the shape may be, the ultimate truth is that God, Sadguru and the Soul are one and the same. The realization of one leads to the realization of the other two. The Ultimate Power, which we call *Parambramha*, has manifested Himself as human beings through a process of evolution—inorganic and organic. These human souls go through incalculable number of births and deaths before they reach their original state of God, the Almighty. All souls will ultimately have to go back to the original state. Thus, the evolution of the human souls is nothing but souls going back to their original state.

Some of these souls, because of the kindness of the Sadguru, develop spiritually faster than others and experience God while in a human body. After leaving their human body, such souls retain their memory and knowledge of past lives. They die consciously, which means they do not experience the state of death experienced by an ordinary individual, whose awareness of the gross world vanishes totally after death. The others, who always retain their consciousness, whether with a body a without a body, are known as *Jivanmuktas*, that is, persons who have got out of the cycles of birth and death. They are in a state of pure consciousness. Having experienced miseries and tribulations of mortal human existence, they try to impart knowledge, and render help to the other souls to realize their original God state, so that they can also get out of the cycles of birth and death. Because of their infinite compassion, they descend on earth in a human body, out of their own volition, just to help the suffering humanity. They draw other human souls to themselves by certain methods yet undiscovered by science, and go on evolving them life after life, till they reach the ultimate destination, that is, God. This is what Shri Sai Baba used to do, sitting in that unknown village called Shirdi.

These great souls are called the Sadgurus or Perfect Masters or Qutabs or Adepts. Shirdi Sai Baba was not only the *Param Sadguru* of His time, but is the incarnation of this age. That is why, even after departure from physical existence, His influence is spreading all over the globe. Highly self-motivated devotees are performing yeomen service in propagating His preachings. Sai is as He was. Today, under His beneficial influence, the Sai Age has dawned and this is what every devotee has to understand.

The role of the incarnation is more expansive and spreads over thousands of years. We should celebrate Guru Poornima as a token of love for these great souls who sacrificed themselves for the evolution of mankind, and ameliorate the sufferings of crores of human beings who come in direct or indirect contact with them. The least one can do about these infinitely merciful entities is to remember them, pray to them and follow them.

– Guru Poornima, 2000

The Advent of the Sai Age

Shri Sai Baba of Shirdi is called *Sadguru, Fakir, Awalia, Maha Yogi* and, most importantly, 'the Incarnation of the Age'.

During the stay of Baba at Shirdi, some spiritual personalities used to pay a visit to the place. Once, on seeing Baba as a young person at Shirdi, one such personality, Shri Gangagir, commented that the young Sai was like a jewel under a heap of cow dung and also that one day His divine illumination will bring glory to Shirdi.

Meher Baba, a disciple of Upasani Maharaj (who was a prime disciple of Baba), has commented that Shri Sai is like the beginning and end of creation. Upasani Maharaj has spoken a lot on Shri Sai, saying that Shri Sai is the *Satchidananda* God.

Thus, a lot has been spoken and written on Shri Sai. Hundreds of epithets have been used for His name. The *Sai Nam Astottarasata Namahvalih* (108 names of Sai), glorifying the names and divine qualities of Shri Sai, are recited in most of the Sai temples. People, during His time and as also today, have exhaustively written on this majestic and unfathomable divine personality, the past and present miraculous deeds related to Him and on the emotional attachment of the devotees with Him. Millions of people have been drawn towards Him and thousands of temples have been built all over India, and some in other countries, too, in His name. His photographs and images can be seen everywhere — temples, houses, shops and vehicles. The process of such expansion continues.

Today, He is the Sai — the Master and Father to so many. The number of devotees is ever on the increase and this 'Sai Wave' is slowly but surely engulfing humanity.

Speculations apart, the fact remains that the divine status of Shri Sai has not been exactly defined as yet. The Hindus use all kinds of terminologies and epithets, quoting from their scriptures, to explain the divine attributes and *leelas* of Shri Sai. Thus Shri Sai is worshipped as Sai Maharaj, Sai Bhagwan, Sai Ram, Sai Krishna, Sai Vithala, Sai Mauli (*mauli* means mother), Sai Param Bramha, Sai Shiva, Sai Dattatreya, Sai Vishnu, Sai Shankara, Sai Avatar, Sai Ishwara, Sai Ganesha, and so on. If anyone analyzes these divine epithets, he would be drawn to the conclusion that although Shri Sai Baba played the role of a Sadguru, that is, a Perfect Master, while at Shirdi, He is much beyond that.

Shri Sai left His human embodiment long time ago, without institutionalizing his movement and without leaving any heir-apparent, unlike what most of the Gurus do. He came to serve His devotees for their spiritual evolution, although He also rendered temporal benefits to all of them through His kind words and kinder actions.

An analysis of the visible personality of Shri Sai would indicate that He was totally detached from all material needs, was sometimes in a *jalali* (spiritually intoxicated) state, used His spiritual powers for the benefit of His devotees in abundance, treated all equally irrespective of the difference of caste, religion, creed, language, temporal status, and so on; was divinely compassionate to all, including animals. Although He was a God-realized soul, yet He behaved like an ordinary man in a village, without any assertions of His divine hierarchy (as many Gurus do). He lived at the same place for sixty years and left His body, having served whosoever came to Him, without seeking anything in return.

Today Shri Sai is a name known to most of the people of India. Shirdi has become a *tirath*, with devotees from all over the world making a bee-line there. The 'Sai-ism' as many call it, is expanding very fast. Such expansion, by sheer self- motivation of His devotees, indicates the power that Shri Sai is, even ninety years after His Samadhi. This is what happened to all the incarnations in the past.

Let us pray to Shri Sai, 'the Incarnation of the Age' on the New Years' day to guide and bless us.

– New Year, 2005

Sai Movement

Baba took Samadhi eighty-two years ago. In the case of Spiritual Masters, departure of the soul from the body is not termed as death but as *samadhi*. For these great, divine souls, *samadhi* represents a voluntary process of leaving the body at will at a pre-decided moment. It also means that during the process of moving out from their gross human bodies and entering into their body-less divine state, they are in a state of full consciousness. This volitional act of departure indicates that the gross body is no more an effective instrument for them to carry on their responsibilities and, therefore, they have decided to leave it. There are numerous examples to establish that Sadgurus, in some way or the other, had given prior indications about their departure.

Shri Sainath had given a clear indication, in 1916, on the day of Vijaya Dashmi, that His departure was not far off. Also, His premonitions on the death of Tatya Kote Patil and the breaking of the brick, which was a gift from His Guru and His lifelong possession, were indicators. *Shri Sai Satcharita* has given a vivid account about Shri Sai Baba's last days.

So far so good, but does the *samadhi* result in the end of the role of the Sadguru in relation to the souls that He had drawn towards Himself from far and near and with whom He had *rinanubandha*, a Karmic relationship established during many past lives? Although many religious and spiritual people hold the view that a Master, after leaving his human body, cannot help the disciples, yet in the case of Shri Sainath the experience of the disciples has been quite different. I have had the opportunity of knowing some of the devotees of Baba who had been with Him before His departure. I have spoken with some of them and also got recorded their experiences through some ardent devotees. All of them categorically confirmed that many unexplainable and miraculous events with relation to Baba are still happening around their existence, just as they used to earlier, when Baba was there in His physical body at Shirdi.

Most of the books written on Baba's life history and devotees' experiences undoubtedly establish the occurrence of many miracles experienced by Sai devotees, not only before the departure of Baba, but even today. Earlier, there were thousands of devotees, mostly confined to Maharashtra. But today, the increase in the number of Sai devotees is an astounding phenomenon, which is difficult to explain and more difficult to deny. More than a thousand temples of Shri Sai have come up in India and hundreds are in the process of construction at various stages. Where it is not possible for devotees to build Baba's temples separately, small or big statues have been installed in the precincts of temple complexes housing other deities.

In states like UP, Bihar, Odisha, Himachal Pradesh, Punjab and others in North India where there were only one or two temples earlier, a large number of temples have come up within the last ten years. In far-off places like Pithoragarh hills of UP, Andaman and Nicobar islands and the remotest places of Odisha, Himachal Pradesh, Madhya Pradesh and so on, Baba's temples have been constructed. Abroad, in many countries like USA, UK, Canada, Cuba, Malaysia, Australia and New Zealand, His temples and places of devotional congregations, and numbers of devotees, are on the increase. A number of websites on Baba can be visited on the internet.

At Shirdi, the average number of visitors per day has crossed sixty thousand. The Shirdi Sai Baba Trust at Shirdi, in order to cope with ever-increasing number of devotees, has totally changed the face of Shirdi through suitable modifications and additions. The Shirdi of today is a different place from what it looked like a few years ago.

The number of books written and being written on Baba and also the number of journals and magazines published by various Sai organizations in different languages is very large. Except the Shirdi Sai Baba Trust of Shirdi, which is an official body, most of these activities are carried on ceaselessly by the devotees and other Sai Trusts out of their sheer love for Baba. Most of these institutions, besides carrying on regular religious activities in the temples, are contributing immensely towards societal requirements like education, health and other humanitarian activities.

The activities concerning Shri Sainath, today, are so multi-dimensional and spreading all over the country and abroad that one cannot comprehend their total impact on the lives of the devotees and their effect on the religious and spiritual life of India and other countries. The researchers on Baba, from India and other countries, who have written a number of books on Him, need to take up thorough research on this aspect.

This, logically, brings to mind one question — if after His departure, the spirit of Shri Sai is not active, then how are all these happening? Can it be a mere chance occurrence or is there a bigger or subtler law of nature which is manifesting through these activities? Any sensitive mind, with some amount of understanding of the spiritual history of the world, will surely perceive the reality of a quietly emerging Sai movement.

This Sai movement is based on the principles of humanism, universalism, tolerance and mutual cooperation of the highest order. These are principles on the basis of which any civilized society exists and any religion continues. We are all waiting for dawning the Age of Sai who, I believe, is the 'Incarnation of the Age'. In the current decade, the world will see the emergence of international Sai movement and hundreds of temples will be built in a number of countries. History shows that the role of the incarnations has been more pronounced after they had left their gross body.

The world needs someone to lead it and bring about unity among the strife-ridden and mutually intolerant religious, social and racial groups. Shri Sai preached and practiced the unity of the highest order, based on the principles of love and tolerance in the nineteenth century and the early part of the twentieth century. In this new millennium the Shri Sai Movement will lead the world to the path of peace and progress.

– Maha Samadhi, 2000

9

Emergence of Sai-ism

The Master of the Age

One day, while sitting in His dilapidated durbar named *Dwarakamai* at Shirdi, the aging Fakir, Sai Baba, in His typical mood of divine ecstasy blurted out before His devotees, '*Main guli guli mein rahene wala hun,*' which means, 'I will be seen in every lane everywhere.' He said this in 1911 and I am writing this article it is 2011, a century later.

Since the last two decades, I had the opportunity and privilege of working for the cause of Shri Shirdi Sai Baba in its varied aspects in India and abroad. Being only a small part of the mighty and global Sai Movement, I am surprised at the exponential growth of this movement the world over. Leave aside the metropolises and major cities of India, Shri Shirdi Sai Baba's temples have come up in small towns, semi-urban and rural areas, and even in far-off places of India like Assam and Sikkim. Not only have Shri Shirdi Sai Baba's temples come up in towns and cities, but in some states, for example in Andhra Pradesh and Odisha, such temples have come up in remote areas as well. In many places in India and abroad, in the existing Hindu temples, they are installing the statues of Shri Shirdi Sai Baba. This is a clear indicator of future, of things to come.

The total volume of literature pertaining to Shri Shirdi Sai Baba in terms of books, magazines, journals, periodicals and other publications is beyond all calculations. The spread of Shri Shirdi Sai Baba's life history, philosophy and teachings propagated through internet, movies, television, radio channels, media (print, audio and video) in English and most of the languages of India, is phenomenal. The charitable work like hospitals, schools, feeding the poor, financial aid to the weaker and disabled people of the society, carried out in His name is immense.

More than this is the fact that Shri Shirdi Sai Baba has penetrated into the lives of millions of His devotees. The more surprising thing is that Shri Shirdi Sai Baba never created any organizational structure for propagation of His own philosophy or name. The Shri Sai Baba Sansthan at Shirdi is doing its best to cope with the ever-growing number of visitors to Shirdi, which touches about fifty thousand persons (and climbing) on an average per day. This Sai miracle or phenomenon is transparently perceptible from the fact that most of the devotees are self motivated and carry out Baba's work with missionary zeal.

Not only in India, but in other countries like the United States, United Kingdom, Europe, Australia, Africa and even in places like New Zealand, Singapore, Malaysia and so on, a number of temples have come up and more are in the process. When I inaugurated a temple in a remote village of Odisha called Tigiria, or a big temple at Dehradun, the state capital of Uttaranchal, or at Delhi, the capital of India, or at Sydney in Australia, or at Chicago or Houston in United States, the involvement of the devotees there was basically the same, with slight difference because of local conditions. All the devotees of Baba feel closeness with Him in some form or the other. Some of them are emotionally driven to do more and more work in His cause. Thus the Sai Movement goes on with a poetic spontaneity and lucidity.

When I got drawn into this movement two decades ago in 1990, I had a premonition that, in the future course of time, the Sai Movement will engulf the whole globe. I had also foreseen a new spiritual approach of the confused humanity which can be termed as *Sai-ism*. Today, when I look back, I find that what Baba said '*Main guli guli mein rahene wala hun,*' is coming true.

Let us, then, welcome the Sai Age and be a part of *Sai-ism*, as He is the Master of the Age.

May Shri Sai Baba of Shirdi lead us all towards light.

— Ram Navami, 2011

The Omnipresent Sai

Most of the devotees of Shri Shirdi Sai Baba are reported to have been receiving spiritual experiences, many of which are in the form of miracles. Such experiences of actual or perceived miracles not only enhance their faith in Baba, but also spiritually uplift them personally. If one goes through such similar experiences of the devotees as depicted in *Shri Sai Satcharita* and other literature on Sai Baba and compare them with the experiences of the present-day devotees, one would find a close similarity between them. Shri Khaparde, a prominent advocate of Amravati, a town near Nagpur, who used to visit Shirdi frequently and Kaka Saheb Dixit, who devoted the later part of his life to the service of Baba at Shirdi, have recorded details of many such experiences in their diaries which they used to maintain.

When one hears about some of the common experiences reported by devotees, one's mind is transported to the time of Baba at Shirdi. Imagination becomes vivid, all worries cease to exist and time seems to stand still. Most devotees have reported that they used to get spiritually charged at the very sight of Baba; disturbing and uncontrollable thoughts of their mind used to vanish, and a feeling of purity, calm and love engulfed them.

Baba had a unique way of communicating with his devotees through words, look and touch, besides the extremely strong and vibrant spiritual thought waves He used to send. He used to send His thought waves even from afar. These powerful thought waves used to appear in the form of vivid dreams and ideas in the minds of His devotees and used to convey certain impulses, directions, forewarnings, future happenings and love of Baba. Those who followed these directions with an open mind benefited amply. When such directions were related by Baba in the dreams of His devotees, the results were seen taking shape suddenly or in due course of time in the actual realities of their worldly life. For example, one devotee saw Baba giving him yellow rice grains in his dream. When he got up, he found yellow rice sprinkled all over his bed. Similarly, another devotee found a coconut in his bed when awakened from sleep after having seen Baba in his dream.

Another direct experience, as depicted in the *Shri Sai Satcharita* (Chapter 40), was in 1917, when Hemadpant had a dream in which he saw Baba in the form of a Sanyasi, promising to come to take a meal at Hemadpant's house on that day. At lunchtime, just as the family was about to begin eating, two men, Ali Mahomed and Moulana Ismu Mujavar, appeared at the door and handed over a picture of Sai Baba to Hemadpant. Hemadpant was much moved at the thought that Baba, as promised, had indeed blessed him by gracing his house for lunch.

There are numerous experiences about Baba appearing in a physical form in different and distant places, while He was actually in His human form at Shirdi. Devotees have reported that Baba, while sitting in front of the Dhuni (fire) in the morning at the mosque, would often refer to His visits to distant places and other worlds He had visited during the night, despite being physically present at Shirdi.

A famous incident that took place in 1910 is narrated in *Shri Sai Satcharita* (Chapter 7), when Baba, sitting near the Dhuni, was pushing firewood into it. Suddenly, He pushed his arm into the Dhuni, as a result of which His hand got burnt. Some devotees, who were sitting near Him, forcibly pulled His hand out of the fire. On enquiry by the shocked devotees, He replied that in a village a little away from Shirdi, the wife of a blacksmith was working at the furnace, with her child tied to her waist. When her husband called out to her, she got up suddenly and the child slipped into the furnace. She called out to Baba to save the child. As a spontaneous reaction, Baba thrust His hand into the Dhuni to take out the child from the furnace. Later, the couple visited Shirdi with the child and thanked Him for having saved the child. Another devotee, B. V. Deo, had sent a letter to Bapu Saheb Jog in Shirdi, requesting Baba's presence in a group lunch he had arranged. Baba promised to attend the lunch with two other persons and did so by appearing in the form of a Sanyasi with two followers.

The greater miracles of Baba show instances of control of natural forces like fire, air and water (rain). *Shri Sai Satcharita* (Chapter 11) narrates about an evening when torrential rain, accompanied by lightning and thunder, hit Shirdi, flooding it entirely. This terrified all the people of Shirdi. Devotees, animals and birds, all took refuge at Dwarakamai Masjid and prayed to Baba for help. At their request, Baba commanded the clouds, in a thunderous voice, to stop their fury and to allow His children to go to their houses. Within minutes, the rain stopped and the storm died down.

Another instance documented in *Shri Sai Satcharita* (Chapter 11) is about an incident when flames from Baba's Dhuni rose up to the roof of Dwarakamai Masjid, threatening to burn it. Baba took his *satka* (stick) and started hitting a pillar, commanding the fire to calm down. At each stroke of the *satka*, the flames started coming down gradually. Soon, the situation became normal. Baba gave numerous other types of experiences to His devotees, but it is not possible to codify or cite all these examples here due to lack of space.

The more surprising and interesting fact to note is that, even after departure from His bodily abode in 1918 and till the present day, devotees continue to report similar experiences relating to Baba, some of which are in the nature of miracles. On the day Baba left His body and thereafter, devotees have been experiencing such unexplainable events. Such experiences of Baba are not limited merely to the gullible and uneducated rural folks of India, but cut across the intelligentsia of the society, including lawyers, professors, officials, doctors, scientists, and many others.

It is interesting to observe that even in this era of science and technology dominated individualism, with population (the number of devotees) having increased manifold, where rationality and objectivity rules the minds of the people, such spiritual experiences, at times bordering on miracles, continue to affect millions. Cutting across the man-made differentiations of race, religion, caste, socio-economic diversities, and so on, all are making a beeline to Baba's Samadhi at Shirdi, as Baba had once predicted in a state of spiritual ecstasy.

Despite the modern day youth's affinity with the western culture, Baba's message remains ever relevant and appealing to them also. Today's youth and children, with all their scientific temperament, are staunch believers of Baba and find Him to be the solution to all their problems. That is why so many temples have come up across the globe. Sai Baba not only crossed the boundaries of humanism, but also gave shelter to all living creatures. *Shri Sai Satcharita* narrates numerous instances of His acts of compassion towards dogs, snakes, horses, goats, tigers and even birds.

Today, on an average sixty thousand people visit Shirdi every day and on weekends the numbers go up to lakhs. The phenomenal growth in the Sai movement can be seen in the astronomical growth in the number of temples, literary publications, devotional music CDs and numerous TV coverages. The number of devotees dedicated to spreading the name and message of Shri Shirdi Sai Baba is mind-boggling. The Sai movement is no longer limited only to Maharashtra, as was the situation during the time of Baba. Within decades of His departure, it has crossed the national boundaries to become a global movement. This new era of *Sai-ism* does not only touch on the religious aspects of the devotee's life, but also affects and permeates all other aspects of his life — family, culture, social behaviour, and so on. For the devotees, Shri Sai Baba is not a just part of their life, but He is their life itself in all its aspects.

The spirit of Sai is more active and alive today than what it ever was. This raises a fundamental question — Who is Sai Baba? Some address him as a Sadguru, some as a Fakir, some as a Yogiraj, some as a Saint, and most of the devotees address Him as 'God, the Almighty' Himself. He has been accepted as an incarnation — *Saguna Sakara Avatara*, which means, God who walked on the earth in human form.

History has shown that the expansion of religions and faiths started by the incarnations expands phenomenally after they left their human embodiment. This was the case with Jesus Christ, Buddha, Mohammed and Shri Krishna. The Sai movement is on the increase exponentially in a similar manner, which goes to reinforce the faith that Sai Baba was an incarnation of God (Paramatma). It further goes to prove one of the promises of Baba that after leaving His body, He will be ever active from His tomb to protect and guide His devotees. As Baba had once promised, He continues to exist in a subtle form (*Mahakarana* sheath), as a unifying force, to spread and re-establish compassion, love, truth and tolerance amongst human beings and among all living entities on earth.

Let us welcome and embrace this Age of Sai, Who is the panacea for all the evils of the present world, torn asunder by forces of regionalism, racialism, economic and social differences, religious bigotry, fanaticism and lack of faith in God. Let us look forward to a happier tomorrow; let the name of Shri Sai resonate in all corners of the globe.

– New Year, 2007

10

Divinity in Sadguru

Guru and Guru Poornima

Guru Poornima is an auspicious Full Moon day, celebrated all over India by every sect of Hinduism, to pay respect to the gurus who impart religious and spiritual teachings to the disciples. The word *guru* here indicates a *Sadguru*, otherwise known as a Perfect Master or by the sufis as *Qutab*. Ordinarily, the word *guru* is used for any teacher imparting training in any field of knowledge, like a professor in a college or a music teacher. However, the word *Sadguru* denotes a personality so vast and universal that it is beyond the comprehension of an ordinary human being. Only spiritual seekers get a glimpse of the magnanimous personality of the *guru*, gradually, as they advance in their spiritual journey.

A Sadguru is one who leads the created to the Creator. Being himself beyond the multiplicism and dualism of nature, He has the power to pull human beings out from the illusions and limitations of nature imposed on them from birth till death. Some people think that training under a living Sadguru is essential for spiritual evolution in one's life. However, history reveals that even after leaving the body, a Sadguru continues the activities of protecting, nurturing and spiritually evolving His devotees in a subtle and inscrutable manner. Thus the Sadgurus play a vital role in the life of the devotee and thereafter as well.

Shirdi Sai Baba has categorically assured His devotees that He would be active from His tomb to render help to them and that even His bones will speak. It is because of this that the Sadguru is known as the Qutab in Sufism. Qutab means an axis around which the wheel rotates. Similarly, around Sadguru, the spiritual axis in the very existence of the devotee, rotates the life of the devotee. A beautiful depiction on the importance of the Sadguru in the life of the devotee is given below:

Dhyan-moolam Gurormurtih,
Pooja-moolam Gurorpadam,
Mantra-moolam Gurorvakyam,
Mukti-moolam Gurorkripa

It means that for the devotee, the Guru is the very basis (focal point) of meditation; the feet of the Guru are the object of his worship; the utterances of the Guru are his mantras and the *kripa* (grace) of the Guru is the basis of *mukti* (salvation). If one were to believe that spiritual progress is impossible without a living Guru, then how does a devotee do all that is prescribed in the Guru mantra mentioned above? History of different religions shows that after the *Maha Samadhi* (physical death) of the Guru, devotees still meditate on the Guru, worship the symbolic representation of His feet (made of metal or wood, etc.) and seek His kindness through prayers.

Even if the Sadguru is in a disembodied state, his *vakyam*(sayings), written and codified by disciples in the form of holy books, continue to have the same effects on the followers. This is not only true for Hinduism, but also for Sikhism as well. In Sikhism, after the Maha Samadhi of the last Guru, Guru Govind Singh, the Sikh religious scripture Guru Granth Sahib has taken the place of Sikh Gurus.

The experience of the devotees, in relation to Shri Sai Baba of Shirdi after He left His gross body on the 15th of October, 1918, is a witness to this eternal game of *Guru-shishya* interrelationship. Innumerable people are getting help by praying to Baba, at times even miraculously. Being in a state beyond the limitations of nature, a Perfect Master or Sadguru is as much alive without a body as with a body, in the time-continuum.

A Perfect Master is at first a perfect man, a *Satpurush*. A *Satpurush* means one who does not suffer any imperfections or limitations which the other creations of God, including other human beings, are subjected to. Only God is perfect and everything else is imperfect. The Sadgurus, evolving life after life, from the state of a normal human soul (*jivatma*), spiritually culminate to the state of complete divinity (*shivatma*). When this state of realization dawns on them, they are in a state of pure consciousness or pure divine state and are known as *Soham* (I am He), *Brahmosmi*, (I am the *Bramhand*) or *Anal-Haq* (I am God). Pain and pleasure, life and death, heat and cold, and such other varied attributes of the phenomena of the world do not affect them. As Divine personifications, they have infinite knowledge, infinite power and are in a state of infinite bliss.

The seventh spiritual stage of the Paramhansa is the highest level in the spiritual journey of the soul. At this stage the gross, subtle and mental bodies are totally annihilated. When they undergo annihilation of mind (*Manonaasha*), they are called by various names such as *Bramha-nishtha*, *Paramhansa, Turiya, Jivanmukta,* and so on. No matter how much one may try to understand or imagine about such a spiritual state intellectually, it is not possible to realize it without actually reaching that state.

Most of these *Shivatmas* remain in a state of perennial bliss of Divinity, even after leaving their body. They are *Jivanmuktas*, but that again is not the ultimate stage. This stage, which is also known as the *turiya avastha*, is not the final stage of the divine journey. A *Jivanmukta* has conquered the life-death cycles of nature, but he is yet not free from all the forces of nature (*prakriti*). The higher stage is that of a *Parammukta* or *Turiyateeta* (beyond Turiya state) or *Kaivalyateeta*. It is at this stage that the soul reaches its highest goal. He is beyond *prakriti*. Only the *Param Bramha* (the God Eternal) is beyond *prakriti*, as *prakriti* is the power of God through which He manifests in gross, subtle or mental forms.

The creative will of God to manifest is known as Ishwar or Bhagwan and the actual manifestation is known as Shakti. However, those in the stage of *Parammukta* have the highest divine power of creation, preservation and destruction. They carry out the universal work of God in the form of man on earth. It is these souls that come down to earth in human form to bring about spiritual evolution of the human beings. When embodied in human form, they remain simultaneously in the state of God and also in the state of man. They do not move around like mendicants, and are not bound by any scriptural injunctions. Their actions are universal and based on Dharma, cutting across religions, nations and all divisions of society. Even animals and birds are not treated differently by them. They are a law unto themselves and establish new ethical norms for upliftment of the society.

Shri Sainath Maharaj of Shirdi is in this stage of divinity. Let us, then, surrender to Him and worship Him for our spiritual evolution

— Guru Poornima, 1995

On Sadgurus

The Sadgurus or Perfect Masters are born at different times in different places and different cultural backgrounds. Their external situations may be widely different, but their actions in their embodied stage display a common theme and common approach to solve human problems through spiritual evolution. I have studied very extensively the methods adopted by the Sadgurus to solve human problems and to evolve themselves. One thing very certain about all of them is that some of their actions are extremely mysterious and beyond the comprehension of ordinary human logic. For example, at times they display extreme anger without any apparent cause, even to the extent of inflicting physical injuries on others, and the next moment suddenly calm down and shower their blessings as if nothing had happened. Many a time they seem to be restless, but nevertheless they maintain an inner calm even in the face of danger to life.

Shri Sainath, the *Param Sadguru* of our times, as also Swami Akkalkot Maharaj, Baba Tajuddin of Nagpur and other Sadgurus, used to go into tantrums and throw objects at their disciples who, strangely, used to get benefited after tolerating such activities of the Sadgurus. This goes to prove that even such so-called unsocial acts only benefit and do not harm the disciples. This is so because Sadgurus do everything with a divine intention, only to benefit others. *Shri Sai Satcharita* is replete with of such examples of kindness of Shri Sainath Maharaj.

The Sadgurus are generally surrounded by a swarm of devotees. At times, when they are expected to be vocal, they resort to silence or may even leave the place. It has been established that such incomprehensible activities have something to do with much wider issues attracting the attention of the Sadguru.

Sadgurus are unconcerned about social appreciation for their activities, because they are fully aware about the ultimate good that results from their actions, which no one else, however intelligent, is able to appreciate. However, the fact remains that whatever they do is ultimately for the benefit of mankind, because they are absolutely compassionate by their very nature.

Sai Baba

Old photo of Gurusthan

Baba at Chavadi

ORIGINAL PHOTOGRAPH OF SHRI SAIBABA
IN THE YEAR 1914.

Baba going in procession

Baba reading a book

Baba's love for children

Baba seeking bhiksha

Old Photo of Baba's Samadhi at Shirdi

Old Samadhi Mandir

Samadhi of Shirdi Sai Baba, 2014

श्री:

साईंनाथप्रभा.

SAINATHPRABHA

Kiran 1.

किरण १ लें.

साईंनाथ-प्रभा ही प्रकटुनि हृदयीं मावळो अंधकार ॥
मायेच्या संभ्रमाचें घन-पटळ उडो जें महा दुर्निबार ॥
श्रीच्या दिव्यप्रभेचे किरण नवनवे भक्तहृदांतरंगीं ॥
फांकोनी, चित्रकाशीं स्थिरतुं जनमता सर्वदा आत्मरंगीं ॥

प्रकाशकः
दक्षिणाभिक्षा संस्था, माईंआबाद-ऊर्फ (शिर्डी.)

किंमत ८-६-०]   [एप्रिल १९१६.

Front cover of the first issue of SAINATHPRABHA from the personal library of Shri C.B. Satpathy

Their divine consciousness is so universal that it encompasses within its fold all kinds of living beings on this earth and beyond. Many people think that the Sadgurus are aware of their divine power but pretend to behave like ordinary people. The truth is that they are in a state of pure consciousness, not affected by the three *gunas* (*tama, raja* and even *satwa*). They are like pure mirrors. When a person approaches them, his entire personality and his past, present and future are reflected in their mind.

As the mirror reflects exactly what the person is, but does not add anything, we call it only a mirror. The Sadguru is in the state of consciousness only. This means only existence. Therefore, whatever we project to the Sadguru, good or bad, will be accepted by him. He, being in a state of only consciousness, would absorb negative or positive traits of mind falling within the realm of three *gunas,* and would return pure consciousness, as He is nothing but pure consciousness.

That is why, always think of Sadguru, keep Him in mind in every small or big act you do in your life. At each step you take while walking along life, make Him a companion, for He is the only companion who walks along with the devotee during life and beyond life.

— Guru Poornima, 1996

Sadguru as Sakshat Parabramha

The ultimate God, the Ancient One or the *Paratpara Parabramha* is the non-manifested aspect of God and the non-realized aspect of Divinity. The manifested aspect of God, known as *Prakriti*, continuously goes through the triune cycle of creation, sustenance and destruction. Although

the three aspects are the parts of the same Divine cycle of
time, yet, due to functional division as conceived by limited
human intelligence, they are characterized as separate divine
personalities called *Bramha, Vishnu* and *Maheswar*. As far as
I understand, the same generative energy of divinity called
Bramha changes to *Vishnu* to sustain His own creation and
also later, as *Shiva* or *Rudra,* to bring it back to its primordial
substance, from where again to regenerate as *Bramha*. This
is called the 'Beyond State of God', whereas the *Paratpara
Parabramha* is called the 'Beyond Beyond State of God'.

Very few people in the path of spiritual evolution, spread
over hundreds of lives, reach the state 'Beyond State of God'.
Having reached that state, only a few of them, as a player in
the Divine game, come to the earth in human embodiment.
Some such souls, known as *Shivatmas,* remain in the God state
or the *Param Bramha* state, with all the attributes of God, that
is, unlimited power, unlimited knowledge and unlimited
love. It is this attribute of unlimited love or kindness that
forces some of them to come down to earth in human form
and ameliorate the misery of life-forms on earth. Such a soul
is known as a Sadguru.

When the Sadguru leaves His body, the same Divine 'love
aspect' operates through another body, ready for the purpose.
Someone may ask as to where does the soul of Sadguru go
after He leaves His body. The soul of Sadguru is eternal, all
pervading and always in the state of *Parabramha* or *Almighty*.
All Sadgurus are the same spirit and are within one another
as much as they are within God or in a State of God.

There are five Sadgurus guiding the affairs of the
Universe at any point—even today, and at all points of time
to come. For example, if an ant were to move on the body of
one Sadguru, the sensation will be felt by the other Sadgurus.
Their personalities may seem to be different, but their egos
are one—the ego of the Oversoul or God. Being in God State,
whatever they say becomes the Command of God for that
time, as also for all times to come.

While thinking of Shri Shirdi Sai in the context of His Maha Samadhi day, we must remember that Shri Sai, as the *Param Sadguru* is God, is in God and will always remain as God. He had embodied Himself for the suffering lot, and His kindness is unfathomable. His job is to carry out certain Divine duties of creation, sustenance and destruction, and to lead souls in their spiritual journey towards salvation. Even after leaving His body, He looks after His devotees and children as much today as He used to when He was at Shirdi. His devotees may be reborn, but Shri Sai will always be there to help and guide them towards their happiness and spiritual evolution.

We must, therefore, make Him our mainstay of life and pray to Him with our heart and soul.

— Maha Samadhi, 1998

God and Sadguru

Who is God or the Sadguru? This is a question on which people generally ponder, particularly the devotees of Baba. Through the medium of books, *mantras*, temple priests, pandits and saints, they try to get their answers. Hinduism proclaims that through *Karmayoga, Gyanayoga, Bhaktiyoga* and *Rajayoga*, God can be realized and be understood through a process of spiritual evolution.

The more the pain and misery in society, more the people seek divine compassion. Some people approach Mantrics, Tantrics and Astrologers to understand their future. Taking advantage of this situation, some characters are offering new pseudo-religious solutions and giving wide publicity to attract simple people. Some have given advertisements to say that they can rouse the Kundalini Shakti of anyone immediately. Others are selling various amulets and similar items, which, they proclaim, can solve the approaching human problems and ensure spiritual evolution rather easily. Without the least understanding about the lofty, difficult and sadhana-based path of Hindu Yoga Sastras, some characters are deceiving the people with self-created concepts, some of which are adopted from Indian and Western occult vocabulary. All the great saints had always warned people to be careful about such characters. Those who come under the influence of these characters waste a lot of precious time and money.

Even when the knowledge of God had not flowered in our minds, human beings did exist in God's creation. They were experiencing God at the level of their consciousness and experience, even though human language had not been created to codify them. Surely, the men of the Stone Age must have experienced God in them as much as the men in the Iron Age. The people of Mohanjodaro must have experienced God in a certain way, as did the Aryans who tried to experience Him through *yagnyas* and rituals. Even today, simple human beings are experiencing God at the level of their perception, even though they do not possess the language to describe their divine experiences. All this indicates just one thing, that God is what each person experiences. When we evolve tomorrow, we will perceive and experience Him differently. Anyone who has achieved some supernatural powers through Yoga practices will experience Him in yet another manner.

All other knowledge of God gained through heresay, or reading of books, etc., can be termed as *relative knowledge*, because it is not experienced. Since relative knowledge is not the real knowledge, it does not benefit substantially till *direct knowledge* is gained. The lives of saints like Kabir, Shri Sainath and Nanak, etc., became simple and pure because they had direct experience of God.

It is true that all rivers taking different paths, straight or crooked, will ultimately meet the sea. Similarly, all the paths that human beings adopt will ultimately lead to God. But will a traveller moving through a crooked, difficult and long journey reach the destination easily and safely, when moving along with a band of thugs and cheats? There is every possibility that the traveller will be waylaid and still more are the chances of his being robbed by the thugs, both of his money and time. Since such people know the art of attracting the travellers, there is a great chance that their spiritual evolution will be impeded. Hence a true guide is needed.

We worship our Sadguru Shri Sai Baba of Shirdi because, even after leaving His human form, this great divine soul continues to give us many divine experiences and bliss. He came only to give and had nothing to take. If we closely study the life history of Shri Shirdi Sai Baba during His stay at Shirdi for nearly sixty years, it becomes evident that He continues to give the benefits to His devotees, just as He used to do when He was in Shirdi in a physical form. Devotees of Baba, when constructing temples or doing any work in His cause or name, should not be proud of their doership, as the faith and strength to carry on such activities are given by Baba only.

The relation of the Sadguru with His devotees is not limited to one life but spreads over a number of lives. When a person is attracted towards the Sadguru, it is for sure that he must have accumulated a lot of merit in his previous lives. The most important role of the Sadguru lies in his great vision to convert the whole world into a family on this earth. Experience has shown that those people who render maximum possible help to others and who have created Sai organizations are the best recipients of Baba's blessings, if they have done so without seeking any returns.

Shri Das Ganu Maharaj spread the name of Shri Sai in every corner of India. Kaka Saheb Dixit contributed his best in forming the Shri Sai Baba Sansthan, as it is known today, and brought harmony among people through the *Sai Leela* magazine, which he started. Shama used to take part in functions arranged by many organizations and individuals on behalf of Baba. Mahalsapati and Tatya Kote Patel rendered immense service to Baba, being with Him always, and Shri Anna Saheb Dabholkar spread the name of Baba throughout the globe through his magnificent book *Shri Sai Satcharita*. Sai devotees take the names of these people today with devotion and respect, notwithstanding the fact that some of them did not have any formal education or degree.

But those unfortunate souls who, even when working in Baba's temples and getting the blessings of Baba, are not able to clear the mental cobwebs of negative thinking, surely create differences among the devotees and disturb the pious vibrations in the temples. Some of them are more demonstrative in their Bhakti to impress others, while nourishing ill feelings towards them. They will get inner happiness only if they correctly follow the path of Baba as reflected in *Shri Sai Satcharita*.

I may advise that people should focus their thoughts on Baba and His sayings as depicted in *Shri Sai Satcharita*, instead of running around here and there in search of God or for the evolution of their soul. Under all conditions of happiness and unhappiness, they should always remember and depend on Baba, as advised by Him. If they continue to do so with faith and concentration, slowly the deeper inner knowledge about Baba will be revealed to them and they will receive divine experiences. Only then their contribution to the human welfare will be distinctive and others will learn from them. A candle will light many other candles.

— Ram Navami, 2002

Justice and Compassion

God descends on this earth in different forms from time to time. He came as a king in the form of Rama, as a devotee in the form of Hanuman, as an annihilator of the oppressors in the form of Parasurama and even in the form of persons in the lowest rungs of society. God that manifests in the form of the Sadguru is the same God that manifests in the form of a devotee. When a devotee is paying obeisance at the feet of a Guru, God is a giver as also a receiver of the obeisance. Therefore, God and His devotee or the Guru and disciple are complementary to each other. The Guru and disciple together achieve the form of divinity and one without the other cannot represent divinity. If the devotion of the devotee and the acceptance of the Master are not working in the same frequency, then there cannot be a relationship.

The universe created by God is broadly ruled through two principles or systems. The first principle is the Law of Justice. It works like the Newton's Law of Motion of Matter, which propounds that to every action there is an opposite and equal reaction. This Law of Physics can equally be applied to the world of meta-physics and spiritualism, although in a subtler way. Such subtler principles of action and reaction taking place perceptibly or imperceptibly in the metaphysical world, are generally not understood by human beings due to the limitations of their cognitive faculty and brain capacity.

While holding that every action would necessarily have an equal and opposite reaction, Newton did not say that the reactions to such actions would necessarily be instantaneous. The reactions to such actions can be potentialized, to be kinetized later. This is similar to winding a coil, which stores potential energy and releases it in the form of kinetic energy later.

This mechanism of potentialization and kinetization of the impact of the actions of human beings is guided by certain invisible principles of nature. In Hinduism, this principle of Justice is stated as *Sanchita-Kriyamana-Prarabdha* theory of Karma. The *Prarabdha* Karmas are like a debit in a Chartered Accountant's books. They are supposed to be the reactions to the actions (bad, good or neutral) done in previous lives. However, the total quantity of such actions carried forward from past lives cannot be mitigated in one life. This total quantity of 'carry forward' is known as *sanchita*.

It may further be mentioned that the reactions to all the past Karmas cannot be measured in terms of the total volume of past Karmas. Such Karmas of past life mitigate item-wise. Since each and every action has to generate an equal and opposite reaction, it has to be highly specific in nature. Let us examine the reactions to two actions such as murder and ingratitude. A man who has murdered someone will be killed by the same person in one of the ensuing lives. Doing harm to a person who has done good is like double jeopardy in law. The first part is that the good done by that man will not be repaid and second part is the harm that we are doing in addition to the ingratitude. Human beings also commit good or evil deeds in the current life when suffering the reaction of past lives' Karmas. This Karma-syndrome is very complex and nobody has been able to understand it completely. As a result, human beings go on having an incalculable number of life cycles.

To save human beings from a cyclical fate, God created another principle of nature, namely the Principle of Compassion. God is the ultimate reference point in the universe. A state of being a Master or a Guru is a state of perfection to which human beings aspire to evolve. The Law of Compassion is the principle under which mothers give birth to children and rear them. All the so called *devatas* (deities) in Hinduism work through the Principle of Justice as stated above. Only Sadgurus, Qutabs, Perfect Masters, Pirs or Fakirs are the embodiments of this Law of Compassion. That is why we surrender to them and worship them.

May Shri Sai bless you all.

– Guru Poornima, 2009

11

Efforts at Spiritual Evolution

Atma Chintan

We often see people planning for their spiritual evolution. Some of them are of the view that spiritual practices required for evolution can only be initiated or started after attaining a certain age and physical condition. From my own experience and going through some of the available spiritual literature, I can say that spiritualism cannot be planned in this manner. We can plan for our personal and professional progress, but we cannot plan love or experience of God with such methodologies. Spiritual evolution is like a spontaneous organic growth which generates from love and is not built on logic alone. The entire human society has still not managed to produce a single Perfect Master from the intellectual class. Intellect by itself is a self-protecting, self-limiting and self-expansive propensity because of ego or 'I' factor. Therefore, man should try to shun his ego and mentally request the Master like Shri Shirdi Sai Baba to lead him on the spiritual path. ,

We can all see that ego in every form is self destructive and limiting in nature. Of all forms of ego, spiritual ego is the worst. We often see people starting to do pious work for Baba out of sheer love, but gradually the achievements take the form of ego and become a deterrent in spiritual progress. For example, while serving in the temple, if we nurture ego in our mind, then the temple becomes a place where the quality of love and togetherness is disturbed. Sometimes it is also seen that people show off their special relationship with Baba, which should definitely not be the case. Spiritual evolution cannot be based on a competitive spirit.

In the present times, a modern man cannot do Yoga or Yagya; so the simplest approach is to be in a constant mental communion or to keep Ishta or Guru closest to one's consciousness to engage in *swadhyay, atma chintan* and *satsang*. A lot of literature is available on Baba in which Baba's advice towards the adoption of these methods is clearly prescribed. One should read *Shri Sai Satcharita* every day before going to sleep for this purpose, so that one can keep Baba in one's consciousness.

Atma chintan means thinking on one's self. There must be some time during the day when one can muse over what one has read. One should consciously strive to find time to think about the Master and His sayings. The intensity of desire to read about the Master and to know about Him slowly brings out perfect love for the Master. Once love for the Perfect Master becomes unshakeable and established in one's heart, then anything can be achieved.

Satsang means being together and exchanging ideas with similar minded people. When a mass of devotees pray intensely, one can find a pouring of divine blessing from the Master. Therefore, the importance of the temples as instruments to encourage and provide a platform for group prayers, is clear. The *aartis* sung by groups in temples are indeed intended to invoke the Master by the group of devotees.

Swadhayaya, Atma chintan and *Satsang* create the right state of mind by evolving the required qualities of a devotee according to the Master's wish.

– *Maha Samadhi, 2009*

Absolute Consciousness

The Absolute Consciousness or the divine form of the *Divine Player* is the real entity behind the manifestation, sustenance and transformation of this phenomenal world. Whether we consider the created world to be the reflection of God's unlimited intellectual brilliance and enlightenment or simply a Divine Play, the created world is based on this Divine Super Consciousness, which manifests itself at different levels and in vivid forms. Everything that exists in this world, whether inanimate or animate, object or non-object (*vaastu* or *avastu*), all the species, existent or non-existent, are amalgamated or embedded within the Divine Super Consciousness.

Since pre-Vedic times, India's *seers* gave prominence to concentrating or meditating on *Tat Twam Asi* or 'Thou Art That' or 'You Are That.' The evolution of civilization may also be termed as the evolution of consciousness. The presupposition of the creation of the entire phenomenal cosmos is borne of that *Aham* or *I* of that Divine One. However, this *Aham* or *I* is not the same as commonly understood, but it is the fundamental power which is the root of the process of creation. 'I am in everyone, everyone is Mine, and therefore, everything is within Me.' This is what Lord Krishna preached Arjuna.

The human being is a very tiny particle of the Super Consciousness or the Absolute One. Generally, a person's life is based on a very narrow thought process and he remains caught within the extremely limited boundaries of his self-centred role in life — himself, his family, his desires, his achievements — and that is all. Growth of God

Consciousness occurs in the human being only when he expands his horizons beyond this limited boundary of his own and his family's needs and desires. Once this happens, his concerns and sensitivities extend beyond himself and his family and include other human beings and creatures. Then the awareness of divine existence and power are awakened in him. This awareness enables this small particle of the vast universe to become a part of the creative process and a part of the galaxies and even travel into and walk in space.

As soon as human concern and sensitivity, based on the power of love and power of desire, arises to work for the whole of God's creation, all conflicts come to an end and the *jiva* attains pure divine consciousness. This stage marks the end of the cycle of creation, sustenance and dissolution along the time continuum.

After transcending the concrete phenomenal world, the human being enters the world of *Vijñayan* or knowledge and then, transcending the world of knowledge, he finally enters the world of *Bliss*. Then, the individual *self* exalts itself to a state of Cosmic Consciousness, which is the state of *Paramhansa, Bramhastha, Jivan mukta, Tureeyaateeta,* and *Trigunateeta* (the Self emancipated from the bondage of the body despite being in the body) and attains the state of *Satchidananda,* that is, the *Real*, the *Consciousness* and the *Bliss*. Once this happens, the dialogue between Krishna and Arjuna in the *Gita* becomes meaningful, '*I* am in all, and all are *Mine.*'

This is the real form of Sai Baba of Shirdi. Let us meditate upon Him all the time.

— Ram Navami, 2009

12

Ethical Living and Conduct—The Essence of Spiritualism

Follow High Moral Principles

Devotees of Baba may remember that on one occasion, Shri Shirdi Sai Baba advised one of His devotees, working as a Magistrate, to maintain probity in personal and professional life. This is mentioned in *Shri Sai Satcharita*. The word *probity* means a high standard of moral behaviour and adherence to the highest principles and ideals—in short, uprightness in whatever one is engaged in doing. People from all walks of life, such as government servants, magistrates, revenue officials, tehsildars, mamlatdars, police officials, lawyers, artists and pilgrims used to flock around Baba at Shirdi, seeking His divine blessings, help and guidance in both the mundane and spiritual aspects of life. Baba helped everyone according to his need, without any considerations of religion, caste, creed, temporal status or social position.

Of all the advice that Shri Sainath Maharaj rendered to His devotees, the most important and common advice was to maintain uprightness and honesty in all aspects of life—religious, social, professional or personal. By asking the Magistrate to exhibit moral conduct in his profession, Baba gave the message that demonstrating the quality of righteousness in only one sphere of life, that is, in religious activities only, is not conducive to spiritual growth of an individual. Probity has to be practiced or adhered to in every sphere of life. It has to be a holistic approach. It has to be built in the personality of the seeker to be righteous and truthful.

In our ordinary life, we come across many people, who exhibit the quality of piety by donating a lot of money to temples, but shirk away from rendering any such help to their poor domestic servants, even if he or she may be in dire straits due to any reason such as the sickness of his or her child, etc. There are others who spend a lot of money and time on their pet dogs, but do not think twice before hurling abuses and even beating up urchins begging on the street. Such examples are too numerous to be described within the limited space of this article. Such people show contradiction between their thoughts and actions. They display their virtue selectively and at times simply for personal gain. Thus, the qualities of uprightness, probity and honesty are applied as mere utilitarian principles and not moral principles, as Baba had prescribed. One need not be surprised at such examples, because to be successful in the worldly life of today, most people take recourse to such behaviour. However, this approach is not conducive to those who are desirous of inner evolution. The method that Shri Sai Baba of Shirdi prescribed was to uphold the qualities of tolerance, compassion, uprightness, sacrifice and non-attachment, and to practice these resolutely in every sphere of life, be it professional, personal, religious or social.

Those who followed the preachings of Baba in letter and in spirit gained spiritual progress at a much faster rate than those who did not follow them. *Shri Sai Satcharita* cites stories of many such evolved souls during Baba's lifetime, such as, Megha, who maintained his qualities of truthfulness, faith and simplicity till his demise; Bala Saheb Bhate and Kaka Saheb Dixit who renounced the worldly life entirely on the bidding of Baba; and Mahalsapati, who maintained his non-attachment to materialism, till his end. These exalted and noble souls, and many others, who never faltered in sustaining their moral principles in life under the guidance of the Master of Shirdi, have been praised in *Shri Sai Satcharita* and elsewhere.

Therefore, it behoves the true Sai devotees to consciously try to improve upon and evolve the best qualities in themselves and put them in practice in all the activities they undertake. No doubt, this is not an easy thing to achieve, but steadfast love, devotion and unwavering faith towards Baba gradually brings out the best qualities in devotees. May Shri Sai bless us all, so that we are able to follow the path of righteousness and uprightness.

A number of Judges, Magistrates, Police officials, Revenue officials, Advocates and rich businessmen were Baba's devotees. Nanasaheb Chandorkar, Shri Hari Vinayak Sathe, and Bala Saheb Bhatte were Executive Magistrates; Shri Rege was a Judicial Magistrate who was elevated to the status of a High Court Judge (posted at Indore), Dada Saheb Khaparde and H. S. Dixit were prominent lawyers who fought cases in favour of Bal Gangadhar Tilak, Shriman Buti was the richest man of Nagpur and Das Ganu was a police officer.

Many other persons of prominence were ardent devotees of Baba. Their official activities were vital for the welfare of the society in which they used to operate. If they were corrupt and insensitive people, then the justice they were supposed to give to the general public would have been defective and harmful for the social good. On the other hand, by committing sins in being unrighteous, they would have added to the *papa bhandara* (store house of sins). Thus, it would have been a peculiar situation when Baba, the Master, would be trying to cleanse the negative and unrighteous qualities of their minds, but they would be trying to continue with their unrighteous practices and yet loving Baba. It is to take these out of such conflicting situations that Baba used to advise and even force them to maintain the qualities of probity and uprightness in public life.

For the devotees of Baba living in today's world, which is full of corruption and greed, it may be difficult to be absolutely honest in the personal life while adjusting with the society. However, they can and should try to maintain as much steadfastness and probity in their professional life as possible. While doing so, they may have to face some opposition from the dishonest ones, but my experiences in life convinces me that if one continue to pray to Baba when holding such high standards of conduct and character, one will always succeed in the end and gain everyone's respect. The devotees of Baba should never fail in moral values.

— Ram Navami, 2008

Essence of Spiritualism—Ethical Living

An in-depth analysis of the path shown by Shirdi Sai Baba leads to certain obvious pointers essentially required for spiritual evolution of human beings. Baba, during His interaction with a very large number of devotees of different religions and paths, had repeatedly brought out certain common emotional, psychological and physical parameters to be followed by the devotees. Although specific instructions were given directly or indirectly to most of the devotees to solve their immediate or mundane problems, yet the general parameters for ethical living and spiritual evolution were more profound and long term.

After Baba left His human form, those who followed the parameters and advice for the rest of their lives benefited immensely. Others, who deviated in the absence of interaction with the Sadguru, did not evolve much. This is the conclusion one is bound to draw when lives of the prominent devotees of Baba are examined as a whole.

These general parameters for a contented and evolved life have been brought to the fore extensively in *Shri Sai Satcharita* where it narrates devotees' real-life happenings at Shirdi, as also the anecdotes and interpretations pertaining to Shri Sai Baba. Most of the other books written on Baba have also tried to bring out these parameters in different ways. Thus, for a good disciple, the examples and anecdotes from the life of Baba and His percepts, as mentioned in *Shri Sai Satcharita* and other published materials, should work as the best reference points for guidance for ethical conduct and spiritual progress. This is why I always prescribe reading of *Shri Sai Satcharita*, in particular, and other related materials, in general, to the devotees and others following any path or religion. Whenever in doubt about his thoughts and actions, the devotee should try to relate them with the information on similar situations provided in *Shri Sai Satcharita*. He should always evaluate to find out as to how far he is able to progress with reference to the parameters such as the permanent principles of an ethical existence.

Baba has spoken about the loftiest principles in the simplest way while exemplifying these principles through his own conduct as well. For example, let us take the case of a man who spoke ill of another devotee to Baba when He was returning from Lendi Bagh. Baba told this man that pigs will only eat dirt even if they are given the best of food. The meaning of this sentence is too obvious to be explained. In another situation, while giving two rupees to a person who had helped Baba with a stepladder in going up and coming down from the home of Radhakrishnamayi, Baba demonstrated that one must pay for the labour rendered by any person. In fact, the entire gamut of all his advice reiterates the principles of ethical conduct reflected in *Shrimad Bhagavad Gita*.

The problem with some of the devotees is that they read *Shri Sai Satcharita* more intensely for its stories depicting miracles rather than for understanding the applied principles of ethical living as prescribed by Baba. Further, while carrying on their mundane deeds or misdeeds, they often forget Baba's advice at that moment. Therefore, they are prone to ask the same questions on various issues again and again over the years, whenever in trouble. What Baba wanted the followers to do is more to practice these principles than only to read about them. As Baba's intentions reveal, the question is not as to how many times one has failed while trying, but as to whether he is determined and remembers to apply these principles while doing any act, good or bad. Each devotee needs to ask this question to himself and find the answer. *Shri Sai Satcharita* can only give them guidelines.

– Maha Samadhi, 2004

Positive and Negative Thoughts

Any attempt to understand and value the spiritual world on the basis of the purely materialistic knowledge of the mundane world is an exercise in futility. On the other hand, one who has trodden along the spiritual path and has gained direct knowledge can handle the material world in a much better manner. Even if both spiritual and materialistic paths emanate from the same God, the spiritual path is finer and purer.

It is not possible for any worldly man to leave the material world and enter the spiritual world suddenly by his sheer will and volition. Such a path is for the true spiritual practitioners, known as Yogis, Munis or Sanyasis. The spiritual depth and value of these true spiritual practitioners cannot be assessed by seeing the examples of frauds who can be found everywhere these days. Yet, most of the gullible people get attracted to them because of their attractive attire and speech. Since most of the people live in this world of illusory greatness with a limited and distorted mindset, they easily get attracted to such actors. However, human beings who are purer and simpler in nature, instinctively do not get attracted towards them. Such people generally get attracted and attached when they come in contact with some purer souls like the genuine saints and Sadgurus. The impurer ones generally accept the impure persons projecting themselves as spiritual characters or Gurus. The purer souls accept only the true Saints as their Gurus. This obviously leads to the conclusion that one's Guru is what one wants and selects him to be. Or it may be said that the Guru is what one thinks him to be.

There are two types of people. Some of them are capable of seeing the positive side (*shubha*) of everything and there are others who are capable of seeing the negative side (*ashubha*) of everything. A man with an impure mental vision can cause much harm to himself as his mind gets contaminated with the negative traits of his own thoughts progressively. He ultimately becomes a prisoner of his own thoughts and sees the worst in everyone and everything around, even when he is in a temple or in association with the other purer souls. As the worldly people going through the experience of negatives and positives in life try to evolve themselves out of their negativities, so also the spiritually evolved souls — even those with a lot of positive qualities — continuously strive to eradicate the remaining negative qualities in them. Thus, all human beings, the evil and good alike, who are at different stages of consciousness, are in a continuous process of evolution.

The theories of different religions, as also the different theories of Psychology, agree on one point that ultimately a man's nature gets conditioned by what he thinks continuously. One who continuously thinks about the bad qualities in others, ultimately develops those qualities in himself. The same is true of continuous good thoughts. One finds an interesting story in *Shri Sai Satcharita* about this. A person used to speak ill of another person at Shirdi when Shirdi Sai Baba was there. Later, when he met Baba, He asked him to look at the pig devouring dirt with relish and commented, 'Look how happily he is eating the dirt. You have been speaking ill of your brother to your utter satisfaction and so your nature has become as evil.'

Thus, in this world of material illusions, even educated people, coming in contact with people harbouring evil thoughts against others, get easily contaminated. Far from achieving spiritual evolution, such an approach towards others ultimately leads them morally downwards. The best way to save one from such a situation is to pray to Baba when a negative thought comes to mind or to recite His name silently or read *Shri Sai Satcharita*.

– Guru Poornima, 2005

The Route to Purity

It has often been observed that some of the devotees and spiritual practitioners, whether they are followers of Shri Sai Baba of Shirdi or other Gurus or any Deity of the Hindu pantheon, enter into the subtle and sensitive world of faith, with certain convictions in mind. Such convictions do not get infused into the minds of the devotees in a perfunctory manner. When a new thought, inspires one to adopt a fresh approach to life, it takes the form of a mission. In the case of belief in God or Guru or Divinity in any form, it usually takes an extremely long period of time for the belief to settle down in the mind before one truly tries to convert the belief to an existing reality of life.

Let me try to clarify my statement. Let us try to examine the case of a person who has very little conviction about the existence of God or a divine force, even though he visits temples and willingly follows the prescribed rituals. He performs his actions as a socio-religious habit inculcated from childhood because he was born in a traditional Hindu family. He had learned all this from his parents, priests and others during the course of his childhood.

A majority of people of our society belong to this category. Nothing is wrong with them, but they are like this because the existing social milieu considerably conditions their minds. Such devotees can be seen in most of the temples, religious functions, ashrams and in large religious congregations like the Kumbh Mela. While performing religious rituals, they feel a sense of self-purification in themselves. They think that because they perform such religious activities, the stock of their *paap* (accumulated evil deeds from the past) will automatically get depleted. They feel free from their mental tension, having downloaded their past sins, present worries and future concerns to the guru or deity in whom they believe. Such a frame of mind, exhibited in temples towards the deity and for self purification is good.

But this is as far as it goes, because, generally, as soon as these persons leave the temple, the promises made before the deity or guru are conveniently forgotten. Many people, sooner rather than later, display the same evil propensities which they had earlier, when they go out of the temple. A few days later, they return again for the mitigation of their new sins and evil acts. In such a state, the relationship of the devotees with the God or guru becomes conditioned by their expectation from the God or guru to play the role of a benevolent provider and protector, notwithstanding their self-created and oft-repeated evil activities. More often than not, their feeling of repentance becomes as transient as their kindness towards the poor people on the street.

Such people, at times, display melodramatic exhibitionism about their spiritual attachment with the deity or guru. However, such pretensions do not build within them the inner strength to support them at the time of distress. This is so because they don't try to inculcate the qualities of *Shraddha* (faith) and *Saburi* (patience) so essential and required for spiritual evolution as prescribed by Shri Sai Baba of Shirdi.

The first step to evolve in the spiritual path is to truly repent for the mistakes done, not to repeat them and undergo self-imposed penance, howsoever severe. There are no short cuts to evolution, be it the evolution of nature around us or the nature within us. Therefore, realization of the weaknesses within himself is the first step towards self-realization by a devotee. A person may read all the scriptures, visit all the temples, practice all the religions or even worship all the deities, but spiritual advancement will delude evade him till he consciously tries for it.

At Shirdi, the old Fakir was ever vigilant about the thought processes of His devotees and used to influence their minds through various gross and subtle methods, day-in and day-out. One day, Baba taking the name of a certain devotee told the devotees around Him about what would happen to that person if He (Baba) was not awake to protect him.

May Shri Sai protect us from evil thoughts and lead us towards purity.

– New Year Message, 2014

13

Further Research on Shirdi Sai Needed

Sai Library

Shirdi Sai Baba has become a phenomenon today. This can safely be stated on the basis of the unexpected and innumerable gamut of activities taking place in India and the world over towards the propagation of the path and preachings of the Sai Baba of Shirdi. It is seen that, in the last few years, Shri Sai Baba Sansthan at Shirdi has expanded its activities manifold to cope with the ever-increasing number of visitors to Shirdi. This rate of expansion is very much expected, given the fact that on an average of about sixty thousand devotees visit Shirdi daily. On important days it goes up to a few lakhs.

What is amazing is the construction and opening of hundreds and hundreds of Shirdi Sai Baba temples and other related institutions in India and abroad through the self-motivation of the devotees. Shirdi Sai Baba had never set up any institution or mission. If one examines the way in which temples have been created by devotees following other paths or religions, it becomes clear that usually the main trust opens its branches at other places as the first step. Then the main trust and the branches take up temple construction projects which includes planning, financing, constructing, supervising, and so on. But in the case of Shri Sainath Maharaj, self-motivated devotees and groups are themselves arranging resources, constructing temples and carrying out a number of other religious and charitable activities, without any main organization controlling them. No doubt, such self-motivation is a result of the existing spirit of Shri Sai.

Most devotees of Baba are emotively linked with Him and are prepared to undergo any amount of hardship and sacrifice to perform a task in His name. The rate at which the number of His devotees and institutions are multiplying is simply mind-boggling. There are a number of publications about Baba in various languages in the form of books, journals, magazines, booklets, and their numbers run to thousands. Devotees are ever keen to know more and more details about Baba when He was at Shirdi and also the happenings of today, relating to Him. There are a large number of websites on Baba on the internet, created in India and abroad.

Notwithstanding these multi-faceted activities, one important aspect which is seriously required to spread the name of Shri Sai Baba is prominently lacking. Serious research on Baba, using modern research methodologies, is much below the desired requirement. Some scholars from India and abroad, independently or through research institutions, have made substantial contribution in the form of research and publishing books and research findings in the form of articles. However, a study of these volumes would indicate that the researchers or authors have not had access to many of the important documents published during Baba's time and thereafter. This is because, initially, most of the books and articles written on Baba were in Marathi language and English versions or original writings in English came to the market later. There is no library which has a comprehensive collection of literature on Baba.

To undertake serious research, a good library, which has the required documents like books, journals, newspaper articles, manuscripts, hand-written notings, photographs, paintings, sketches, maps, research papers and a well-maintained bibliography is a must. Unfortunately, no such library is in existence to enable the researchers on Baba to undertake serious study. Some devotees, particularly the writers, are in possession of some of the important documents, but what is needed is to create a single forum or body that possesses and maintains these for posterity. It should be the endeavour of each devotee to collect all such records of the past and maintain them properly for use by future researchers. This would be a great contribution for Baba's cause. Let us resolve to work towards this end in the New Year to come.

– New Year, 2006

Research on Shirdi Sai

Literature is a reflection of the times in which it is written. Good literature truly manifests the happenings and thoughts of its time. It works as a link between yesterday and today. Of all the literature that exists, that pertaining to different religious and spiritual movements on this earth is the most valued and permanent in nature. This is because the spiritual and religious movements are spread over millenniums, unlike other movements like social, economic, political, and so on. As history has shown, agrarian economy has changed to industrial economy; autocratic systems of government have changed to democratic systems of governance; monarchies have changed to republics; and closed societies have given rise to open societies. Notwithstanding all such social changes through thousands of years, Shri Krishna remains Shri Krishna and Jesus Christ remains Jesus Christ. They, or for that matter all such spiritual leaders, would always remain as the guiding forces of human civilization.

Given this backdrop, let us consider the vast amount of literature composed on Shri Sai Baba of Shirdi for over a century now. Shri Shirdi Sai Baba left His human embodiment in October 1918, and most of this literature has been produced after this. However, some literature, in the proper sense of the term, and some documents relating to Shri Sai, which later became part of literature, were available even before 1918.

These are:

- *Bhakta Leeleamrit* and *Sant Kathamrit*, the writings of Das Ganu Maharaj in Marathi Ovi poetic metre.
- Personal diaries of daily happenings at Shirdi maintained by H. S. Dixit, G. S. Khaparde and others.
- Correspondence between different devotees on Baba and Shirdi related issues. It is written in *Shri Sai Satcharita* that many devotees used to write letters to Shama, to be presented to Baba and would get their replies.
- *Sainath Prabha*, a bilingual magazine in English and Marathi, which used to be printed in Pune (then called Poona), was being published from Shirdi by Hari Vinayak Sathe.
- Literature by individual devotees like Bhim, Savitri Tendulkar, Upasani Maharaj, Vaman Rao Patel (Sai Sharan Anand), and so on, in the form of prayers, *bhajans, aartis,* etc.

In 1923, *Shri Sai Leela* magazine was published for the first time in Marathi by Shri Sai Baba Sansthan. In 1929, Govind Raghunath Dabholkar (Hemadpant) brought out a compilation of his notes and other devotees' experiences in the form of *Shri Sai Satcharita* in Ovi poetic metre in Marathi language, which has become a classic text on the life and teachings of Shri Sainath Maharaj.

In 1935, B. V. Narasimha Swami interviewed the then surviving devotees of Shri Sai Baba and published *Devotees*

Experiences under the auspices of All India Sai Samaj from Madras, in Tamil, which was later translated into English and other languages. Over a period of time, *Shri Sai Satcharita* also got translated into English and all the major languages of India.

During the last few decades, a host of Indian and foreign writers have written on Shri Shirdi Sai Baba. Some of them, like Antonio Rigopolous (Italy), Kevin Sheperd (United Kingdom), and Mariane Warren (Canada) have done research for their writings as part of their academic curriculum. However, original research on Baba was first undertaken by Das Ganu Maharaj, followed by Govind Raghunath Dabholkar and later by B. V. Narasimha Swami.

Yet, there is lot of scope for further research, not only at the personal level but also at an institutional level, by using the available modern research methodologies in various languages. Such research can be carried out by creating Chairs in universities, creating research institutes, academic research by scholars, publication of research papers in various languages, and so on. Sai Devotees would do well to encourage and contribute towards research on Sai literature.

— *Ram Navami, 2012*

14

Guru- Shishya Relationship

Learning Aptitude

The acceptance of the essentiality of a Teacher or a Master or a Guru is a universal concept in all human civilizations and at all points of time. This concept holds good for most of the aspects like education, research, music, dance, and so on, that is, anything and everything linked to the education of a human being from birth till death. Such teachers can be of a formal or an informal nature. For example, Lord Dattatreya, the Mahayogi and Siddha, proclaimed that he had twenty four Gurus from whom he gained knowledge. The twenty four Gurus in his case were not necessarily human beings, but included living and non-living entities like bees, elephant, moon, fish, python, fire, etc. However, by projecting these different entities as his Guru, Lord Dattatreya tried to impart a valuable message to the world. This message is so deep and universal that it cuts across all religions and all cultures. If one analyzes his statements, one finds that Lord Dattatreya has laid more emphasis on the learning capabilities of a student than on the teaching capabilities of a Teacher or Guru.

Let us talk, for example, about a bee being a teacher of a human being. No one can say that in the ladder of evolution, a bee is more evolved than a human being so as to be able to teach him. Why bee alone, if all the species on the earth are put together, they cannot match the intelligence of a single human being. In this case, the student's (Shri Dattatreya) mental faculties were so evolved and his thirst for knowledge was so focused that even from a less developed species like a bee or an element like fire, he could pick up important learnings about life.

This obviously implies that the importance of the student in the learning process is greater than the teacher. If the student or *shishya* has the passion to learn, the patience to pursue knowledge and the right attitude towards the Master, he can learn even from a distance. The story of Eklavya, in *Mahabharata,* is a unique example of a student who had truly and devotionally accepted Dronacharya as his Master. He could not be accepted by the Master as a disciple due to the existing social and caste divisions. But Eklavya was undaunted in his spirit and keen to learn, with the right attitude towards his Master. So he created a *murti* (symbolic representation) of his Guru Dronacharya, placed it in a certain place in the jungle and started worshipping in earnest faith. From this place, he used to observe the training imparted by Guru Dronacharya to the Pandavas in archery, with full concentration. Such was his potential that soon he excelled in the art and science of archery and became even better than the Pandavas. Such again was his faith in his Guru that, later, when his Master, Guru Dronacharya, wanted the thumb of his right hand as *dakshina*, Eklavya gave it happily, knowing fully well that without the right thumb he would not be able to practice archery for the rest of his life.

In Indian Hindu mythology, we find magnificent personalities excelling in their roles as *shishyas* (students). Some people are of the view that in the field of knowledge, both the teacher and student are equally important. But then, knowledge is meant for whom? It is meant for the one who does not have it and who has a need for it. The

Teachers (Masters) already possess what the student needs. The attitude of the one who needs the knowledge is more important and so the student should know the best way to extract the knowledge from the teacher.

Therefore, in order to gain any kind of knowledge, more so spiritual knowledge, the student needs to develop the right aptitude, sensitivity, strong determination and an intrinsic faith in the Master. This a vital and pious tradition of Guru-*Shishya* or Master-Pupil relationship is continuing in the spiritual tradition of India since long.

– Guru Poornima, 2011

Guru and Shishya

Some devotees are often heard to be saying that Shri Sainath Maharaj or Baba is either angry with them or is not taking care of them as He used to earlier, for reasons which they fail to comprehend or appreciate. Such an attitude indicates a highly personalized approach towards the Master.

It is a unique feature of the Sai faith that the devotees experience the personality and form of Baba even though His physical form is no more there. Psychologically, they depend a lot on Shri Shirdi Sai for solace, guidance and, more importantly, for getting a solution to their day to day mundane problems. For most of the devotees, He is a part of their lives. They worship Him, they read about Him, they meditate on Him, they do His *Naamjaap*, they talk about Him all the time without getting tired, hold *langars* in His temples and donate alms to beggars in His name. Some of the ardent devotees, before taking any food or drink, offer it to Baba mentally. Like children, they collect all sorts of photographs, trinkets and other articles related to Baba and show these to other devotees as their proud possessions. Such activities are a pointer to the fact that they are ever in search of Baba in their mind and soul and wish to establish an intense relationship with the Master.

It has been observed that when a devotee at first enters into the fold of Shri Sai Baba's divine and magnanimous personality, he gets attracted to Him quickly, in a manner that our ordinary human reasoning cannot explain. When Baba was in Shirdi, many of the devotees used to go into a state of spiritual trance or a sort of emotional hype at the very look of Baba. Such examples find a depiction in *Shri Sai Satcharita* and many other books, like Khaparde's diary. Such was the attraction of the Master that when a non-believer like Balasaheb Bhate met Baba for the first time, he looked at Him and just decided to stay back and settle down in Shirdi forever. Later, he resigned from government service, only to serve Baba for the rest of his life. Having renounced the world, he served Baba till the last day of his life and passed away at Shirdi.

Most of the devotees hold Baba's relations with them as their most prized possession. Before departing from His physical embodiment, Baba had assured His devotees that He would continue to protect them from His invisible abode. He had even said that whenever His devotees would call Him earnestly, He would make His presence felt in some way or the other and also render help to remove their difficulties. Incidents happening in the lives of most of the devotees after Baba had taken Samadhi show that Baba continues to keep His promise and help His devotees till today.

Thus, Shri Sainath Maharaj continues to render love, assurance and protection to all His devotees. At times, being busy tackling their earthly problems, the devotees are not in a position to remember Baba as much as they used to do in earlier times. In such a situation, they start feeling an emotional vacuum in their hearts. Let's compare this sense of void created in the devotee when the feeling towards the Sadguru reduces in its intensity with the example of the sun and sunlight. Rays of light continuously emanate from the sun and fall on earth. When the sky is clouded, the sun's rays cannot be seen but, nevertheless, the electromagnetic waves do fall on earth, having penetrated the clouds. Similarly, Baba's love and protection towards the devotees flows continuously, but some of the devotees do not experience it when their mind is engulfed with the worldly clouds.

Shri Sainath Maharaj often used to tell devotees at Shirdi, in no uncertain terms, that whoever offers prayers to Him with intense faith would certainly receive His grace, help and certain experience relating to Him. Once the emotional rapport between the Guru and the pupil is established, then the pupil is bound to go through a series of varied emotional experiences. Sometimes he will be flooded with loving emotions towards his Master and sometimes he will feel a sense of emotional void. This bipolar emotional oscillation is not due to the Master's changing mood affecting the pupil, as perceived by devotees, because a Perfect Master is a perfect soul. The reason for such a feeling in the devotee lies in the devotee himself. Hence, whenever such a situation arises, the devotee should not get bogged down under his own emotional pressures and feel frustrated. Instead, he should pray to Baba to stabilize his emotional faith towards Him.

Every devotee should try to understand that a Perfect Master has a thousand things to do at the same time for the benefit of innumerable devotees staying at different places. Therefore, to expect that the emotional needs of each devotee would be immediately fulfilled by the Guru is not the correct approach. Such an illogical mental state of the devotee only indicates a lack of faith in the Guru. If the devotee is convinced that the Sadguru is always busy in helping a large number of His devotees at the same time, he (the devotee) should take care to see that he does not disturb the Master on his frivolous issues. The best support a pupil can render to the Master is to leave Him to carry on His magnificent and universal work. This understanding on the part of the devotee will make the Master comfortable.

— Guru Poornima, 2007

15

Imbibe the Sai Spirit

Significance of the New Year Day

The beginning of a New Year does not really indicate a sudden change in anything in the life of an individual, society or nation. We all celebrate the First of January simply because it is beginning of a western calendar which has been accepted the world over as a reference point for measurement of time. Different days have been adopted as new year by the Hindu, Chinese, Muslim, and such calendars of the world. Nonetheless, the new year day gives the satisfaction of having completed a year and also raises hopes of a better tomorrow. However, wishful thinking alone for a better tomorrow does not automatically create anything good for anyone, unless one strives for it in right earnest. To create a better tomorrow, we have to forgive and forget the mistakes and pains of yesterday and go ahead. The happiness of a person lies in his capacity to learn from his past mistakes and remodel his life accordingly.

Therefore, we must muse on our mistakes and imperfections of yesterday and try to evolve, even if it is only a little, during the new year. Knowing that no ordinary mortal is totally perfect, we should try to find a model of perfection, which we can find in a Sadguru or Perfect Master, because the Perfect Master is, at first, a perfect man.

Shri Sai Baba of Shirdi, the Perfect Master of the Age, is our model to follow for many reasons.

He taught us that by loving our fellow beings and even the other species, we can create a healthy and happy society. He also taught us that rigorous and complex ritualistic methods need not be practiced for spiritual upliftment. All that is needed is to bring about a qualitative change in our way of thinking and acting in this mundane world.

He brought about a cohesive theme amidst the opposing themes of inter-cultural, inter-rèligious and inter-sectarian groups.

This He achieved by allowing each group to carry on with its own mode of living, religious and cultural practices, without disturbing those of the others. He created a way of life at Shirdi which reflected a confluence of different cultures and religions.

His simple act of accepting a piece of stale bread from an old, diseased and poor woman, when the more affluent devotees were offering Him the best of food, justifies the dictum that 'God loves the poorest of the poor.' His deployment of Bhagoji Rao Shinde, a leper patient, to take care of His body by applying balm to His wounds, indicates His love for the rejected groups of society. His residing in Dwarakamai Masjid and participating in Hindu and Muslim functions at the same time, indicates his equal respect for all religions.

This, then, is the real Sai spirit. If we are true Sai devotees, we must try to imbibe the Sai spirit. The best pledge we can take in the New Year is to decide to flow along with this Divine spirit that a confused and battered world of today needs.

— New Year, 1996

Love and Sacrifice

Time is a continuum. Therefore, there cannot be segments of time. However, human beings have created time sections called years, months, days. There are different calendars in different systems. The Chinese linked their calendar with harvesting and Indians linked it with trade practices. For the Sai devotees, New Year has a different connotation. For them, it infuses a new hope to start new ventures for a happier tomorrow. As tomorrow becomes a fact, yesterday becomes a fiction. Such is the game of illusion that facts become fictions and, at times, scientific fictions becomes facts. With physical death, life ends for most of us, whereas the fiction of our past existence continues for some generations. The entire endeavour of the spiritual seekers is to be in a continuous state of fact or reality (truth and *dharma*) and get redeemed from the fiction (illusion or *maya*). But at the start of the New Year, do we consciously plan to put in adequate efforts for making the year more meaningful?

Experience shows that mere intellectual endeavour, however potent and mighty, does not evolve any ordinary human being spiritually, without the support of a Spiritual Master. Most of the Spiritual Masters were uneducated in the formal sense of the term, for example, Shri Ramakrishna Paramhansa, Shri Shirdi Sai Baba, Namdeva, Tukaram, Paltu Maharaj, and so on. This obviously means that dry intellectualism has something self-limiting in it to evolve one in the path of spiritualism. All that a Spiritual Master spreads among His devotees is *bhakti* or devotion. *Bhakti*, in the general sense of the term, means love of God in any form. Since God can't be seen manifestedly in a form, therefore it is very difficult to generate devotion towards a formless entity. This is where a Sadguru or a Spiritual Master helps.

What we learn from Shri Sai and the examples of His lifestyle is that He went to no temples, followed no rituals, followed no specific religion or cult, but only loved His people and sacrificed Himself for them. Love, therefore, leads to sacrifice. The self expands from its state of esoteric or micro individualism to a more universal and macro state. Our New Year's Message, if it should mean anything, is, 'To love Shri Sai and love all the humanity He served.'

– New Year, 1997

Eternal Truth

A n analysis of the life of Shirdi Sai Baba would indicate that the advice rendered by Him and the examples set by Him can be considered to be the easiest path to spiritual evolution in the present world, in case they are followed in the correct perspective. As described in the Hindu scriptures, during the *Satya Yuga* the majority of people trying for spiritual evolution resorted to the path of meditation and righteous living. During the *Treta* and *Dwapar Yuga*, practices in Yoga and Yagya were adhered to as methods of spiritual evolution. In those times, people endeavoured and opted for a life of purity leading to *mokshya* (emancipation) and God-realization. Shri Krishna was born in the intermediary period between the *Dwapar* and *Kali Yugas*. For the spiritual evolution of the people in Kali Yuga, Shri Krishna has prescribed various methods described in the *Gita*. Would one try to find the actual application of the principles enumerated in *Gita* in the life of anyone, he can find it in the life of Shri Sainath Maharaj.

During the *Satya Yuga*, a majority of the people accepted spiritual life as the real life and did not give much importance to the worldly life, considering it to be illusory, temporary and painful. The realized souls of that time, known as the

Great *Rishi*, established a social order which contained inbuilt norms and principles for the spiritual evolution of each and every person.

After the *Treta* and *Dwapar Yugas,* the number of people consciously striving for spiritual evolution gradually reduced and the people afflicted with worldly desires increased progressively. On completion of the *Dwapara Yuga,* the realized souls had to prescribe simpler methods for the people of *Kali Yuga,* towards their evolution. The social, economic and ethical norms having undergone a sea-change during the last few centuries all over the globe, difficult methods like Yoga, Sadhana, etc., prescribed earlier would have certainly been difficult for most of them. *Kali Yuga* has crossed more than 5,100 years of its age and during this period the number of persons with evolved spiritual potentiality has greatly reduced in its materialistic world.

Even though the path needed for spiritual evolution in the present age has been made simpler, yet the intellectual potentiality to understand the subtle world of nature or of God is greatly lacking in the people as their minds are more worldly oriented. Under these conditions, the easiest path is *naam smaran* or 'Remembrance of the name of God or the Sadguru,' constantly. Sai Baba once told His devotees that 'I went on repeating the name of Hari and my troubles ended.' He used to advise the devotees visiting Him to read books on different religions and spiritualism, to remember the name of God constantly and to have a righteous living.

Although the population of the world has multiplied manifold, yet the number of true and spiritual persons, in comparison to the last three *yuga,* has reduced substantially. On the other hand, the number of people afflicted with family and worldly miseries has increased substantially. There are examples of many saints who had families but were also spiritually realized, in the earlier *yuga.* The ancient *rishi* like Atri and Gautam had families, but maintained their spirituality through rigorous spiritual practices. But today's man, engrossed deeply with the worldly problems, is painfully convinced that he cannot get out of these problems and, hence, cannot evolve. He is desperately trying to find a path, a direction, which would give him an independence from the worldly encumbrances. But he is not able to find a way. In spite of all the technological and scientific facilities provided to him, a feeling of hollowness, restlessness and desperation goads his life.

An evaluation of the role of Shri Sainath Maharaj, as depicted in *Shri Sai Satcharita*, would show that He tried His best to pull these household people, having mundane responsibilities, into the path of spiritual evolution through many perceptible and imperceptible methods. No doubt, some Sadhus, Fakirs and Yogis used to visit him often, but even at that time their number was much less than the number of household people visiting him.

Most of the families of Shirdi were connected with Shri Sai Baba. For example, all the family members of Shama, Tatya and Mahalsapati were attached to Baba. Some families even constructed rest houses (*wadas*) at Shirdi to stay for long periods. Many people like Megha and Vijayananda came from outside and even breathed their last at Shirdi and all those who came from outside were taken care of by Baba.

These people came from different strata of society, with different professional backgrounds and also used to believe in different traditions of worship. Yet all of them used to gather around Baba for His guidance and support for the fulfilment of their temporal and religious aspirations. Thousands of families, from many different places, used to visit Baba regularly, just as many do today, with an ever increasing number. However, a study of the available literature on the contemporary activities at Shirdi would show that comparatively very less number of people have been approaching Him purely for their spiritual evolution.

Yet, the lives of all these people had become simpler, purer and peaceful after they came in contact with Shri Sai Baba. In spite of their struggle for existence, they did evolve spiritually to different levels of their consciousness under the close guidance of Baba, the all knowing Master.

Today, the number of such family members have multiplied a thousand times, but the number of devotees seeking purely spiritual evolution has reduced substantially. I am not mentioning here about those handful of people who are quietly striving for their spiritual evolution and that of the world as a whole.

Today millions of people in India and abroad are trying to follow the advice and precepts of Baba, having accepted him as their Master, within the limits of their intelligence, faith and capacity. It has been experienced that if a person develops faith in Baba, gradually his negative qualities like restlessness, selfishness, etc., reduce and good qualities like kindness, tolerance and honesty increase.

The greatest contribution of Shri Sainath Maharaj is that He stands like a beacon-light in the tempestuous and darkened ocean of this *Kali Yuga,* singing to His devotees a soothing melody of loving assurance and keeping His compassionate hands on them. He is saying, 'When I am with you, why do you fear?' To those who are lost in the whirlpool of worldly sufferings, Shri Sai Baba is assuring that 'You can have spiritual progress and even in this evil world, full of trials and tribulations, you can realize God and emancipate.' Baba further tells us that 'For this you do not have to strenuously practise Yoga, *Tapa, Dhyana, Hathayoga* and so on; only take my name, meditate on me with or without my form, follow my advice and make me the very basis of your existence, with faith and patience, believing that I am always with you.'

Baba proved what He preached through his own examples. What He means to tell all His devotees can be put in the following words: 'You see me in this world in the poor you help; you see me in the kindness you extend to the distressed; you see me when getting rid of debts; you see me when getting rid of hate and anger; you see me when caring for your children; you see me in loving your neighbours; you see me in fulfilling the promises you have made; you see me in getting out of greed and you see me in every religion, every guru and every pure thing around you.' The gist of all that He said in *Shri Sai Satcharita* is that while staying in the society a person should look at Him and should test the level of his faith and purity with reference to the ideals set by Him.

In today's world, it is not easy to follow and practice all that has been mentioned earlier. Baba knew that His devotees would fail many a time and, therefore, will feel without hopel and restless. To encourage them, He said: 'Do not be desperate, my child. If you take one step towards me, I shall take ten steps towards you. It does not matter how many times you fail, but try to proceed step by step towards your goal. As I am your mother, I shall, therefore, accept both your virtues and sins, your purities and impurities, equally. Therefore, till the last moment of life, depend only on me. It may take a few lives, but do not be desperate because whatever good acts you do, will never go unrewarded.'

In order to convince His devotees about the continuity of life cycles of human beings, He spoke about the past lives of many of His devotees (mentioned in *Shri Sai Satcharita*) and has promised that in all their lives, He will be responsible for their protection and evolution. We do not know whether His devotees like Kaka Saheb Dikshit, Shama or others are born again and, if so, where they are, but we believe that in whatever form they are, Shri Sai Baba is taking care of them. Then what is there to fear? When the Sadguru is with us life after life and keeping His promises, then why should anyone be desperate, why should anybody feel hopeless and agonized?

In today's world, it is difficult to go through the four stages of life (*ashram*) as prescribed by Hinduism. The *ashrams* are— *brahmacharya, grihastha, vanaprastha* and *sanyas.* Therefore, Baba had shown the way to His devotees to go through these four stages of life even when staying in the family. Baba held that the institution of family is one of the most difficult *ashrams*, but even being a family man one can carry on the activities of all the four *ashrams*. Upasani Maharaj, who was a married person, was asked to stay for years in Khandoba Mandir at Shirdi. Kaka Saheb Dikshit, whose family was at Mumbai (called Bombay in those days), was asked to stay at Shirdi. Similarly, many other devotees came, from time to time, and stayed at Shirdi and had spiritual evolution and emancipation.

It has been experienced that one can evolve out of his miseries, hopelessness and desperation of the domestic and worldly life and evolve spiritually even in this *Kali Yuga,* if he follows the simple path prescribed by Baba, with faith and patience. The fluttering flag atop the Shri Sai Samadhi Mandir at Shirdi announces this eternal truth, saying:

'Do not fear when I am here.'

— Guru Poornima, 2002

The Sai Spirit (Vasudeva)

Ever since the phenomenon of Shri Shirdi Sai caught public attention in India and outside, there has been a relentless stream of speculation as well as concerted effort to answer the question whether He was born a Hindu or a Muslim. The result of research by different researchers has turned out to be either speculation or controversy, since it is based more on circumstantial evidence, as opposed to primary data. However, my efforts are channelized into finding out who and what Baba is rather than what was His parentage or where He was born.

There can be no denial in any quarter that Shri Shirdi Sai Baba is a divine personality of the highest order Who demonstrated magnificent qualities of selfless service to all who came in contact with Him, with least consideration of His self. He was not constrained by the limitations of any organized religion or path, as is amply evidenced by His acceptance of disciples from all religions, cultures, castes and paths. There was no question of economic and social differentiation in His scheme of things. Besides non-possession and non-attachment, He was divinely magnanimous and empathetic towards the poorest of the poor among His devotees, as well as animals and birds. He also possessed wonderful powers of miracles, which He often used to help His disciples in distress, even from a distance.

Given this universal theme of His approach, one can safely conclude that Shri Sai Baba demonstrated the highest qualities of Hindu philosophy in His actual life, notwithstanding whether He was born of Hindu or Muslim parentage.

When one speaks of Hinduism, at first one has to understand as to what Hinduism stands for in its essence. Some historians comment that the word *Hindu* was originally *Indu* representing *Indus Valley Civilization,* but some foreigners say *Hindu* represents *Hindukush* mountains. Hinduism, in its quintessence, is 'a way of life' rather than merely being a Hindu path of worship of deities. It prescribes numerous paths to its people and leaves them free to choose any one. It prescribes the worship of a number of divine forms (*devatas* or *devis*) and also the worship of the formless (Bramhan — the ultimate God).

Hinduism does not insist or force conversion of people to its fold and, failing that, their extinction. It has never believed in religious expansion with the help of sword and always believed in the peaceful coexistence of all religions. This highest level of tolerance of the Hindus has led to the absorption of many conquering or colonizing races, each following a different path, into its all-embracing fold. Sufism, which truly believes in the unity of souls and tolerance among people following different paths, therefore, found a strong base in India – the soil of the Hindus.

Basically, what Shri Shirdi Sai Baba practiced and taught is spiritualism and humanism, as against bigotry, obscurantism, blind faith and intolerance. To that extent, He was a genuine Hindu and a genuine Sufi, amalgamated into a single human form. He often used to say 'Allah *Maalik hai'* or 'Ishwar *achha karega'* or '*Sabka Maalik ek hai'*, that is, the one and ultimate God called Ishwar or Allah is the sovereign power who controls everyone and everything. This is the monistic *advaitya* philosophy of the Hindus.

On the other hand, He never deterred His Hindu devotees from going to any temple to worship any deity of their faith. Similarly, he never stopped the Muslims from taking out the Tazia procession, or doing anything prescribed by their religion, at Shirdi. Indeed, He encouraged both religions and ensured, at Shirdi, tolerance towards the religious sentiments of devotees practicing various faiths, through mutual participation in one another's festivals.

Not only to the residents of Shirdi, but also to the outsiders who used to visit Him in great numbers, He was not only a Guru, but a part of their entire existence. Shri Sai had permeated into all aspects of the lives of His devotees – religion, family, festivals, way of earning and spending, social conduct, moral conduct, cultural activities, births and deaths, diseases and cures and even regarding the rearing of children and pets. Baba's influence has been so strong and wide that often two or three generations of family members would come to Shirdi, together, to seek His blessings and advice on various matters.. Everyone looked up to Him as a God in human form and also as the head of the family and surrendered to Him.

The way of life, not only for the natives of Shirdi, but those visiting Baba, metamorphosized to a new way of looking at life, which Baba taught them through His conduct and precepts. Thus, like Hinduism, the path shown by Shri Sai has become a way of life for His devotees, rather than a religious and ritualistic path alone. Even today, the same Sai spirit pervades the lives of millions. It is because of this universality and simplicity that He is accepted by all and He is being worshipped.

This is what explains the unimaginable expansion of the Sai path, not only in India, but in other countries, too. Shri Sai remains, as promised by Him, a living Master, with His all-pervasive spirit that controls the entire life of His devotees. Such a magnificent, universal and timeless divine personality is termed as *Vasudeva* in Hinduism. And the spirit of Shri Vasudeva is eternal.

– Guru Poornima, 2006

16

Lessons from Some Animal Habits

Lessons to Learn

From the welfare of the universe comes the well-being of the self. This statement is difficult for an ordinary man to understand, because he is intelligent and also has an ego. However, in our world where human intellect is not so evolved, this truth becomes evident. Moving in single files, ants organize their work. The honeybees live harmoniously together in one beehive. When an ant collects any food material or when the honeybee collects nectar from flowers to make honey, it, at that point of time, it does not think that it is merely for itself. If one minutely ponders over the behaviour of the ant, then the question arises — what if the ant decides to eat the collected grain itself, or store it for its own use in future in the ant nest? Then, what would be the fate of the ant community? If that happens, neither would it be possible to be able to help one another in a state of emergency, nor would it be possible for them to protect themselves when invaded by other pests and insects.

The purpose of this reference is that the life of living beings is based on social and community living, which is the law of nature. However, man behaves in a way that is unlike the natural lifestyle of other beings. Using his intelligence, man's vision of survival is diverted from caste, religion, country and is aimed at his own natural self. Conflicts, wars and other incidents continue to take place when one overlooks the universal interests.

It has been observed that the flight of birds in the sky or a herd of animals roaming in the jungles takes place in a definite pattern. They do not require any written guidelines or laws, because they naturally modify and adjust themselves according to the requirements of nature, which we call discipline. On the other hand, in spite of being more intellectually sound, though man has created many rules to be followed, yet he remains essentially disorderly. In the human community and history, the terror of wars repeatedly reminds us that, till the time human race continues to move without understanding the laws of nature, and moves merely self centredly or with restricted thought processes, till then there shall be no peace established on earth. No matter how much intellectualism human beings demonstrate, until they follow the edicts of nature, they cannot take pride in calling themselves civilized.

The value of human civilization cannot be considered greater than the value of nature. In reality, following the guidelines of nature spontaneously, the animal world is far more civilized than the so called intellectuals or humans. While a dog can give up his life to save his master from assaulters, yet when the same dog ages, it has also been seen that the same master does not take care of it and lets it go unattended. The greater irony is that, in some countries, with advancing age, those beings who are of no more use to man, are poisoned or shot dead. If the same principle of conduct is applied in the case of human beings, then should all the disabled and aged people be killed? In the town of Sparta during ancient times, girls were sacrificed, as they did not have enough physical strength, due to which they were unable to fight wars as their male counterparts could. Hence they used to be exterminated. Should and can this principle be applied today?

Was it right for Hitler to kill the Jews due to their religion? Human society, which is controlled by the mental trait of selfishness, has been continuously committing major sins. The strange part is that it is being justified with doctrines based on faulty reasoning. Even historians have recorded it all with a very narrow vision. At times, it seems that even history has not been written truthfully.

This is why, instead of limiting man's lofty and expansive consciousness to humanism alone, it has to be extended towards other living species as well. Mere animistic practices would not be enough. It is also incumbent on us to protect the entire creation, and balance must be maintained with it, as per the laws of nature. Therefore, it has been said *ahimsa paramo dharmaha* (non-violence is the greatest virtue). But this belief in non-violence should not be restricted to merely man or other beings; it should also be extended to trees and plants. Since plants also have life, they are sensitive to violence, a fact that has been scientifically proven by the great Indian scientist Shri Jagadish Chandra Bose. The main reason behind the disasters like land erosion, earthquakes, floods, air and water pollution in today's world is that man has not adopted the right perspective towards holistic welfare, for thousands of years.

Shri Sai Satcharita mentions an incident that took place in Shirdi. Shri Sainath was physically hurt when His horse Shyamsunder was caned. And when the hungry dog was beaten up and chased away, Shri Sainath Maharaj had told Upasani Maharaj that He was in that dog and had come back hungry from Upasani's place. If we evaluate these two events in detail, then we get to know that He has put forth a great and expansive principle of animism before us.

If, (on this Guru Diwas), we wish to see the real Self of the Sadguru, then we must look into each living thing — be it a man, a creature or nature — the Sadguru must be seen in all.

— *Guru Poornima, 2001*

17

Sadguru and Shakti Pooja

On Maha Shakti Pooja

Durga Pooja or Dussehra is basically a day of *Shakti Pooja*. *Shakti* is the manifested and creative form of God. It manifests from the *Param Bramha* and rests in *Para Bramha* in a dormant state when not manifested. Thus, there is no difference between the *Para Bramha (Purusha)* and His *Maha Shakti (Prakriti)*. Adi Shankaracharya, at the height of his spiritual realization, came across this truth and realized the power of the *Maha Shakti*. *Maha Shakti* takes different forms, symbolically represented by the various *devas* and *devis* (called *Daivi Shaktis*). In the Hindu mythology, each of these *Shaktis* has a specific role for the fulfilment of the Divine Will in the cosmic cycle of creation, sustenance and destruction of the Universe.

In front of these *Shaktis*, human beings are too small to be mentioned. A human being becomes miserable if any of these *Shaktis* abandons him, for example, speech, hearing, and so on. The *Shaktis* work both at micro as well as macro levels in everything in the universe. They operate in atoms (Quantum Theory) and also in the space (Relativity Theory). Goddess Kali is said to be the ruler of *Kala*, that is, the time-dimension and Goddess Tara is said to rule the space-dimension of the Universe. It is said that Bhadra Kali (Kali in a certain mood of action), is said to be yelling because she feels hungry even after swallowing a few universes.

The beginning of the universe is said to be the beginning of time or *kala*. However, no one knows when time actually started and why. Similarly, the form of Durga, or the activities of Durga, indicate the force which, having annihilated the destructive forces of nature, established supremacy of the creative forces of the universe. Durga *Shakti* contains within it many other *Shaktis* like the Dasha Mahavidyas, eighteen Matrukas and sixty four Yoginis, etc. It is difficult but necessary to please these *Shaktis* to be able to live a meaningful life. Many fraudulent persons are seen these days to be bragging about possessing some such *Shakti* through certain *sadhana*. Innocent people fall into their trap and lose their money and mental peace as well.

Those who make self-advertisement through various media about possessing tantrik powers are the most dangerous of the lot. I have seen many innocent people being fooled by such tantrics. Please be assured that to find a real tantric in India is one of the most difficult things today. After Shri Ramakrishna Paramhansa, who practiced tantra, there has not been another person like Him in India. The *Shaktis* or Powers can be acquired only through rigorous practices of *Raja, Gyan* or *Hathayoga* under a spiritual master.

The Sadgurus are the repository of all *Shaktis* because they fulfil the wishes of God on earth as His medium. Therefore, all *Shaktis* of the *Pura Bramha* assist them. Whenever we surrender to a Sadguru, the support of whatever *Shakti* is necessary is provided by Him, whether it is for material benefit or spiritual upliftment. Shirdi Sai Baba has shown Himself in the form of different Deities and *Avatars* to some of His devotees – Vishnu, Maruti, Krishna, Shiva, etc. On the day of Dussehra, He is to be worshipped as Durga or *Maha Shakti*. Whatever He is, for us He is our most dear, most loving and most caring Sai. He is our father, mother, friend and Guru.

– Maha Samadhi, 1997

18

Meditation

Purify the Mind

The word *meditation,* as is generally understood, means to focus one's mind for a period of time for spiritual purposes. It also means to think carefully about something, in the sense of contemplation. In the Spiritual Science of India, meditation is prescribed as a method of spiritual contemplation of God (with form or without form) and Guru, the Spiritual Master. Some people, at times, use the word *concentration* as a synonym for the word *meditation.* The generic meaning of the word *concentration* is to focus all of one's attention on a certain thing. This thing can be a book, or a piece of music, or anything else of our everyday life. While enjoying or doing something for which we have a passion, we do concentrate. Sometimes, when reading a book of interest, we are so intensely focused that we lose the sense of time.

However, in the spiritual world, one does not say that he concentrates on God, even if concentration is the most essential component of meditation. Meditation can be said to be concentration plus something more. The plus factor here means a divine or spiritual aspect.

When one says that he meditates on God, or practices meditation, it means that (a) the practitioner has stationed or seated himself in a certain place, (b) he focuses his attention on God, Guru or *Ishta* (personal deity) with form or without form (*saguna* or *nirguna*), (c) he continues with the activity for a certain period of time as desired or prescribed, (d) during such period of meditation, he starts losing awareness about the surroundings and his own self, wholly or partially.

It is extremely difficult for a person to meditate, in the true sense of the term, when he is walking, although one can meditate when lying down in a sleeping posture. Only the God-intoxicated persons can meditate even when walking or standing as they are, at times, oblivious of their physical existence.

That is why the Hindu Spiritual Science (Yoga) prescribes certain physical *asanas* (postures) like *padmasana, siddhasana,* etc., as a *sine-qua-non* for Yogic meditative practice. Generally, the practitioner is advised to meditate, sitting at a particular place (on the ground), using a mat made of wool, cloth, grass, etc. Some Yogis, who are at an advanced stage of evolution can meditate sitting on a chair or bed. Some people even use tiger skin or deerskin for the purpose. Yoga also prescribes doing meditation while facing a certain direction, mostly towards East or North. With some exceptions, meditating while facing South is not prescribed. The practitioner is supposed to wear a clean and loose garment (to avoid tightness and avoid physical discomfort), after a bath, etc., so that during meditation his mind does not get diverted due to physical discomfort.

The *Sadhaka* (Spiritual Practitioner) is supposed to meditate quietly in a place without noise or commotion, as the mind is prone to get diverted. However, some devotees, sitting amid the hustle-bustle of a temple, are found to be struggling for concentration, with loud pitched music (*aarti, bhajan* or *naam smaran*) going on in full blast. No doubt, there is a science of meditation and the pretentious act of meditation does not bring any benefit.

Another factor that the Hindu Yogic Science adds to the acts of meditation is *pranayam*. In short, *pranayam* means control of *prana* (the vital force of a living organism) through a method of breath control. *Pranayam,* if done properly, helps in concentration. It also gives good health and longevity, which helps the Yogi to carry on his practices for a long period of time. In *Hathayoga,* usually *pranayam* is practiced intensively.

Sai Baba does not seem to have prescribed practices in *pranayam,* although He has never spoken against it. Nor did He ever ask His devotees to practice *Hathayoga* and other types of Yoga. He only asked His devotees to simplify and purify their mind through reading of religious books, listening to and participating in spiritual discourses and music (*aarti, bhajan, naam smaran,* etc.) and meditation. He has also spoken about the method of meditation on Him (with form and without form) as mentioned in *Shri Sai Satcharita.*

Without being aware of the prerequisites of meditation, some people seem to be satisfied with their own system of meditation. Such practices may yield some benefit, but they may not lead to the right path as desired. Let us, then, meditate on Shri Sainath Maharaj, as advised by Him and as mentioned in *Shri Sai Satcharita.*

Jai Shri Sai!

— *Maha Samadhi, 2011*

19

Navadha Bhakti

Navadha Bhakti and Ram Navami

A lthough no one knows for sure about the day on which
Shri Sainath was born, as per the traditions adopted
by the devotees, Ram Navami (ninth day of the bright half
of *Chaitra* month in Hindu Calendar, that is, March–April)
is celebrated as Baba's birthday. Shri Ram epitomized
moral excellence as against Ravan, who displayed moral
degradation. Through millennia, such personalities have
been using their Divine powers, either for benevolence, that
is, doing good to others, or for degradation, that is, using evil
forces to harm others. No other species, except the human
race, can reach such heights of good or evil because they are
endowed with superior intelligence. There is a saying that
'God built human beings in His own image' and also that
'There is a God and a devil in every man.'

Shri Shirdi Sai had reached a state of consciousness which
was beyond the limits of the space and time dimensions.
His personality is universal and reflects the quintessence of
human virtues of compassion, truthfulness, protection of
others—the same virtues present in Maryada Purushottam
Shri Ramchandra. Hence, this logical correlation of
celebrating His birthday along with the birthday of Shri Ram
by the devotees.

But, what are the examples and precepts exemplified by Shri Sainath Maharaj for unfolding the spiritual excellence among the devotees? Baba used to take the name of Shri Ram frequently when talking to His devotees and used to advise them to read books like *Ram Vijai* and *Ramayana*, etc. He used to advice His devotees to imbibe, to the extent possible, the noble qualities of Shri Ram, the Maryada Purushottam.

Navami means the ninth day of the Moon. It is an astronomical reference point in the Hindu almanac. We will understand the spiritual significance of Ram Navami better by interpreting Navami as *Navadha Bhakti (nine types of devotion)* to bring spiritual evolution.

Navadha Bhakti means nine-fold devotional approach to God or *Sadguru*, that is, *Shravan, Bhajan, Smaran, Dhyana,* etc. There is a long description in *Shri Sai Satcharita* about this. At the time of His Maha Samadhi, Baba had given nine rupees to one of His ardent devotees named Laxmi Bai, as a symbol of *Navadha Bhakti*. This may well be taken to be His last advice to the devotees to whom He wanted to give spiritual evolution. On this day of Ram Navami, this is what the Sai devotees should try to follow.

— Ram Navami, 1996

20

Necessity of a Guru

Divine Role

Hindu scriptures have extolled the virtues and role of the Sadgurus and Gurus extensively. In Buddhism, Jainism and Sikhism also, the role of the Gurus in evolving the devotees, in ushering in a better social order and their spiritual and miraculous powers, has been accepted. In Christianity and many other religions in the world, the divine role of these magnificent personalities, variedly known as Apostles, Perfect Masters, Masters, Qutabs, and so on, has been accepted.

Ever since human civilization developed its consciousness, there have always been some who opened the treasures of knowledge in different fields, including the spiritual field. The methods of imparting such knowledge have not always been formal. This is why parents, who teach the infant, are considered as the first Gurus of the child and are held in the highest esteem in Hinduism. Parents have been eulogized in Hindu literature and scriptures. In the formal systems of education, starting from the stage of a baby sitting in a nursery to the stage of super-specialization in any field, imparting knowledge has been made the responsibility of the teachers and professors.

The Hindu society, in earlier times, also had a formal educational system under the Gurus. We had *Gurukul*

Ashrams. However, the modern education system does not prescribe the need for such Gurus. The difference is that, whereas in the earlier Hindu system of education a lot of religious sanctity was attached to these Gurus, in today's society, such religious sanctity is not there. The Gurus of the past have been depicted as highly honourable personalities of a lofty nature. Besides opening the different vistas of knowledge, the teacher or the Guru was supposed to be a role model for the pupils. Even today, good teachers are highly appreciated by the students and the society. Thus the Guru has been a universally accepted and respected concept of the society and the society draws wisdom from them.

In a way, one can say that a society will be what its teachers are. History lends evidence that the best societies of the world had the best teachers and the worst societies had the worst teachers or Gurus. However, except the spiritual Guru, the job of the other Gurus ends with the imparting of knowledge in their respective fields. But the role of the spiritual Gurus or Sadgurus is much more expansive and is much above that of the ordinary Gurus. A Sadguru or Guru is a unique phenomenon of nature. The Kul Gurus, Siksha Gurus, the Mantra Gurus, etc., impart knowledge within their limits. The Sadguru, on the other hand, using his spiritual powers, can evolve the human souls by leading them through a path of piety, discipline and proper conduct.

Not only this, but by awakening the inner spiritual potentialities of the pupils or devotees through a method called *shaktipaat*, they prepare the devotees to become the instruments of God, to serve others. Whereas in the formal system of education, the teachers are paid for the duties they perform, in the spiritual field these highly evolved beings do not want any material returns. The only thing they seek is evolution of the souls of the devotees so that they become the agents to carry out God's will. When they start taking care of any devotee, they give them training through a series of direct experiences.

Formal education, when compared with the knowledge imparted by the Gurus, is very limited. Formal education is basically meant for giving knowledge, skill and an attitude (an exercise in the personality building of the students). Such teachings are basically meant to help the students earn a livelihood or to enhance their intellectual creativity in a certain field.

The Sadgurus give direct knowledge to the devotees through a chain of experiences, leading to the purification of the souls. These Masters are themselves evolved souls, having gone through a process of evolution through a series of births and deaths and, therefore, are absolutely competent to lead the devotees in the path of God realization.

Some people have a wrong concept that these Gurus, who sometimes do not adorn the garb of a modern man, are unintelligent and emotional propagators of an imaginary concept of God. What they fail to understand is that these evolved species of the human race will not be governed by the rules of a society which they had left far behind in time. Further, their consciousness is highly evolved, which enables them to comprehend any issue on which they focus. Their powers of concentration and performance are the highest and their brain capacity is immense.

Every human being not only wants to learn the biggest things of life, but also the smallest ones. To get the best results from the Guru's teachings, some factors are necessarily required. They are: the time spent both by the teacher and the pupil together, the eagerness of both the student and the teacher to learn and teach respectively, the emotional relationship between the teacher and the pupil and, most important of all, the capacity of the pupil to receive the teachings.

When one wants to specialize in only one out of the thousands of streams of knowledge, one spends a considerable number of years in different academic institutions. From this, one can imagine how much of time it would take to learn and practice spiritualism and what quality of relationship is required between the Guru and the disciple. It is because of this reason that, in the early Hindu society, the pupils and the Gurus used to live together for a number of years, tied together in an emotional bond.

The outer forms of societies may go on changing, but the inner spiritual essence of human beings always remains the same. The real Spiritual Masters of today are playing the same role, but in different forms, adapting to the existing societal ethos. All the creations of God are changeable, but the essence of divinity never changes. Therefore, the vital and divine role of these Sadgurus, the agents of knowledge and compassion, will never change. Human society will always need them.

— Guru Poornima, 2003

Shri Sai after Maha Samadhi

The very act of worshipping a Sadguru or a Perfect Master is termed *Bhakti*. The two major attributes of Bhakti, as defined by our Master Shri Sai Baba of Shirdi, are faith (*shraddha*) and patience (*saburi*). The history of different Bhakti movements has shown us that the maintenance of steadfast faith in the Master is, perhaps, easier when He is in a bodily form and not so easy after He leaves His body. This is so because a Master in a human form can communicate and carry on with numerous visible activities over and above His subtle and invisible activities. When in a bodily form, the Sadguru can be communicated with by the devotees through the different cognitive instruments of the body (like ears, eyes, mouth, etc.), but the same is not possible with the Master's statue, photograph or painting.

Those devotees who, during the period of human embodiment of the Master, evolve spiritually and establish a subtle mental communication with the Master (even when physically away from Him), don't find it difficult to continue such a communication with Him even after His taking Samadhi. However, those devotees who did not evolve when the Master was physically there or had never seen, heard, touched or smelt the Master's body or items (through the use of their gross physical instruments), find it difficult to maintain their devotion and faith as steadfastly as earlier, after the physical departure of the Master. There is a possibility of their devotion and concentration on the form of the Master getting affected gradually. The devotees usually get what can be termed, as a 'spiritual feeding' or 'spiritual vitalization' when directly in the presence of the Master. Once His body is entombed (Samadhi), they worship the tomb not because of its aesthetic value but because underneath the tomb lies the body of the Master, whom they continue to love.

For devotees who are born after the Samadhi of the Master, it is a different issue altogether. Their devotion emanates from the knowledge they receive from the old, experienced and direct devotees of the Master. They also get a lot of information from the print media (books, magazines, etc.) and audiovisual media (movies, TV, radio, etc.) about the divine personality, qualities and noble deeds of the Master. Today, they can get the requisite information through the internet. Thus, when they start following a Master, they start reading the available literature on Him, asking questions about Him and participating in discussions on Him. Once influenced by the superior divine and humane qualities of the Sadguru, they start worshipping Him. In this process, they establish a mental and emotional connection with the omnipotent spirit of the Master and also realize that the spirit of the Master, even without a physical body, can guide them in the path of spiritual evolution and protect them from worldly miseries.

However, there is another school of thought which holds that a Sadguru can guide and protect His devotees only while in a mortal body. Once a Sadguru leaves His body, he cannot actively help His devotees. Therefore, they insist on following, what they call, a 'living Sadguru'.

Let us take the case of our Master, Shri Sai Baba of Shirdi. Before leaving His body, Baba gave certain assurances to His devotees in unequivocal terms, popularly known as the Eleven Sayings (*Gyarah Vachan*) of Baba. The gist of these eleven sayings is that Baba will protect and guide His devotees (old or new) from His Samadhi, where His body is entombed.

Once, when in a mood of divine ecstasy, Baba made a forecast to a group of devotees that in the future, Shirdi would be visited by an unimaginable number of devotees, both big and small, and they would make a beeline to His tomb and also that He would be present in *'guli-guli'* (correct pronunciation is *gali-gali* in Hindi, which means 'every lane'). This finds a mention in *Shri Sai Satcharita*. Let us examine whether Baba's forecasts have come true ninety years after His Samadhi.

During the last ninety years, and particularly during the last twenty years or so, the spread of the name and fame of Sai Baba and the increase in the number of His devotees is phenomenal. There has been a mushrooming growth of temples and other related activities (medical, educational, social and religious) in the name of Baba, all over the country and abroad. The number of books, magazines, souvenirs, etc., created exclusively for spreading the name and preachings of Baba in different Indian and foreign languages is too numerous to be listed here. Not only are hundreds of new temples coming up all over the globe, but in many existing temple complexes, His statues and images are being consecrated. Television channels and internet are regularly displaying various shows of His life and His preachings. Many devotees are experiencing His kind divine intervention in times of distress, as a result of their prayers even today. Thus, the Sai Movement is an intensely dynamic process, which is flowering and prospering day by day.

This naturally leads to the belief that a Sadguru or a Perfect Master is as potent without a body as He is with it. Therefore, the devotees of Shri Sai Baba of Shirdi do not have to regret that they could not experience the physical presence or the divine activities of the Master when He was in His mortal embodiment. He is omnipresent and omnipotent, and the mere lack of a physical manifestation of His Self need not make His devotees lose faith and hope. Baba had promised His devotees of protection even after leaving His body and He has kept His promises, feel His devotees.

On this New Year day, I pray to Shri Sainath Maharaj to bless the millions of His devotees, grant them health and happiness and lead them on the path of spiritual evolution. May the year 2009 bring them closer to Baba.

— New Year, 2009

21

Purpose of Life

Happy and Satisfied

Human beings carry within themselves the two opposing aspects of nature: good and bad. Usually, that which gives pleasure is considered good and that which gives pain is considered bad. In this context, pleasure includes both pleasure of body as well as of mind. Our bodies and minds need satisfaction at every moment, from the smallest things, for example, adding a little sugar to our morning cup of tea. At the mental level, a person may be inspired by the photograph of a film hero in a magazine and wish to become a hero like him.

All the time, human beings are seeking instant gratification of their wants in the multi-dimensional aspects of their lives, at the desired level and in the desired style. If we make a daily assessment of the number of physical and mental activities that give us pleasure, then we may find that at least some of these desires never get fulfilled. This area of dissatisfaction becomes an area of deficit—a sort of an emotional hole.

At the end of the day, some people often forget their fulfilments and remember the areas of deficit only. Let us, for instance, place all the activities of life under twelve categories, namely, parents, brothers, sister, wife, children, health, job, money, property, fame, religion and God. With certain rare exceptions, most people want the greatest possible satisfaction in all desires in these categories or aspects, which they nurture simultaneously.

Satisfaction of the temporal status of human beings is not material in this situation because all the aspects mentioned till now are human aspects and are common to all human beings all over the world. History tells us that no person on this earth, however powerful or great, has ever been fully satisfied in all aspects of his life. Let us take the case of someone who has complete satisfaction in ten or eleven aspects of life and incomplete satisfaction in one or two aspects. Even in such a situation, we find that this person will spend more time and energy in brooding over only those two aspects of life which he lacks. Often, such deficits or unfulfilled aspects are taken too seriously. Sometimes, the wastage of time and energy on the smaller areas of life cripples or even destroys the other happier and vital aspects of life. Let us take the example of a person who has everything else, but has a crippled body due to an accident. History is replete with examples of such people who achieved many things despite their physical disabilities.

However, some people, due to their pessimistic outlook, have a propensity not only to disturb their own lives but also that of everyone around. Because of their peculiar mental state (sometimes magnified due to their imagination or selfishness), they become a liability for others. Such a state of mind often creates complex psychological conditions or even adverse health conditions. Many of these people even become self-destructive, leading to suicide, such as in cases of failure in love and exams, etc. Some people consider such extreme reactions in them with a sense of idealism and believe that to remain dissatisfied is a great virtue. They are often shocked to find some other people happy despite great adversities in their lives. Sometimes, they look at such balanced people as insensitive beings or as persons who are escapists or careless.

Thus, in the ultimate analysis, it will be seen that the enjoyment of life depends on the level of one's satisfaction. Life gives some things and denies some things to all living beings. Therefore, one should not be over-happy when life offers certain desired pleasures and should not break down when certain things are denied by life or go wrong in life. Shri Shirdi Sai Baba often used to tell his devotees to be happy and satisfied with whatever God has given them and to patiently watch the changing patterns of life dispassionately. This, then, is the key to a happy and meaningful life.

— Ram Navami, 2010

Who to Blame?

I realize that everybody's life comes to a full cycle between birth and death. Life is a dynamic process consisting of multiple activities—physical, mental and spiritual. The spirit of life, which for our understanding at this stage may be defined as the soul (*atma*), is said to be the root cause of human birth. This soul force in each living being brings along with it impressions of past lives. When this soul force creates a living entity like a human being, it becomes a *jiva*. This *jiva* or human being is endowed with certain mental and physical instruments in the form of mental and physical *indriyas* in order to carry on the worldly activities (both physical and mental) in accordance with desires, either created in this life or brought forward from the past lives.

Using the different faculties of mind and body, a person calculates and strives to achieve his desired objects. While doing so, at times he succeeds and at times he fails. When he achieves whatever he desires, he feels happy and when he fails to achieve his desires, he feels unhappy. His life goes through a series of achievements and non-achievements till death.

Besides the inherent capabilities of the mind and the body, it is the circumstances in which the person tries to achieve his goals which contribute immensely to achieving success or failure. Human beings do try to use the circumstantial advantages to their benefit and control the unfavourable circumstances to the extent it is possible for them to do so. However, no person, the mightiest and the lowliest alike, has ever been able to do so to the fullest extent, in accordance with his desires. History indicates that even some mighty rulers had a miserable death.

The greatest limitation of the living beings is that they cannot control their circumstances beyond a certain point. When circumstances become favourable sometimes, a person achieves more than what he anticipates and when circumstances become unfavourable, he achieves less than his expectations. A saint or a wise man accepts such limitations and, therefore, lives happily, whereas others who fail to accept such a reality, suffer agony. Take, for example, a child who has genetic disorders, as a result of which his physical organs are defective or his mental faculties are limited. In such a situation, who is to be blamed? Should we try to blame someone else, including the parents, nature or God for this miserable state of affairs? Again, for example, when many people perish due to a landslide on a mountain, then who is to be blamed? Can one get a solution by blaming the hills or the forces of nature? Even if a person makes such factors responsible for his misery, does it bring a solution to his satisfaction? Blame the deities one worships or the non-manifested sovereign energy force called God? Many people do so, but I do not know if this brings about a solution to their problems.

The Hindu Vedic *seers* have explained such happenings through the theory of Karma. The theory of Karma, elucidated exhaustively in the *Bhagavad Gita*, simply states that 'as you sow, so you reap'. This reaping of the seed of Karma can be of this life or the earlier lives. According to the Karma Theory, visible reactions are not always commensurate with visible actions. The blueprint of the invisible action-reaction syndrome is carried forward by the human beings (*jivas*) from their past lives. This seems to be a good spiritual solution, but, except for the highly evolved souls, an ordinary man is not capable of mentally accepting such a concept in its totality and continue holding a stoic attitude to life. In such an eventuality, who is responsible?

Some human beings have a tendency to blame others, which includes other human beings, society, circumstances and even God, for all their miseries, simply because they cannot accept the realities of life. They forget that God or nature has created human beings of widely different varieties and has given a right to each person to complete his lifecycle as ordained by destiny. Some of them often hold on to their so-called moral standards and blame others for not coming up to their level. This is another type of self-created problem of the so-called good people. 'If I am so good', they say, 'Why should I suffer?' or that, 'Why should the bad people enjoy life?'

Therefore, it would be wise to avoid such an attitude of blaming others, as no human being is even near perfection (spiritually speaking) on this earth. One needs to learn to accept certain realities, however painful, and make the best use of whatever is good and favourable to achieve reasonable standards of happiness and success in the life cycle.

May Shri Sai bless us all.

– Guru Poornima, 2010

Life Infinite

All of us are aware of the fact that the lifespan of every living entity on this earth is extremely limited when compared with the flow of infinite time. Since human existence is bound to meet its end at some point of time, we are, therefore, known as mortal beings.

In the past, some mighty rulers, as in the case of ancient Egyptians, tried to gain immortality. The pyramids of Egypt are nothing but odes to immortality sung by history. The rulers of the ancient times imagined about returning to their human bodies of the past life at a later point of time, through a process of alchemy and magic. In Hinduism, we often read about *Puranic* personalities who achieved immortality, like Lord Dattatreya and others. Even if we believe in the existence of timeless saints, they have to be exceptions within nature's general framework of birth and death of the living beings.

So, for lesser mortals like us, life is limited and we live that limited life with a lot of limitations. There are three somewhat meaningful things that remain when a man winds up his mortal coil and departs from his physical existence. The first is children, if he has any. The second is his name — good, bad or neutral. And the third thing is his material and intellectual property.

With the process of time, say about five–six generations after his death, his name is forgotten. The material property that he builds around him goes to other hands, from generation to generation, if he is lucky. Even the people who build temples and charitable organizations go in to oblivion. If we revisit the history of great men, we find that in the process of time there has been no value addition to the great products they claimed to have created on this earth. We only remember these people through codified literature, generally known as history. As yet, we don't have a list of the brilliant Hindu intellects who created the *Vedas*. However, we are thankful to them for the knowledge they have left behind for posterity. This has not only been the situation for the Hindu civilization, but is true for all civilizations on earth. These great men lived a finite life, but left behind the essence of their existence for a far greater period of time. The knowledge they gave sustained itself through centuries. What I mean to say here is that only knowledge has the capability of sustaining itself. The material forces cannot survive themselves without the knowledge that creates them and sustains them for some period of time. Such material forces may be defined as kingdoms, power in any form, property, and so on.

Thus, the perceptible life forms on this Earth will always be finite in their existence, no matter how much they try to achieve immortality. Spiritual Science, at times, speaks about the immortality of the soul. Even if one agrees that the soul is immortal because it is a part of the Over Soul or God, yet it cannot be called 'life infinite' on earth with a human embodiment. In the backdrop of such an assumption, I am inclined to believe that we should make our finite living existence happy and meaningful, to the extent it is possible.

May Shri Sai Bless us all!

— New Year, 2011

22

Sadguru Sai as Ishta

Spiritual Evolution

Of all the religions in the world, Hinduism alone believes in the symbolic representation of various energies of nature in the form of *devis* and *devatas*. As per Hindu scriptures, *Ishta*, or the Ordained Deity of a devotee, is the main deity worshipped, besides other deities in the Hindu pantheon. It is generally believed that there are thirty-three crore *devi-devatas*.

The five most important deities are known as the *Panch devatas*. They are Shiva, Vishnu, Surya, Ganesh and Hanuman. Again, there are *upa devatas* and *adhi devatas*. Most of the people are not clear which deity or deities they need to worship and why. As a result, in different temples, they worship one deity or the other, as suggested by the priest. In some temples, multiple deities are worshipped, catering to the needs of the devotees of different deities. At times, devotees downgrade the deities they don't believe in and extol the virtues of their own deity as the supreme. To add to this problem, are the different methods of worship of different deities. The Shaivaites and the Vaishnavites are seen to fight on the issue of superiority of their respective deities. But the devotees in some other religions, like Buddhism, have the advantage of focussing on the preachings and form of one diety like Lord Buddha alone .

Incarnations, have been born from time to time, to re-establish a society going downhill on the path of moral degradation. The activities of the Incarnations reveal that their divine activities go through a certain well organized process. Leaving aside Lord Krishna, whose divine activities started even before and immediately after His birth, in the case of some other Incarnations, the earlier parts of their lives went through many trials and tribulations. At times, such trials and tribulations have been extremely strenuous, but the Incarnations, with their spiritual powers, could overcome them. During the initial stages, the Incarnations experience themselves—God experiencing Himself in a human form. Even if they are Incarnations, at this stage they have to come under the tutelage of a Sadguru, for example Vasishtha Muni to Lord Rama and Sandeepani Muni to Lord Krishna. During that period, some of the other spiritual souls, who were already born or took birth during the period of the Incarnation, also had some similar experiences.

At a predetermined point of time, under the leadership of the Incarnation, a crisis gets precipitated, often in the form of a great social crisis or war. Handling that crisis with divine foresight and in a manner which no human being can dare, the Incarnations ensure that the evil forces are ultimately annihilated and virtuous forces are established. The history of Hinduism, in terms of *Ramayana* and *Mahabharata*; Muslim religion in terms of wars conducted by Prophet Mohammed; Sikhism in terms of the bravery of the Sikh Gurus against the Moghul Rulers; are all pointers towards the powerful roles played by the Incarnations or Prophets. For them, destruction is as much a divine role as creation. After this powerful action of destruction of evil, a new order or society is established based on principles of *Dharma* (rules of balanced sustenance), and thereafter the Incarnations leave their human body, according to their own will.

For an Incarnation, even after He has left His human embodiment, one aspect of His mission continues, in which

He guides people on the path of *Dharma*. They also play the additional role of a Sadguru at the same time. Shri Krishna, as an incarnation, changed the social order through *Mahabharata*, but thereafter, His role remains till today in the form of a teacher or Sadguru in *Gita*. While following *Gita*, millions of Hindus are following the path laid down by the Sadguru aspect of Shri Krishna. Similarly, through *Bible, Koran* and the *Guru Grantha Saheb*, Christ, Prophet Mohammed and the Sikh Gurus continue their divine roles.

Unlike the Hindus, the followers of some of these religions don't worship numerous deities. They only pray to one God, the Almighty, and follow the path prescribed by the Prophets or Sadgurus. Search for God, search for self and peace need not necessarily be turned into a difficult or complicated process. The Incarnations or Sadgurus have always tried to offer the simplest path for spiritual evolution to humanity.

The easiest way to spiritual evolution is:

1. To believe that there is one God for all human beings, who is called by different names and worshipped through different methods.
2. To believe that the Sadguru or Perfect Masters, as Divine Incarnations, will lead the devotees on the path of spiritual evolution.
3. To follow the path laid down by the Sadguru, as reflected in their preachings and try to emulate their noble conduct.
4. To understand that man, howsoever he strives, cannot progress in the path of spiritualism beyond a certain point without the kindness and help of a Sadguru. Even incarnations like Shri Krishna and Shri Rama, in the process of experiencing the state of incarnation in them, had to be helped by Sandeepani Muni and Vasishta Muni, their respective Sadgurus.

5. To focus the entire spiritual consciousness on God through the medium of the Sadguru, both in *Sakar* (with form) and *Nirakar* (without form), and worship Him.

6. To believe that the Guru is the repository of all divine powers and, therefore, He alone should be made the mainstay of one's life. All needs, worries and questions should be placed before Him and prayed for a solution.

7. To believe that the quality of surrender is the ultimate requirement for spiritual evolution, as experience shows that people devoted to Sadgurus evolve faster in the spiritual field than those following other methods, because such devotees believe in surrender to the Guru and God.

Every devotee of Shirdi Sai, on this New Year day, should decide whether he wants to hold Baba as his *Ishta* – the only one to be prayed, worshipped and called in times of distress and need. Personally, for me, Shri Sai is the only one and the ultimate. I don't seek anything from elsewhere. Who would like to join me?

– New Year, 1999

Focus on Sadguru for God Worship

Devotees speak volumes about their Master. They speak about the Master's glory, personality, activities, miracles, their personal experiences and of other devotees with the Master, their group activities and so on. Particularly, when it comes to Shri Sainath Maharaj, devotees speak more about dreams with relation to Him, their own experience which they call miracles and on their inner and emotive communications with Baba. In short, they experience Him as a Personal God, who can be a Sadguru or a deity.

Some of the devotees worship a number of Personal Gods at the same time and, therefore, find it difficult to focus on only one. In any case, the One and the Ultimate God, the Almighty, has to be beyond all the Personal Gods. A Personal God, by whatever name, is called *Saguna* (with certain qualities and powers) and *Sakara* (with a form which a human mind can ordinarily comprehend). A finer understanding of God is *Nirguna* (beyond such limited qualities and powers) and *Nirakara* (beyond all form). *Nirguna Nirakara* — this means seeing or experiencing the essence of God or that Ultimate Reality or Bramha in all its creations, that is, in the devotee himself and in the entire manifested and non-manifested creation around him.

By this logic, all statues or paintings, structures (like *samadhis*), names, *aartis, mantras, charan padukas,* etc., are symbols of God and certainly not God, the Ultimate. Such symbols are generally worshipped and contemplated on as it is easy for the limited human mind to comprehend them.

The question is whether the human mind should necessarily be limited, or a path should be chosen which keeps it limited. If any path or any religion prescribes such an approach, it itself is limited. Hinduism prescribes certain methods by which a devotee can graduate from a *sakara* (limited form) of worship to a *nirakara* (formless) worship.

Religion means both ritualism and spiritualism. Unless one transcends ritualism, it is difficult to enter the arena of spiritualism in the true sense of the term. Spiritualism means to follow the true diktats of the spirit within. Generally speaking, 'the spirit within' means the soul, which is a part of that God, the Ultimate, Who encompasses both the seen and unseen, the living and non-living aspects of nature — from the smallest particle to biggest stars. Spiritualism, therefore, has necessarily to expand the spirit of the soul from its limited body-bounded awareness to a vast cosmic awareness. If sheer rituals like *pooja, archana, yagyna* do not uplift the spirit of the individual or expand his mental horizon, it certainly is not spiritualism.

Usually, it is due to the lack of understanding of what real spiritualism means that most of the devotees spend their whole life doing certain rituals without progressing spiritually. From multiple forms of God, to a single form God, to a formless state of God, is the real prescription for spiritualism. Multiple-forms worship (that is, of deities etc.) does not give focus on a particular form. Since these various symbolic representations of different aspects of nature go with various functions and powers, a person worshipping these forms gets scared to stop such worship even when he understands that he has to graduate to a formless state of worship. For example, Shri Ganapati is for the removal of obstructions, Shri Durga is for protection against enemies, Shri Laxmi is for prosperity, Shri Hanumana is for courage, and so on. No doubt that all the four deities are manifestations of the Ultimate One, but then, on whom does the devotee concentrate? Where then is the question of what is called *ekagra chitta* as a *sine qua non* for subtle experience of God? In such a situation, one has to choose one of the two ways — either worship the Ultimate One (*Nirguna Nirakara*), going beyond the worship of these deities, or evolve through these limited forms to the Ultimate Reality through *gyana marga* (path of knowledge).

All spiritual practitioners, in all ages, of all religions, have gone through this process of leaving the forms and contemplating on the formless state of God or in experiencing the formless state of God through the forms. The Perfect Masters or Sadgurus always taught the same method to their disciples at a certain stage of evolution. Those who followed them and tried to experience the impersonal aspects of God evolved faster than those that remained stuck on only the personal aspect of God.

Baba has clearly stated in *Shri Sai Satcharita* that the best way of worship is to experience Him as a Formless, Universal existence. If not, to worship Him with a form. Therefore, a devotee of Baba, while worshipping Him with a form, should always try to experience Him as the formless one. But then, the big question is, how to be focused and be in a state of *ekagra chitta* when too many forms are contemplated on at the same time? Is not the form of the Sadguru enough!

— *New Year, 2004*

23

Sai Path—Universalism, Humanism, Magnanimity

Universalism and Magnanimity of the Sai Path

God is addressed differently by different groups of people and also differently by individuals through various names. God, the unseen, is thus addressed differently as He does not have a single form. His manifested forms are millions and millions. These forms may be visible to the human eye or may not be. He has gross forms, subtle forms, energy forms, thought forms and feeling forms. But the ultimate form of God is that which no one has seen. All saints, paths and religions, at best, have called it a vast, timeless, spaceless, causeless, attributeless ocean of emptiness or a primordial void.

Whatever God reveals about Himself through the sense and beyond the perceptions to the human beings, is what they understand Him to be. Species other than human beings are not mentally evolved to conceptualize that the movements in the universe and also within them are created by God as their soul-force. The excellence and superiority of the Homo sapiens lies here. Not only do they have the capacity to conceptualize God in myriads of forms, they have also worked through different methods to experience God at different stages of consciousness. Whereas other religions have conceptualized a limited number of these forms of God, Hinduism, being one of the oldest religions on this earth, has created thousands of symbols for millions of aspects of the unlimited God. This has not happened in a day or year. It has evolved through the passage of time of thousands of years, through the experience of practitioners who have devoted their lives completely to the realm of spiritualism.

The universally accepted principle of experiencing God can be explained through the parallelism of a river meeting an ocean or sea. All rivers emanating from different places (locations), meandering through different lands and paths, ultimately merge with the sea. Thereafter, forever, the river is a part of the sea. It merges its total identity in it. When we think of the Bay of Bengal, we do not picturize it as a combination of the Ganga, Brahmaputra and other rivers and thousands of water channels merging in it. Herein comes the concept of multiplism and dualism, leading to Monism (*Advaita*). Since each of these rivers flows on different soils, through different hills and forests, takes different curves and falls, the attributes of the water it carries cannot be the same in content, speed, density, quality and quantity. However, once merged with the sea, all the different qualities merge and become one with the attributes of the seawater.

Different religions and paths that people follow are like these different rivers. It is wrong to criticize any of these religions and paths. A person is free to practice any path he chooses, but is socially and morally not free to demean other religions or paths.

This is what Shri Sainath Maharaj taught his disciples through His own conduct and precepts. *Shri Sai Satcharita* amply elaborates on this universalism of Baba in the backdrop of the day to day happenings at Shirdi. Following the Master, Sai devotees should, therefore, develop the highest amount of religious tolerance. As Baba used to say, all are the children of God and He is the only and ultimate Lord.

– Ram Navami, 2005

Sai Humanism

There are a few major differences between other species and the human beings. Human beings or the homo sapiens race has established itself as the most superior race on this earth because of the superiority of its mental faculties. These capacities grew stage by stage through innumerable phases of evolution. What we call as nature is the limited manifestation of the Sovereign Divine Power called Bramha or God. That Ultimate Power manifested as universe, solar systems, planets, etc. Thereafter, It created the living organisms, birds, animals and ultimately human beings, through different stages of growth in consciousness, to inhabit on our planet called earth.

All other species have instinctive intelligence but what human beings exclusively possess is intellect. This intellectual consciousness of man is a combination of his mental faculties like memory, recall, analytical ability and also the qualities of heart like love-hatred, selfishness-self sacrifice, anger-calmness, intolerance-patience, etc. The highly developed human brain, which is much greater than any computer, takes all these factors into consideration in giving a solution to any problem. It is, again, this intellect that has created the loftiest and greatest systems on the earth — social, economic, religious, political, spiritual, and so on.

Man's intellect has penetrated into the micro world of elements and also the macro dimensions of space. During the last two to three decades, we have witnessed, what is termed as intellectual explosion, in the world. Developments in space technology, cloning of animals, transplantation of human organs, sub-earth discoveries, micro analysis of elements, wireless communication, to mention a few, have revolutionized human civilization and given human beings immense power to control the forces of nature, almost bordering on divinity.

Commensurately, the pressure on human brain has increased tremendously. Newer concepts are entering into our thinking system or thought process, making the old concepts redundant. It is happening so fast that many of the older persons are finding it difficult to adjust to this rapid transition, whereas it is easy for the newer generation to adjust at a faster pace due to the nascent state of their mind. The older generations find the new thoughts to be heavily at odds with their old concepts and style of thinking. This, obviously, is creating a lot of maladjustment in individuals, with different levels of sensitivities and also greater disharmony in the social fabric. Such maladjustments are reflected in the assertion of selfish individualism beyond proportions, discord between parents and offspring, large number of divorce, material approach to emotional aspects of life and a mad race to compete with others in the material world at the cost of the finer aspects of life. This happened in many civilizations earlier and by the law of self-contradiction, these civilizations fell and lost their glory. Such a maladjustment between the material and the emotional world brought the downfall of the mighty Roman, Egyptian, Mexican, Persian and many other ancient civilizations.

The answer to such confusion does not lie in the assertion of atomic egoism or selfish individualism at the cost of greater social good, but to accept the ways of others, with their perfections and imperfections. Love is not acceptance of only the best in the loved one, but is the total acceptance of the entire personality. This is what Baba preached and practiced at Shirdi. Only He was capable of bringing the divergent groups of individuals belonging to different castes, religions, creeds and different socioeconomic status under a single banner – the banner of humanism – at Shirdi. The world needs to follow this concept today, to make tomorrow a better place to live.

– Maha Samadhi, 2005

The Spiritual Training Methodology of Shri Sai

When Shri Sai Baba was in His human embodiment at Shirdi, thousands of people of different regions, religions, languages and categories used to visit Him. The young and the old, married and unmarried, worldly people and spiritual seekers and many others, representing a cross section of the society, used to approach the Master, to get His help and blessings to satisfy their material needs and spiritual aspirations. In *Shri Sai Satcharita,* one finds mention about some of these persons, although there were many more about whom there is no record.

Sadgurus, like Shri Shirdi Sai Baba, operate simultaneously at two levels of consciousness. Some of their activities are visible and some are non-visible. Examples of some of the manifested activities are feeding the poor and the devotees, curing physical and mental diseases, rendering temporal assistance in material needs and religious pursuits of the devotees, and so on. The manner in which He used to give relief was miraculous at times. Hundreds of families of Shirdi and outside used to depend on Him for relief and sustenance in their worldly existence. Sai Baba never refused help to anyone who approached Him. He laboured day in and day out to solve the complex problems of His devotees, even when He was in indifferent health. Once He told a devotee that He (Baba) could not sleep during the previous night thinking about that devotee. 'What would happen to my people, if I constantly do not keep an eye on them?' He used to say. This was the role of a Provider and a Protector.

The other role of Shri Sai Baba was subtle and non-visible in nature, which added permanent value to the lives of the people who approached Him. Shri Shirdi Sai Baba was a Perfect Master or a Sadguru. Being a Sadguru, His divine charter of duties was to train the devotees with a view to evolving their mental and emotional qualities and ultimately to lead them towards emancipation. Such a process of evolution, when left to the disciple himself, is very slow and may take a number of lives to achieve. As ordained by the law of nature, every human being evolves during each life cycle while on the earth plane, by experiencing an incalculable number of events that generate pleasure or pain. Without the help of a Master or Sadguru who has travelled along and experienced the path of spiritual evolution, the seeker has to go through an audacious process of trials and errors, and in this process his evolution slows down. However, if the person accepts a Sadguru as his mentor, and strictly abides by His advice, his evolution becomes easier and faster. The Sadguru, with His divine powers and qualities, has immense capabilities to hasten the process of evolution of all beings that come in contact with Him. Therefore, He is called a Samarth (capable of giving God realization) Sadguru.

However, notwithstanding the ceaseless effort of the Masters, all devotees do not progress spiritually at an equal pace. The pace of evolution of a devotee depends on a few prime factors, like acceptance of the Master – both intellectually and emotionally – as the sole guide and Protector in the spiritual journey, complete faith in and adherence to the advice and commands of the Master and, finally, a lot of patience under all kinds of trying circumstances, stretched over long periods of time, to follow the Master's prescriptions in their true spirit. (Quoted from *Shri Sai Satcharita* Chapter 18 and 19).

Usually, the Perfect Masters like Baba do not force disciples to follow their advice. They suggest the prescriptions directly (through words, actions, direct experiences, etc.) and/or indirectly (through dreams, anecdotes, hints, mediums, etc.) to each disciple or sometimes to a group of disciples.

Baba, at times, used to speak cryptic or broken sentences or utter a certain unintelligible language. The devotees could comprehend its meaning only after a protracted mental effort and deliberation or discussion with others over the issue.

Baba can always give a direct solution to all the problems, but His method has been to lead the devotee through a self-discovery and an analytical mental process. Many a times, He would enquire from some devotees as to what they were talking about when they were together. He would then advise them on how to handle the compulsive and negative thoughts of the mind and how to inculcate a habit of generating positive thoughts. The Omniscient Sadguru used to keep a watch on the negative and positive thoughts of His disciples and numerous examples about this can be found in *Shri Sai Satcharita*.

Baba used to create thought waves in the minds of devotees by His subtle powers, thereby leading them to find a solution to their problems on their own. To many, He used to give directions in dreams as well. He used to render such help with a view to creating a clearer and purer state of mind in the devotees, which is essential and required to progress in the path of spiritual evolution.

The Sadgurus do not believe in keeping their disciples dependent on Them for all times to come, with a view of getting continued personal service from them. Their only desire is to evolve the disciples to the state of a perfect human being (*Satpurush*), with perfect noble qualities so that these evolved souls can further carry on certain subtle and difficult tasks on this earth or elsewhere, in accordance with the Divine Plan. The Sadgurus not only gives emancipation to the human souls under their care, but they also create a few spiritual workers from among the evolved devotees to assist them in their universal and subtle activities. The basic principle they follow is to light a number of candles from a single candle and they expect the process to continue for generations, for all times to come. This is known as the *Guru Marg* or the *Path of the Teachers*.

If we analyse the various methods that Shri Sai adopted while dealing with different devotees, one objective stands out prominently – the qualitative evolution of mind of the disciples. In whatever He did towards the training of His devotees, the moot idea of Baba was to evolve not only the mental qualities but also the thought process itself. For example, when Nanasaheb Chandorkar, sitting near Baba at Dwarakamai Masjid was attracted by the beauty of a woman, Baba never advised him not to look at women. This incident is mentioned in Chapter 49 of *Shri Sai Satcharita*. What He advised was that while looking at any beautiful woman or beautiful object, one should think of beauty as an aspect of God's creation. He further emphasized on the internal beauty of the soul and not on the external beauty of the body. The lesson that Baba gave was that when the mind is attracted to anything, it is better to attach a higher value to the thought itself rather than to struggle with mind to avoid the object of attraction. No one can struggle with his own mind, as it is the most powerful force in human beings, as ordained by nature. The moment one tries to struggle with mind in order to erase an evil thought or enforce a good thought by one's sheer will, it is bound to create a certain reaction and such reactions are likely to lead to further problems. This, then, is the most difficult task for any human being to perform, living as he does in a complex world. Therefore, Baba used to keep a constant watch on the thoughts arising in the minds of His devotees and used to guide them promptly.

In another case, mentioned in *Shri Sai Satcharita*, Baba had asked Kaka Saheb Dixit to stay quietly (*Uge-muge*) in Dixit *wada* at Shirdi and not to mix with others. He told Dixit that he should be wary of thieves in the *wada*, lest they take away everything, meaning thereby the loss of positive quality of his mind and peace. Similarly, Upasani Baba was asked to stay at Khandoba temple and not to meet anyone. He was not even

allowed to meet Baba for a long time, who was sitting a few
hundred yards away at Dwarakamai Masjid. By separating
the genuine seekers from the rest of the world, Baba wanted
them to maintain a purer and positive state of mind and not
to get contaminated by the negative thoughts of others, as it
usually happens in social interactions.

Baba used to render advice in the same or similar
manner to different devotees, for example, to keep one's
promise always, to make adequate payment for the services
received from any person, to tolerate and not to quarrel
even if provoked, to avoid speaking ill of others, to avoid
differentiating between human beings on the grounds of
material or social differences, and finally, to visualize the
presence of God in every living being, every object, every
thought and every feeling.

All religious rituals including *poojas*, *aartis* and *prayanas*,
etc., are methods for the evolution of the human mind to
the first stage. Evolution of the thought process of the mind,
in itself, is the intermediary stage and emancipation of the
soul through realization of God is the third and final stage in
the spiritual journey of the soul. Since the Omniscient Baba
could easily read through the thoughts of all His devotees,
He could prescribe specific methods of thought control and
spiritual evolution to each of His devotees.

History shows that it is the positive forces of human
minds that have built mighty civilizations and it is the
negative forces of human minds that have brought about the
destruction of their own civilizations, as seen in the case of
the Roman, Egyptian and Peru civilizations.

We see the world as our mind visualizes it and our
visualization is limited and often distorted. We see the
world with a fixed kaleidoscope from a certain angle. If the
kaleidoscope is rotated, then different forms and patterns
of life would appear. Since each individual sees life from a
certain fixed angle, each experiences a specific pattern, and

this pattern of life experienced by him seems to be the only truth to him. Leave alone the people with a predominantly evil nature, even people with the best of qualities suffer from this limitation of mental fixity.

It is sometimes seen that the best quality of an individual becomes the greatest block in his evolution in certain situations. For example, there was a kind person who used to help everyone. He had the expectation, as is usually the case with human beings, that others would be equally kind to him and reciprocate in his bad days. But when he was in distress, no one rendered the help needed in the manner and to the extent he had rendered to them. As a result, he started questioning the very foundation of kindness and decided not to help others as he used to earlier. Now his proactive kindness turned to reactive narrow mindedness. His evolved quality of natural benevolence was blocked and the evolution process of his mind slowed down. No doubt, as a worldly-wise person, he went a step forward, but in his spiritual evolution he had gone a step backward. If he had the flexibility of mind to accept that imperfection is bound to exist in others, without passing value judgement over the imperfect conduct of others, he would have been happier and more evolved. The lesson to learn is that howsoever perfect one claims to be, the universal nature (containing both the so called perfect and imperfect aspects), does not give a licence to anyone to condemn others, howsoever, imperfect. Therefore, our *seers* have proclaimed that one may hate sin, but not the sinner. Baba unequivocally declared that when any one condemned anyone else, His feelings were hurt.

Some psychoanalysts hold the view that perfectionists suffer from psychological stress the most, as they find it difficult to adjust with the imperfect circumstances or the imperfect traits in the character of others with whom they interact. Such persons are, sometimes, highly creative because of their sense of perfection, but nevertheless they suffer the most due to the psychological social maladjustment. This problem of human beings is not limited to a category alone. It is more or less with everyone to some extent.

The fundamental problem with the magnificent human beings is that each human being considers himself to be the centre of the Universe — the little universe he has created for himself. Therefore, he desires that everything around him should fall in line with his requirements in that little universe. He is not prepared to visualize himself as an infinitesimally small particle in the vast Universe, with millions and millions of ever-changing patterns. These millions of little universes of human ego, juxtaposed with the social fabric of our complex world, clash with one another and try to pull one another apart by the gravitational force of their individualism or ego. The Sadgurus have always tried to give simple solutions to this complex problem of human society.

If we follow the prescriptions of Baba, as contained in *Shri Sai Satcharita*, our thought process can go through a qualitative change and we can have a clearer picture of the world around and the vast universe. It will not only do good to us, but also to others around us. Therefore, when reading *Shri Sai Satcharita* or other literature on Baba, our thought should always be focused on the aspect of conscious mental evolution that Baba repeatedly taught and exemplified through his own conduct.

— *Dussehra, 2006*

24

Scientific Versus Spiritual Approach

Identify the Root Principles

Some people view and see scientific knowledge as a method of understanding the different laws of nature, with a view to controlling and applying these for the benefit of the human race and others on this earth. They view the scientific discoveries, inventions and newer technologies from intellectual, empirical and utilitarian points of view, which can be cognized directly through the cognitive faculties like the eyes and ears, and indirectly through artefacts created by them (for example, a radio or TV receiving electronic waves and transmitting audio or light waves). Whereas this is not contradicted, there are very few people who are able to correlate their rational approach with the spiritual approach pursued by some other people. These two separate approaches, if not looked at in a holistic manner, would lead to certain contradictions.

The purely spiritual group says that there is a God who cannot be seen and proven in the manner in which scientific evidence is established and He can only be experienced through subtle inner perceptions. On the other hand, the purely scientific group argues that without scientific evidence, the so called God and His mythological concepts and miracles, cannot be accepted. These two approaches, at the extreme, would have rendered the human civilization apart, had not the majority of humanity believed in the existence of a supernatural power called God, Allah, Nature, or called by whatever name. In this world of ours, though human societies have changed, their economic and political factors have changed, yet the concept of God has never changed. For the Hindus, Ram remains Ram, for the Christians, Christ remains Christ, and for the Muslims, Prophet Mohamed remains Prophet Mohamed, notwithstanding the fact that societies propounding such faiths have undergone vast economic, social and political transformations over time.

All such thoughts bring to mind a fundamental question—can there be a God who has created two unrelated and independent principles: scientific principles and the spiritual principles? Is it that scientific principles, like the discoveries and technology created by the human brain, are a mere chance occurrence in the gradual process of evolution or can they be viewed from a spiritual angle or vision?

When Einstein expounded his theory on interconnection of matter and energy in his famous formula, $E=MC^2$, he tried to explain the entire universe through this single equation. He could not, however, succeed, because he could not contemplate the interconnection between consciousness, energy and matter. Nevertheless, Einstein was a genius and he did acknowledge that he experienced an infinite subtle world, much beyond the perceptible matter and energy world, which he was unable to explain. In other words, Einstein, the great scientist, experienced and had the intellectual honesty to express the limitations of his theory to explain the subtle energy field existing in the world beyond. Had a genius like Einstein gone a little ahead and approached the issue from a different angle, as has been explained in many spiritual books like the *Gita* and the *Bible*, he could, perhaps, have been able to connect the apparently diversified theorems into a single formulation. Had he got the sixth sense of the spiritual practitioners and saints, he could have unearthed more about the subtle forms of the universe and nature.

If Einstein is taken as a model, it means that it is possible for the scientific-oriented minds to have a different approach towards the unearthing of the mysteries of nature, in the manner followed by the great *seers* of various religions. But rarely have human beings come across such great personalities like Aryabhatta of India or Pythagoras of the ancient Greece.

When the Spiritual Masters, in different forms, gave a spiritual thrust to the nascent human civilization, they obviously did not jump steps and straightaway start teaching theology and philosophy. At the earliest stages, what they did was to generate certain types of logic in the human minds, without which it would not have been possible for them to understand the complex and finer aspects of nature. Hence, the simple logic generated in the minds of human beings was evolved to grow into a more complex logic at later stages. What they taught was simple arithmetic (relating to numbers) and geometry (relating to shapes) and out of this mathematics, other branches of science developed. Through these symbols, they could explain the different phenomena of the vast world of nature more easily.

In the second stage, they gave the concepts of architectural designs and simple mathematical calculations. Like a newborn child looking at the world around with surprise, the human race started picking up these concepts rather quickly. Once they were ready, their brain cells were geared to make higher scientific discoveries through the use of this logic. A few individuals, who were ready for it, were then systematically given the required thought process and it is these individuals who propounded the theories of science like Marconi's Law of Radio waves, Newton's Law of Gravity or Einstein's Law of Relativity.

Today, such discoveries and the related technology have gone to a great extent of conquering of the space, cloning, genetic engineering, and so on, which, if done by any human being a few years ago, would have been construed as a divine act. Logically, therefore, the secrets of nature are being revealed to the human beings with the purpose of expanding the horizons of their knowledge through the expansion of their brain capacity.

Given this background, it is evident that the very basis of scientific thought has emanated out of the thrust given by these spiritual beings, who were incarnated on this earth with a superior intelligence. Obviously, when the living creatures of the earth had not experienced subtle thought processes, some souls coming from outside stirred them. These superior beings must have carried such superior intelligence from their evolution in their past lives. Commonly defined as *transcendental intelligence*, these intellects could not have achieved such levels of excellence in a single lifetime. The inspirational revelations of many spiritual personalities holding such transcendental intelligence existing in this solar system (of which earth forms a part) is a real possibility.

Today, in science fiction, we can well see the imaginative depiction of such characters or events as inter-stellar warfare, UFOs, etc. The present fourth human civilization is on the threshold of transcending to the fifth human race. More and more scientific discoveries and experiments will be undertaken by a few human beings and this will create a group which will have the potential of controlling the subtle forces of nature, without the help of artefacts. That is, as time progresses, they will depend more and more on their inner faculties of mind to capture and use the subtler forces of nature than depend on the machines created by them. For example, they will communicate with one another through the subtle faculties of their brain, rather than using a telephone or a cell phone.

The sixth sense of the intellectual faculty is bound to expand much more than what it is today. This will force human society to look at the world of religion and the world of science from a totally different perspective. That perspective will be to find the root principles from which both scientific approach and religious approach evolved and thus establish their interconnectivity. If the contradictions between the two approaches can be reconciled, then the benefits of science and technology shall not be used for destructive purposes. Its use would be coloured with the spiritual approach of kindness and tolerance.

– Guru Poornima, 2004

Essence of Spiritual Science—From Matter to Energy to Consciousness

The religious and spiritual concepts of Hinduism have produced an unimaginably large volume of books, treatises, scriptures and other such texts. Carried from the distant past are the most profound religious scriptures like the *Vedas, Bramhans, Purans, Samhitas, Upanishads, Shrimad Bhagvad Gita* and many more, too numerous to be listed here. A study of these works, written primarily in Sanskrit or in vernacular languages, will lead a person to experience a sense of expansion of his knowledge, imagination and consciousness, in areas hitherto unknown to him.

From an academic point of view, these invaluable scriptures deal with spiritual philosophy, spiritual theory and spiritual science. In quintessence, they propound certain vital theories and concepts of the spiritual realm. Understanding of philosophy and theory are the first and basic requirement for a spiritual practitioner. However, it needs to be clearly appreciated that a mere study of spiritual and philosophical discourses is not enough. Any knowledge, which is not put into practice, shall not be of much use as the path of spiritual progress calls for direct experience and knowledge. So it is necessary for the spiritual practitioners to graduate from the mere understanding of spiritual theories to practicing the applied aspects of Spiritual Science. *Rajayoga, Karmayoga, Gyanayoga, Layayoga, Bhaktiyoga, Hathayoga* and *Tantras*, etc., deal with the applied side of Spiritual Science.

How does one achieve spirituality? As mentioned earlier, merely by reading spiritual or religious texts one cannot become spiritual. In its generic sense, the word *spirit* here means an indestructible divine energy form whose continued and unlimited play sets into motion a series of changes in all forms of existence, including in human beings, starting before birth and going beyond death. Different people understand the word *spirit* differently. Some term it *jiva* (living entity), some call it *prana* (life force in the living being), some call it *chetna* (divine consciousness) and some call it *atma* (a part of the ultimate reality called God or Bramha). These four words, *jiva, prana, atma* and *chetna*, are intrinsically related. However, *atma* is the primordial causative factor of *chetna, jiva* or *prana*. In a way, it can be said that a continued state consciousness, beyond time and space, is the very nature of the *atma*.

Paramatma and its parts, *atmas*, are the essence of the divine creation; they are the ultimate realities, beyond time and space. The cosmos is nothing but a manifested form of the Paramatma. Therefore, each created object in this universe contains a subtle and small part of the Paramatma, termed as the *atma*. Since *atma* is a part of Paramatma, it contains all the attributes of the Paramatma. It is omnipotent, omniscient and omnipresent in an unfathomable time continuum, like the Paramatma.

So then, what is God realization? The word *Atma Sakshatakara* (God realization) means realization of one's own *atma* or consciousness. Even though these particles of Paramatma called *atma* may be functioning in a *jiva*, yet the *atma* is never separate from its root, that is, Paramatma.

Therefore, the realization of God is not the understanding of the material manifestation of *atma*, which includes all the living, non-living, visible and non-visible things and forces existing in the universe. Even if a person can travel to all the universes in space and gain knowledge about them, yet he cannot be said to have realized God.

Different types of consciousness, in their varied form, seen on the earth emanate from *atma* or soul or Paramatma. All forms of energy in the universe emanate from consciousness, and all forms of materials emanate from those different types of energies. Thus, consciousness is superior to energy and energy is superior to matter in the universe. Whereas consciousness can explain and control all energy and material forms, the reverse cannot be true. Therefore, all religious worships of any deity in any form may not necessarily spiritualize a man. Any experiment in Spiritual Science means expansion of one's own limited consciousness to the state of a Universal Consciousness. The science through which the human consciousness can thus be evolved is called *Vigyana maya jagata* or the world of Spiritual Science. To achieve this, a person has to introspect (*dhyana*) on his own conduct and thought processes continuously. Idol worship, mantras and rituals are prescribed procedures at the beginning to purify oneself. Once the mind is purified through the control of senses, the consciousness slowly starts expanding. There is no short cut to this.

If one studies *Shri Sai Satcharita*, one would find that the actions of Shri Shirdi Sai Baba reflected this Universal Consciousness. To evolve spiritually, we should, therefore, try to follow His precepts and conduct in letter and spirit.

Om Shri Sai.

— *New Year Message 2008*

25

Seema Ullanghan—Crossing the Boundary

Transgressing the Limits

Vijaya Dashmi is celebrated by the Hindus to commemorate the victory of the benevolent forces of nature, mythologically depicted as Goddess Durga, against the evil forces of nature, depicted in the form of a demon Mahishasura. This day is celebrated joyfully because it gives us the assurance that, ultimately, good prevails over evil and, therefore, there is a meaning to our existence.

For the devotees of Shri Sainath of Shirdi, it is a day of greater significance because Baba left His gross body on this day, the 15th of October, 1918. On the Dussehra day of 1916, Baba had clearly indicated that two years later He would leave His gross body. He had said that He would perform *simollanghan* (crossing the boundary). It was also the day of Moharram. The departure of Baba on such a day was symbolic of His universal approach to human problems, cutting across religions, nationalities, castes, social differentiations and all such man-made barriers.

Dussehra also used to be celebrated by the Hindu Kings as the day of *seema ullanghan,* meaning the day of crossing of the borders. The Kings used to cross the physical boundaries of their kingdoms and start the conquest of other kingdoms from the day of Dussehra. In 1916, on Dussehra day, Baba told a group of devotees that he would undertake His *seema ullanghan* two year later.

Exactly two years later, Baba crossed the boundaries of His physical existence and entered Maha Samadhi. At His stage of divinity, He consciously changed the state of existence, according to His own will, to a different state. In the path of spiritualism, *seema ullanghan* does not mean only a state of physical change, but it means transcendence. We often hear of words like 'transcendental meditation' and 'transcendental yoga'. Transcendence of what? Transcendence of the fetters of body and mind. This can only be achieved by controlling the compulsions of body like hunger, lust and the compulsions of mind like greed, jealousy, anger, hatred, etc., (the six limitations). When, one by one, the mental fetters fall off, the two elements of mind – desire and feeling – pertaining to these compulsions also vanish. The soul, slowly but imperceptibly, then enters into a state of pure consciousness. At this stage, the person goes beyond birth and death cycles. He also crosses the barriers of time and space. The progress in the path of spirituality is the march of the divine consciousness from its primordial state to the original Divine Self.

Through various acts, advices and examples, Baba showed His devotees how to follow the path of *dharma*, which means transgressing the limitations of our small ego. On this Dussehra day, keeping in mind Baba's advice, we should strive to undertake *seema ullanghan* of the limitations of our mind and body, so that we can forge ahead to make a better tomorrow for the posterity.

– Dussehra, 1995

Samadhi and Maha Samadhi

The word *samadhi* is generally understood as a spiritual state of a person, in which he experiences, not his body state and mind condition as everyone else experiences, but a super conscious experience, which opens up before him much wider knowledge and experience of his self in relation to the universe. Regarding such a state of experience, two concepts called *savikalpa samadhi* and *nirvikalpa samadhi* are often used in Hinduism.

Savikalpa samadhi is a state of spontaneous self-knowledge of a Yogi or *siddha*, but such state of consciousness is not uninterrupted. When one awakens from the samadhi, his divine conscious state is disturbed. But in case of *nirvikalpa samadhi*, the state of divine consciousness is uninterrupted. There is a third type of samadhi, called the *sahaja samadhi*, which the Sadgurus experience when in their human embodiment. This is an effortless, spontaneous state of super consciousness, which means that the Sadgurus do not have to try to enter into a state of *nirvikalpa samadhi*. In their case, the *nirvikalpa samadhi* itself is their very nature — *swabhava*.

But the state of *Maha Samadhi* is different. When a saint leaves his body and is capable of remaining in a super conscious state without the body, it is called Maha Samadhi. Spiritual practitioners at lesser levels do not have such post death awareness. Spiritual Masters and *Jivanmuktas* or *Mazoobs* can be correctly said to be in a state of Maha Samadhi, that is, a continued state of samadhi even after leaving the body. The minimum qualification necessary to be a Sadguru or Perfect Master is to be a *Jivanmukta*, that is, one whose consciousness is not affected by death or birth. For them, death is not process of total annihilation but only a discarding of body, which they had been occupying to carry on certain duties towards humanity. They know exactly when to leave their body and also when to be born with a new body. They are capable even of entering into somebody else's body, as was seen in the case of Shankaracharya.

Therefore, the Maha Samadhi day of Baba simply means that on the 15th of October, 1918, He had decided to leave His mortal body, as the work He wanted to perform with the use of the body was over. There is enough of evidence to prove that Baba had known about His Maha Samadhi even two years earlier, on the day of Dussehra in 1916, which Baba had called the day of *seema ullanghan,* which means crossing the boundary of a mortal existence to an immortal existence.

When the consent to construct the present Samadhi Mandir at Shirdi was given by Him, He had said, 'After the *wada* is completed, I will come there to stay.' Before His Maha Samadhi, Baba had sent some money to Shamsuddin, a saint of Aurangabad, for conducting *kawali, mauli* and *nyas,* saying that the light that Allah had lighted will be taken back by Him on 9th Muharram in 1918 which, incidentally, was on 15th October, 1918. Therefore, we can conclude that Baba, the Perfect Master, who was *Jivanmukta,* had decided to leave His body, as His last days and last minute actions indicate.

When the Master was with a human body, He outwardly looked like a man, but internally He was carrying on His universal divine role. But when He left His body, did His divine role end? The all merciful Sai, before leaving His body, had clearly stated about His role after His Maha Samadhi, so that the devotees He had been protecting and helping do not feel like orphans. He had promised that He will look after His devotees even from His tomb and also that they only have to approach Him with their hearts and with love to get His love and support.

Today, the experiences of millions of devotees throughout India and in the world indicates that Baba's divine activities in helping and evolving His devotees continue, with all their manifestations and glory. Reports of thousands and thousands of devotees getting unexpected help for temporal, mental and spiritual development is coming from numerous places in India and other countries of the world. Experiencing His grace, self-motivated devotees are building many Sai temples throughout the world and carrying on various types of activities in propagating His deeds and philosophies across the globe. It seems as if Shri Sai, without a human body, is many times more active in removing the suffering of His devotees than the Sai when He was with a body. Those days the number of His devotees was much less than the number of devotees today and the activities to spread His name have multiplied thousands of times since then.

Sadgurus, as the embodiments of Divine Mercy, are always in a state of full divine consciousness, and beyond the states of life and death. They take a human body out of infinite compassion for the suffering devotees. Sadguru Shri Sainath Maharaj had taken His Maha Samadhi eighty-four years ago. But because of His *Maha Kripa* (infinite compassion), His love and protection for the devotees continues.

– Maha Samadhi, 2002

26

Shri Sai Faith and Reason

Interdependence of Faith and Reason

Many people, of late, are found asking question why and how is the number of devotees of Shri Sai Baba of Shirdi multiplying all over when, at the time of Baba, only a few thousand people used to visit Shirdi. Today, the number of people visiting Shirdi daily is about sixty thousand. The number of temples of Shri Sainath not only in India, but abroad as well, is growing to unbelievable numbers. The magnitude of other Sai related activities, like opening of different Sai Mandalis, publication of reading material (books, magazines, etc.), the number of websites on Baba and other philanthropic and religious activities is mind-boggling. His photographs can be found in *pooja* rooms of millions of devotees and in shops, offices, vehicles, and so on, in all parts of India. It looks as if a miracle has happened during the last two decade or so, resembling the invasion of a spiritual power on this earth — a mighty and sovereign power.

A Master or an Incarnation takes human embodiment as an agent of God to establish a noble path in a decadent human society. He tries to destroy the destabilizing factors and also re-establish the norms of moral and social conduct. Old order changeth giving rise to new — this is the main work of the Masters, one can say.

The world, and for us India in particular, is presently going through a phase of transition, both in the realm of materialism as well as spiritualism. The human society is, without doubt, undergoing a process of spiritual dialectism. Knowledge of science and technology is empowering the human race to discover hitherto hidden and subtle laws of nature, which a few centuries ago would have been taken as miracles or as actions of divinity. For example, space voyage, cloning, transplantation of various parts of human body, communication system, etc., have enabled the modern man to almost play the role of God of earlier times.

All these are based on sound reasoning and intellect but, then, what about faith in God? Human beings, as individuals, at all points in history, have prayed to God in times of crises. But what about a situation where faith in God and reasoning of man can coexist, in a perfect state of symbiosis and be accepted as a normal way of existence? Cannot monism be reinterpreted as a theory of unison of reason with faith, rather than philosophizing as to whether God is a single entity or a multiple entity?

The conduct and preachings of Baba, in the context of the society in which He lived, indicate that He made reason and faith interdependent on each other, that is, faith cannot sustain without the highest reasoning and no one can evolve with mere reasoning, without a faith in some force much more powerful than him. It does not matter by what name that force is called — God, Allah, Bramhan, Nature, Spirit or Soul.

For example, let us examine a simple instruction of Sai Baba: 'Do not take a service from anyone without paying for it,' when He had gone to the roof of Radhakrishnamayi's house at Shirdi. From the point of view of spiritualism or religion, the act of not paying for services is forbidden as it creates a negative Karma called *rina* (indebtedness). Speaking from a rational point of view, one can always ask as to how a society can sustain itself happily and progress, if some people work without getting paid and others enjoy at the cost of those who work. It is such a situation, played on a larger canvas, that had brought about revolutions in France and Russia, where the French Emperor and the Czar had not paid the peasants for hundreds of years for their labour.

A critical study of *Shri Sai Satcharita* indicates that Baba had always tried to bring about a happy and creative amalgamation of faith and reason. When He asked the devotees following different faiths to accept humanitarian concepts of some other religions, was He not putting reason over faith? No doubt, He was trying to bring about a perfect social cohesion, but what about faith in one's religion? On the other hand, when He had told His devotees that to follow the Sadguru or the Master will bring about spiritual evolution in them, was He not asking them to stop reasoning and surrender to blind faith?

The greatness of Shri Sai and the ever increasing relevance of His approach in the context of today's world, is seen in the simple way in which Baba brought about a happy synthesis between reason and faith in His devotees. This led to a healthy togetherness among different groups living in Shirdi.

If these actions are implemented widely across the world, then there can be a better tomorrow for the ever-warring and ever-jealous human groups, existing in a state of perpetual anxiety and confusion. Whatever be the prescription of any religion, the fact remains that a person will have faith in God only when he has faith in Man (as a part of God) and a person will have faith in Man if he has true faith in God. It is God who created man and gave him the knowledge that God exists, and Man used his highest reasoning called faith to perpetuate His existence in his thought process. This interdependence of reason and faith, as amply demonstrated by Shri Sainath Maharaj in His conduct and precepts, is the only way to evolve human society.

– Ram Navami, 2003

Dependence on Miracles

Human mind has a natural propensity to delve into the unknown and the mysteries of nature. What a man already knows does not interest him as much as what he newly discovers. This discovery again loses importance when a newer one comes to his knowledge. If such discoveries are logically explainable through scientific methods to which his mind is attuned, then their acceptance is spontaneous and easier. This is so because the human brain is conditioned to think and understand the world around or solve problems through the use of such reasoning faculties. When a person is confronted with a new discovery, fact or revelation which his logical intellect fails to comprehend or even if it comprehends, fails to accept, there arises a problem.

This is the predicament which most of the devotees face many a time when facing the inscrutable aspects of a Master's personality or actions. Even if they would like to believe in an unexplainable phenomenon happening around the Master, their mind continues to play its favourite game of doubting again and again. At times, they believe that such unexplainable faculties, which are known as subtle powers, creating miracles, are with the Master or they believe that the Master, being at the highest spiritual level reached by a human being, is capable of using such powers in a subtle way, not known to ordinary human beings.

When in a state of devotional, contemplative mood, they experience and accept these unexplainable phenomena more easily than when they are operating in their normal state of mind, guided by the common human intellect. Thus, they waver between acceptance and rejection and are unable to be in a stable state of mind.

There is an incident mentioned in *Shri Sai Satcharita*. When the grocery shop owners refused to give oil to Baba on a Deepawali day, the Master lit the lamps throughout the night with water, in the most miraculous way. As to why on that day and at that time Baba wanted to demonstrate His power, is a separate issue, but the fact remains that it is not easy for an ordinary human being to accept such an unexplainable and inscrutable phenomenon as reality. Those devotees, who were a witness to this miracle, suddenly realized that Shri Shirdi Sai was no common sadhu, but was a divine personality with occult powers. Such was the electrifying effect of this miracle at that time that the suspicious and mischievous village folks immediately turned into a group of committed devotees. This is the typical human reaction to anything surprising, sudden or unexplainable. However, this does not mean that the devotees' minds had fully accepted the fact and that they had no further questions to ask to Baba, having accepted Him as the all powerful divine entity.

If one goes further through *Shri Sai Satcharita*, one would see that hundreds of events and activities around Baba were happening in the most miraculous way. In fact, at the first stage, it is the news about the miracles that spread like wild fire and brought many devotees to Him from far and wide. Once they came to Baba, the great Master started guiding and helping them, both through visible and invisible methods, in the path of spiritual evolution. The treatment given to each devotee was in accordance with his requirements, which the Master knew through His powers.

No doubt, many of the devotees coming from outside and some belonging to Shirdi, who were in daily contact with Baba, witnessed and experienced His miracles and divine play as a daily affair at Shirdi. Faith was generated in them because of the immense help they used to receive from Baba, sometimes in the ordinary way and at times in the most unexpected manner.

When a man, after a long period of distress, feels desperation and then suddenly help comes from the most unexpected quarters, he thanks God, calling it an act of divine mercy. Baba's devotees, in thousands, staying in different parts of the country, used to get such help at the most crucial moments of their lives. Such divine interventions can be called the grace of the Master or compassion or *kripa*. For example Shama, an ardent devotee of Baba at Shirdi, was bitten by a snake. Baba, without use of any medicines, saved him only by a command. Nainatai, the daughter of Nanasaheb Chandorkar, was at Jamner and had serious complications during delivery of her child, but a man sent by Baba reached the house of Chandorkar, with the help of a mysterious *tangewalla*, with Baba's *udhi* at the most critical moment. Chandorkar, a Magistrate, with all his pride and intellect, was hugely amazed.

Hundreds of examples regarding Baba's help, received by his devotees unexpectedly, far away from Shirdi, not only when Shri Sai was in His physical embodiment but also after His Maha Samadhi, have been recorded. A very large number of these devotees belong to the intellectual and educated group, who would never have believed what they experienced if such miracles were told by someone else.

Herein comes the main question about the faith in the Master. Should miracles be the only factor or the foundation of faith, even if a Master is capable of creating such miracles?

The first problem that arises when faith is dependent only on miracles created by a Saint or Master is that the devotee becomes miracles-dependent. I have seen some devotees not doing what they are ordinarily supposed to do and then praying for help in the resulting crisis. For example, if a child is not studying properly, instead of taking care of his education through the available means and time, the parents run to the temples more frequently to get blessings for the child's success, as if a miracle would solve their mundane problems.

Nature, which is the manifested spirit of God, tells human beings, 'I have given you a body, a mind and a soul. I have created the facilities on this earth. Put them to the best possible use for your good and that of others.' The house in which we stay, the food we eat, the electricity we use, the doctor we consult, the temple we visit, are all created by God. First, not doing what God has empowered us to do, but merely wishing for miracles to happen, is treading an illusory path. Secondly, those devotees who only depend on the powers of miracles of a Master will lose faith if the miracle prayed for does not take place. After all, miracles are also dependent on the laws of Karma, that is, they are a result of a person's noble deeds of the past and take place only if he deserves to get such miraculous help. The worst is that if some problems are solved through miracles, but later the desired help does not take place, faith gets easily shaken. It is, again, in the nature of the mind that human beings are prone to think more of a single negative quality of a man, even if he has many other positive qualities. They lament on a single failure, forgetting that they had many successes in the past. Undoubtedly, if the faith is based on these powers of miracles of the Master, then such a devotee actually loves the Master's miracles more than the Master Himself. This is conditional devotion, whereas true devotion or love for the Master, in the real sense of the term, cannot be conditional.

On the other hand, the true devotees, even when they are experiencing the acts of compassion of the Master or miraculous help, neither pray for it nor depend on it. Tolerating the pleasures and pains of life, they continue to do their best for the cause of the Master. To them, the biggest miracles happen slowly but steadily. They conquer their weakness of mind to depend on miracles and stand out on their own in the world, as great personalities of faith in their Master.

— Maha Samadhi, 2003

27

The Gifts of Shri Sai

Gifts of Sai–And Their Misuse

Prior to Baba's Maha Samadhi on Vijayadashmi day in October 1918, thousands of devotees, from near and far, used to visit Him frequently. Some of them, like G. S. Khaparde, Kaka Saheb Dixit, Upasani Maharaj, Nanasaheb Chandorkar, used to camp at Shirdi for long periods of time, living in close association with Baba.

Baba used to receive numerous kinds of offerings and gifts from his devotees every day. Such gifts used to be made by the devotees out of their love and reverence towards their Guru. The list of these gifts is too long to be covered here. However, a number of examples can be found in *Shri Sai Satcharita*. From His side, Baba used to give away these gifts to other devotees. Some close devotees of Baba, who were residents of Shirdi, like Shama, Tatya Kote Patil and others, were the lucky recipients of such gifts.

Different devotees used to get different types of presents for Baba, like cloth, *kafni*, *phatka*, footwear, *satka*, flowers, food items like fruits and sweets, tobacco for *chillum*, coins, books, and so on. As explained in *Shri Sai Satcharita*, He was also given gifts like a horse, palanquin, embroidered umbrella, a wooden bed and many such items which suit the regalia of a ruler. Although all these gifts used to be assembled and displayed by one ardent devotee named Radhakrishnamayi in a manner so as to project Baba in the style of a Maharaja, it hardly had any significance for Sai Baba, who was truly a Fakir.

On some occasions, Baba used to return some gifts to the donor himself and ask him to keep it in his shrine for worship. Sometimes He used to retain a very small portion of the gifts like food or fruits, etc. Baba distributed the rest as charity, in varying proportions, to different persons, as He was fully aware of their needs.

There are numerous examples of Baba giving to devotees gifts like coins of different denominations (for example, Laxmi Bai Shinde received nine coins on the day of Baba's Maha Samadhi, Baba sent a coin and *udhi* to Captain Hate in Gwalior, with blessings), *udhi* or sacred ash (Baba sent *udhi* to Nanasaheb Chandorkar in Jamner at the time of his daughter Nainatai's childbirth), food (Baba used to personally buy ingredients, then cook and distribute the food to all those gathered), cloth (Baba bought and gave gold embroidered *pheta* or headgear to Tatya Kote Patil), statues and pictures of deities (Kaka Saheb Dixit received silver *padukas*, Shama was given the coin that had the figures of Ram, Laxman and Sita engraved on one side and Maruthi engraved on the other side), footwear (Abdul's family is still known to have pair of Baba's shoes). Some people received the *kafni* that Baba used to wear (families of Hemadpant and Abdul are known to have Baba's *kafni*). Some devotees are also reported to have Baba's tooth, hair, etc.

Most of these gifts given by Baba used to be maintained by the recipient devotee as their most valuable possession. They used to worship them with reverence at their places of worship in their homes or in temples of Baba built later. From generation to generation, it became a custom in families of most of such devotees to worship these items.

Each action of the Sadguru, including the giving of such gifts to devotees, contained an futuristic spiritual angle attached to it. In the process of my research spread over the last two decades, I have been able to collect and collate information about more than a hundred families residing in different corners of India, who possess valuable gifts received from Sai Baba of Shirdi. Most of them have maintained these with the love and respect they deserve. Of course, Shri Sai Baba Sansthan at Shirdi maintains the largest number of such precious items. However, the number of such items possessed by other devotees, if put together, would be much more in number than what the Sansthan possesses.

Some devotees carry such items with them to different places in India and abroad for their own satisfaction or for showing them to other devotees, with a purely non-commercial angle. However, some other possessors of these items, handed over to them from earlier generations who had received them directly from Baba, are reported to be using them for a commercial purpose. To my mind, this can perhaps be avoided, as any item given by a Master to the devotee is basically not given from a materialistic point of view and is much beyond its materialistic value. Therefore, display of such items to others should always be done purely with a devotional attitude towards Baba. No doubt, Baba's devotees feel extremely happy to see or touch any such items given by Him.

Jai Shri Sai.

– Guru Poornima, 2012

28

The Laws of Motion and Karma Theory

The Laws of Motion

Everything in this universe, living or non-living, visible or non-visible, is changeable and mutable because everything is in motion. This law of motion operates in the smallest particle of nature called atoms and sub atoms, as also in the Milky Way, the Universe and beyond. Whether on this earth or in the vast space beyond, everywhere divine energy, in the form of uninterrupted motion, is present. Therefore, the first and foremost principle of the divine manifestation is uninterrupted motion.

There is motion in birth, there is motion in death. Any action means motion, because motion is the *swabhav* or nature of nature itself. Therefore, anything created by God has motion. In fact, the whole universe, with all its aspects, is God in motion. For example, when we think, there is a motion in the mind, when we do not want to think and resist, there is, again, a motion in the mind. Even when we go to sleep, the motion continues in the subconscious state of mind and we see dreams.

The brain of human beings contains millions of cells which are in motion, even without our knowledge. It is said that in seven years the cells in the body are replaced by new ones. Even if we do not know or are not aware as to how the changes take place in the gross body or in the subtle mind, such changes are taking place continuously and in a specific manner, as ordained by nature.

In short, life is a motion, life comes out of motion and life is motion itself. When physical motion stops at the time of death, the soul or the subtle body continues its journey in a certain form and, therefore, it has motion. That is why death is called *jivagati* (*jiva* means soul and *gati* means motion). It is never said that death is *jiva nashtha* (that is, *jiva* destroyed or the actions of the *jiva* are dead). This means that even if the *jiva* or the soul has completed its actions in the gross body in a certain period of time, the mobility of soul still continues. Thus, this motion in a living human being changes to a disembodied state of consciousness. The subtle body particles, like the gross body particles, later get destroyed and go to another body called the causative body. After some time, the causative (which means the cause of creation of all bodies) is also transcended and the soul reaches a state where the cause to be born is not there. Once the causes are destroyed after completion of a time-circle covering thousands of lives, the soul comes back to its original state of causelessness and this state of causelessness is without any motion. In this causelessness state, neither there is a cause nor there is a motion to experience the effects of cause. Neither there is light as we see, nor is there is the *pancha bhootas* (five elements), nor the *devis, devatas,* nor the phenomenal universe. It is beyond anybody's imagination. Only Spiritual Masters experience this motionless, actionless, causeless, spaceless and timeless state of existence.

The universe was created due to some reason, which is called *kripa* or will of God. In order to experience Himself in multiple forms, that the Primordial Energy set a process of motion and that motion created millions of universes. Again, on completion of their time cycle through a process of motion, they go back to the causeless state. Thus, millions of living creatures are created, sustained and are evolved through this principle of motion.

All souls ultimately go back to the original source. This has been going on and shall continue. Philosophy speaks and the saints experience these motions in varied form. Material laws of motion are limited to matter. The laws of motion beyond matter are the laws of spiritual motion. A person who meditates and concentrates to find out the principles of such motions will know about his own past and future, because the laws of motion carry within them the past and also carry the future in a time continuum. The spiritual *sadhana* is, therefore, nothing but a preparation for the understanding and experiencing of these laws of motion, which create ever changing worlds. Happiness is created by this law of motion, and also unhappiness. Even if we do not understand the laws of motion, we are a part of the motion. We can try to witness ourselves as a part of the process of this motion if we develop an objective understanding of ourselves. This is called a *drashtha bhava* or objective look at one's self in relation to all the happenings around us and in us.

The man who has cancer and knows he will die, experiences his body becoming weaker, but does not see exactly how his body is becoming weaker from inside. In this state, he is sure that he will leave the body one day. Therefore, logically, he would be thinking that his body is not a permanent friend as it would die away with the change. He will experience that his soul and not the body is permanent. Thus, the soul can experience the laws of motion as a finer reality.

God is like a pillar and all human beings are like calves, tightly attached with a rope of destiny and Karma. But if we consider that pillar to be the Master, then we will consider that the rope is tied to the Guru and being thus tied, one is moving around on this earth. Sometimes we are pulled near the pillar and sometimes we go far away from it as per our Karma and as per the positive or negative actions of our past lives. When we are near to the pillar we are ground less, when we are far towards the outer side of the grinding stone, we are ground more—that means we suffer the worldly miseries more. As long as we are between the two stones, being continuously ground by the motions of time, we have a chance to go near the central pole, but once we go out of the grinding wheel as a powder, it we will difficult to return. So let us try to be as close to the pole as possible, under all circumstances. Sant Kabirji depicted this situation when he wrote:

> *Chalti chakki dekh ke diya Kabira roye*
>
> *Do patan ke beech mein sabut bacha na koye*

Once someone asked Kabirji if nothing is safe between the two *patans* (grinding stones), what one should do. Kabirji advised that one should be near the pole or the *khunta*, because near that pole the grains are least ground.

Our pole, our protection, is Shri Sainath. We should be as close to Him as possible. In every state of mind and soul, while going through the different events of life, we should always look to Him so that we do not go far away from Him and we are not ground badly by the illusions of the world.

Om Shri Sai!

—Maha Samadhi, 2001

Prarabdha and Karma Phal

All of us are searching for the right path to carry on our mundane worldly existence, every day and at every moment. Each moment confronts us with a new question, a new problem, whether regarding our duties, family, society, body or mind. Then we seek for an answer and a solution. No sooner is one problem over than another one appears suddenly. The problems, the possibilities of which we are aware of, do not take us by surprise, but the ones that manifest suddenly are the ones about which we had not contemplated earlier. Then, we try to find out if there exists any correlation between our actions and these problems, only to find that in certain cases there is none. Then we start blaming someone else or the circumstances, since we imagine ourselves as the victim of the problems, rather than being the creators.

For example, if a car comes and hits one when one is standing on a footpath; or towards the end of one's life one suffers from cancer in spite of all the precautions one had taken throughout life; or one visits a temple in a religious mood and someone starts a quarrel; or a panditji starts his journey for a pilgrimage after having evoked Ganeshji, but unfortunately gets a bone fractured as his bus turns turtle in an accident. Such incidents lead one to an astrologer or others from whom one seeks some answers. Yet one is never satisfied with the answers.

Such situations evoke the question that if in this life one has not done anything which could have been the cause of the troubles, then why do such things happen? Some people even ask that if one is conducting so many *poojas* in the temple and also feeding the poor, then why is it that one's child fails in the examinations or one's wife falls sick? Unlimited numbers of such thoughts, like the waves in a sea, often arise and create mental turbulence.

When one links devotional or religious activities like visiting a temple, with the failing of one's son in an examination or the sickness of one's wife so directly, it surely proves that prayers to the Deity or Guru are not with any other higher intention than simply the desire to be saved from all the troubles and tribulations of life. Such limited type of devotion is an attempt to achieve desirable results and not to spiritually experience the Deity or Guru. Such people, at times, leave the path when their wishes are not fulfilled. They do not understand that the effects of the actions of the previous lives also manifest in this life. Sudden and unforeseen incidents, particularly, are the results of the *prarabdha*, that is, actions of the past lives. Unwise people do not want to accept the unhappy results of their own sinful actions. They aspire only for desirable and good results for all their actions, good or bad. When in distress, one feels miserable thinking that others are not facing the same troubles, but one forgets the brighter aspects of one's life and the sad aspects of the lives of others.

Unhappiness creates many illogical thoughts in the mind. Such limited thinking is like an attempt to stand on the earth and calculate the number of hills on the moon.

As written in *Shri Sai Satcharita*, Baba has advised such people in the following manner:

- 'The reactions to the actions of past lives has to be tolerated in this life.'
- 'As you sow so you reap,' as the saying goes.
- 'You must surely tolerate the happy and unhappy results of your past actions. In case such reactions are not complete in one life, then rebirth will take place.'
- 'I do everything for one who remembers me always with faith and patience.'

Sadguru Sai had also promised that 'I shall help you to bear the reactions to all your past actions easily, if your faith and patience in me is unflinching.' Many such examples can be found in *Shri Sai Satcharita*.

Sadgurus do not break the laws of nature, but they manipulate them in such a manner that their faithful devotees can face the ordeals of life easily and smoothly.

Therefore, let our New Year prayers to Baba be thus:

O Master, the Ocean of Compassion; we promise to destroy the results of our *Prarabdha* Karmas of the past lives by bearing them in this life, but we request You to control our inner thoughts in such a manner that, knowingly or unknowingly, we do not repeat those sinful activities.

– New Year, 2002

The Friend and Foe Syndrome—Karma Siddhanta

When in distress, we look around for someone to help us. We pray to God for quick divine intervention to end our problems. We try to take benefit of the social position of our relatives and friends for this purpose. However, at times, we do not get the desired help, all our efforts notwithstanding. At other times, someone unexpectedly appears in our life and helps us to get out of the problem. When such an unexpected help arrives, we thank God for sending such a helpful friend. Thereafter, while introducing this friend to others we address him as 'my friend'. In this context, let us view the basic principles of Karma theory of the Hindus as propounded in our scriptures and practiced by the Spiritual Masters.

A moot question needs to be answered—Does or does not the cause and effect dynamics operate universally? The Karma theory would say that this helpful friend was an associated character of a certain past life and was to pay back the good act of rendering help, which is known as *rinanubandha* (payment of debts of the past lives). This means that by one's good deeds in the past life or lives, one has earned this good and helpful friend.

Let us also examine the issue with regard to the sudden appearance of an enemy at a certain distressful point of time in life. When such a character suddenly appears, then our immediate reaction starts from annoyance and leads up to anger and maybe revenge. Thereafter, we normally start vilifying the person and address him as 'my enemy'. This is how, in our entire life, we see our life full of 'my friends' and 'my enemies'. But if our friends were created by our past deeds, which we glorify secretly, then is it not logical that our enemies must also have been created by certain inimical acts committed by us in our past life or lives? Let us, therefore, agree to say that in our lives 'my friends' and 'my enemies' have to be dealt with equally, as both have been created by me and are 'mine'. Since both of them have been created due to Karmic *bandhan* (*rinanubandha*) of the past lives, isn't it our duty to neutralize the effects of both in this life, so that we don't carry forward the seeds of cause-and-effect to the next life?

The Karma theory would say that a friend returns the pleasurable experience as we had given same or similar pleasurable experiences to him in a certain past life. Similarly, an enemy would pay back the unpleasant or painful experience(s) because we had given the same or similar painful experience(s) to him in the past. When facing a situation of unhappiness created by the enemy, we have two methods to deal with him—either going through painful experience(s) and neutralizing the effects or reacting adversely to carry forward the chain of reactions to the future lives.

Here comes the wisdom of saints like Shri Shirdi Sai Baba. The story of the frog and snake named as Chenbassapa and Veerbhadrappa respectively, as illustrated in *Shri Sai Satcharita* Chapter 47, is a pointer towards the correct answer to our question. As the story goes, Baba once heard the painful sound of a frog, when He was moving about in the village. Being moved by the painful sound, He searched for the frog and found him on the riverside and saw that a snake was trying to swallow it. On seeing the snake and the frog in a situation of deadly animosity, He tried to separate them by reminding them of their inimical relationship in a past life. Baba told the snake Veerbhadrappa, that he and the frog Bassappa had killed each other in the past life, as the result of a bitter rivalry. He advised the snake to let go of the frog. Listening to what Baba said, Veerbhadrappa (the snake) released the frog (Bassappa), who jumped into the river and escaped. Shri Sai Baba advised His devotees not to react sharply and adversely towards enemies with equal and opposite negativities, but to allow negative effects of past Karmas, reflected through the enemy, to be neutralized gradually.

This highly evolved and critical theory of Karma (cause-and-effect) can perhaps be better understood through a simple example. Suppose one releases an arrow from a bow, then what happens? The arrow at the release point will move with the highest velocity and will gradually slow down due to mid-air friction and take a curving path due to the gravity of earth, before hitting the target. However, the moment it hits the target, or failing which hitting the earth, its force gets neutralized. The more the distance the arrow travels, the lesser is the momentum it creates at the impact point. Greater distance means greater time and less impact.

When we assimilate the basic principles of these two theories of metaphysics and physics, we come to the conclusion that instead of directly reacting to an enemy's wrath, it is wiser to show a little tolerance and allow time to reduce the impact of the inimical act of the enemy. When Shri Sai Baba spoke of *saburi*, it included this aspect of handling of enemies, with patience and consideration. This message of the *seers*, which has been handed over to the human society from time to time is, unfortunately, lost sight of and this is the cause of most of the social malaise that we face today.

Let us pray to Shri Sai to give us the intellect and wisdom to make tomorrow's world a happier place to live in by following His principles of *shraddha* and *saburi*

– Ram Navami, 2007

The Theory of Karma as Told by Sai Baba

Chapter 47 of the *Shri Sai Satcharita*, written by Shri Govind Raghunath Dabholkar (Hemadpant), has the story of the snake and the frog, described earlier. This depiction is in the style of the beautiful parables told to children in Hindu folklores. However, an in-depth understanding would reveal that Shri Sainath Maharaj was propounding the basic tenets of the Karma Theory of Indian Spiritual Science.

The first principle of the Karma theory is that the reactions of actions (both good and evil) committed in the past lives are bound to come into play in the next life (or lives). Those with whom one had good relationship in the past life will be friends in the next lives and those with whom one had bad relationship in life one will become enemies in the next lives. The second principle is that the law of nature, through its unseen ways of working, will bring these people together and precipitate the good or bad events as ordained from the past life. The third principle is that due to the play of maya (human illusions created by the laws of nature), such human relationships will be established in the form of some social relationship, for example, friend-friend, brother-brother, husband-wife, master-servant, father-son, lover-beloved, etc. Such relationship can even be extended to a human being-animals or birds relationship, or animal-animal relationship. Baba was categorical in making the statement that no one develops any sort of a relationship with another person unless a relationship has been brought forward from previous life (lives), even if one is not aware of one's past lives.

In our daily life we, at times, experience that the much desired or admired social relationships sometimes lead to unpleasant or acrimonious events. We also experience that sometimes person(s) with whom we have had no family or social relationships become the best of our friends. History is full of instances of bitter animosity between fathers and sons, brothers and brothers, husbands and wives, leading to a miserable state of existence and mutual destruction. Think of the stories of kings like Ajatashatru and his father Bimbisara, and Aurangzeb and Shahjahan. Unless something is done in the current life of the individual to end this continued state of antagonism, it will spread over a few lives more.

Shri Sainath Maharaj, therefore, prescribed to the snake and the frog that they should not indulge in further actions of rivalry and that they should wipe out the evil thoughts towards each other in order to remove the very seed of antagonism.

This is what most of the Spiritual Masters, like Lord Buddha and Christ, preached and practiced themselves. In short, the principle is to forgive and forget. Many people try to practise this principle, as advised by the Masters, in their life. Nevertheless, problems arise and the entire benefit doesn't accrue to them due to limited or partial understanding of this concept.

In a set of relationships, people usually try to adjust their behaviour because of certain social or economic compulsions and they forgive the actual or perceived injustice which they think has been done to them. Some people, at times, think that they have forgiven when actually they have not. The act of forgiving can never be complete without forgetting. Such acts of forgiveness, without forgetting, can at best be termed as temporary solutions, because usually in unguarded or stressful moments, the old negative thoughts reappear with increased vengeance. It is difficult to forgive others when one thinks that one is totally correct or is less blameworthy than the other person, who is totally wrong or mostly blameworthy. It is more difficult for the person whose memory is more intense and long lived to readjust and forgive the actual or perceived adversary.

It is easier for simple, egoless or light hearted people to clear the feelings of hurt and naturalize or normalize the course of their life. The more the grudge a person carries against someone, consciously or sub-consciously, the more miserable he becomes, cloistered in the caves of his memory. Psychoanalysis reveals that if one person intensely and continuously picturizes another person as his enemy, the other person, even if he is not his enemy, will gradually develop adverse feelings towards the originator of such negative thoughts. This is the most common method of creating enemies through our sub-conscious thought process. Similarly, by generating positive thoughts towards others, one can create friends. 'I can forgive, but I can't forget,' is only another way of saying, 'I will not forgive.' Henry W. Beecher said: Forgiveness ought to be like a cancelled note — torn into two and burnt, so that it can never be shown against one. And Mahatma Gandhi said, 'The weak can never forgive. Forgiveness is the attribute of the strong.'

In view of what has been stated so far, one cannot but agree with the prescription of Shri Shirdi Sai Baba, given out to His devotees while narrating the story of Veerbhadrappa, the snake and Bassappa, the frog. The only way to get mental peace and evolve in life is to control the negative thought processes generated in our mind so that one doesn't create further negative Karma, which one has to suffer in the same life or the next chain of lives.

May Shri Sai bless us all to get out of our negative *samskaras* reflected in our thoughts and consequential actions. Jai Shri Sai.

— Maha Samadhi, 2008

29

Time Dimension and Perspective

Time Dimension

What, in ordinary language is referred to as time, is termed as *Kaal* or also *Mahakaal* in the spiritual parlance. In this connection, words such as *Mahakaali, Mahakaleshwar, Kaalpurush, Kaalraaj,* etc., are seen in literary and spiritual treatises. In a similar context, the word *Akaal* has been used in the Sikh religion and some other religious sects.

Our past, present and future conditions are encompassed in *Kaal.* We call the period from birth to death *Jivan Kaal* (life span) and the period after casting away of the body and acquiring a disembodied form is known as *Pret Kaal* (period in the disembodied form).

Every being or every living matter takes birth to enjoy a specific time period in this universe. The Karma caused due to *prarabdha* begins from the time of birth and a person has to continue to remain in that Karmic bondage till the end of his life. In other words, it can be said that by living in the bondage of *Kaal,* one gratifies the deeds performed in the previous birth. It is for this reason that every soul, which acquires a living form, is in the control of *Kaal.* Not only animals, birds, and trees, but even the vault of the sky extended to the frontier of all directions, is also subservient to that *Kaal.* Crores and crores of Bramhand (cosmoses), *nakshatras* (spheres of heavenly bodies), Akash Ganga (The Milky Way), the sun and planets, etc., take birth in space and merge into it after completing their respective journeys in time. All Gods, incarnations and saints also attain transmigration according to the time ordained by *Kaal*.

Till the Golden Egg (*Hiranyanda* or *Hiranyagarbha*) had not exploded, meaning that till the Almighty had not given up His prime concealed state and had not revealed in the unmanifest or manifest form, energy (*Kaal Shakti*) was also in the subtle state in Him. From the moment the first explosion took place in the Golden Egg and the primordial matter of the golden hue was diffused in a time less than one millionth part of a second because of the explosion, from that point itself the preface to the creative role of *Kaal* commenced. In this way, that primordial man (*Adi Purush*) or primordial matter (*Adi Dhatu*), residing in extremely concealed and subtle state, acquired a luminous form and became the *Kaal Purush*.

This is not a permanent state, but rather a sequential tendency for evolution—an action which is characterized by light or brightness.

Hence, the lifespan of a human being is a valuable factor, because nature has allotted him a specific time period to work out the deeds of his previous births. Every year, every month, every day, every minute, every second also has its own importance. He who has not been able to utilize *the subtle to the subtlest* time period, his journey in time has gone on increasing in the form of life after life. It has been seen that great men of wisdom like Shri Adi Shankaracharya, Isa Messiah and Vivekananda could attain their life's goal within a limited period of time but some beings, in spite of living for a longer period of time, are not able to progress much. The incarnate Shri Ram was merely fourteen years of age when he performed great deeds and Shri Krishna's sport (*leelas*) had started from his childhood days.

Shri Sainath had come in the custody of His Guru at the age of five and at the age of seventeen to eighteen years, when

He arrived at Shirdi, He was already in the state of unison with Bramhan.

All of us should reflect on whether we are rightfully utilizing this important time aspect (*kaal*) through the path shown by the Guru or not. Are we trying to achieve elevation in our lives by using time (*kaal*) in the best possible manner? He who has done this has achieved everything in life. He who has not been able to achieve this has suffered the consequences of his actions of his previous births, life after life. This was Shri Sai's message, which we should try to remember at all times.

— Ram Navami, 2001

30

Appreciation and Projection of Shri Sai

Be a Worthy Ambassador

History has shown that the Divine Incarnations (*avatars*), Perfect Masters (Sadgurus) and other spiritual personalities are capable of bringing about great and long term social, political and other changes at different places and at different times on this earth. Some of them, like Lord Buddha, Lord Christ, Prophet Mohammad and Guru Nanak were instrumental in creating new religions as well. Some others have shown new paths for betterment of the human race and spiritual evolution of the souls coming into contact with them.

When they carry on their Divine and universal duties as ordained by God Almighty, these spiritual entities are automatically supported by the mighty and unseen powers of nature. The possession and use of such powers is natural for them. These powers are far superior in nature to the powers that all others species, including human beings, possess. These are called *divya* (Divine Powers) or *siddhi* (Occult Powers). From the word *divya* comes the words *devata* in Hinduism.

While working in a human form, these spiritual entities are capable of displaying the powers and characteristics of both the human beings and the *devatas* as per their will and requirement. Just as the human beings have superior power and intelligence over all the other species on this earth, so also these powerful divine personalities possess far superior intelligence and vast capabilities, much beyond the capabilities of human beings. Just as a man does not always have to think that he knows veterinary or medical science when treating an animal, similarly, these Masters are not aware of their divine powers when they are helping or treating human beings and other species, whether in their worldly problems or in their spiritual evolution. They use these powers spontaneously, for the benefit of others, without expectations of any material returns.

It is their magnificent quality of kindness that propels them to help others and suffer for them. On the other hand, human beings, when they come face to face with such a mighty personality, are utterly surprised and moved to see the miraculous play of spiritual powers. Further, the kindness with which Masters use these powers for the benefit of the devotees and destitutes brings forth an emotional upsurge in their hearts. This is beginning point of *bhakti*.

This is what used to happen to anyone and everyone who came in contact with Shri Shirdi Sai Baba when He was in His human embodiment at Shirdi. Baba's capability to give immediate and long term redressal of any problem of any person (both temporal and spiritual) was so vast and effective that even the most powerful and capable personalities of that time like Dada Saheb Khaparde, Shriman Buti, Kaka Saheb Dixit, Nanasaheb Chandorkar, etc., looked insignificant before Him. Forgetting their material or social status, they had to surrender at the feet of this kind Master. Being totally overpowered by the personality of Shri Sainath Maharaj and deeply indebted to Him for His kindness, these devotees started spreading His glory wherever they went. They spread the name of Baba, mostly through word of mouth and through varied social interactions, whenever they got a chance to do so. Ardent devotees like Das Ganu Maharaj spread His name in the rural areas of Maharashtra through *kirtans*, ballads and folklores.

During the period Baba is said to have been at Shirdi (between 1860 and 1918), there were a very small number of newspapers and journals in Maharashtra. A study of such newspapers and magazines shows that during that time Baba's name rarely appeared in them. After Baba left His body in 1918, *Shri Sai Leela*, an official publication (magazine) of Shri Sai Baba Sansthan came into existence and this continues to be published today.

The prominent devotees of Baba like Das Ganu, Chandorkar, Kaka Saheb Dixit and many others, who were instrumental in spreading the name of Baba, were extremely cautious and truthful in uttering or writing anything pertaining to Him. The two magazines, *Sai Prabha* (1915– 1919) and *Shri Sai Leela* (1923 till date) were not commercial ventures. Neither the publishers, nor the editors or the writers, had any commercial objectives. It was out of pure love towards Baba and the real life experience they had with Him that they published their experience in these magazines for the benefit of other devotees. They did not boast about the information they shared with Baba or their proximity to Him. They did not write stories on imaginary or concocted miracles purported to have been done by Baba. They did not indulge in bringing out competitive marketing serials based on half-baked truths or speculations on Baba, as is sometimes being done in audio or video channels of today.

Today, nine decades after Baba's Maha Samadhi, His name continues to spread far and wide in India and abroad. As Baba had forecast, Shirdi is thronging with devotees coming from all over the world and the number is ever on the increase. Hundreds of temples have come up in His name in India and abroad and more are in the pipeline. The number of movies, TV serials, magazines, books, audio-video cassettes pertaining to Baba, in different Indian languages, is too numerous to be listed.

Stories on Baba's life, news and views on activities pertaining to the Sai movement today and experiences of devotees can be appreciated through the various audio, video and print media available. Some of them are good. However, what is sometimes lacking is a truthful and correct projection of Baba, after carrying on due research on the subject.

Some people are, perhaps, not aware of the fact that a real Spiritual Master like Baba does not need a commercial venture to attract His devotees towards Him. By their subtle divine power, the Spiritual Masters can draw any soul from any distance by their sheer will. This is what used to happen at Shirdi during Baba's time. Baba has clearly mentioned that He can draw His devotees even from beyond the seven seas whenever He willed. A true devotee, who has full faith in Baba, will avoid projecting Baba through imaginary or concocted stories of miracles. Such false projections send a wrong message to the devotees and work as a hindrance in the correct appreciation of the personality of the Master, His philosophy and His teaching methods. Otherwise also, Shirdi Sai Baba, even after leaving His body about ninety years ago, is a living and helpful divine force for His devotees.

On this day of Guru Poornima, the devotees should pray to the Master to give them the correct emotional and mental capabilities to understand Him through their inner perception. The devotees should not condition their mind through whatever they read, see and hear superficially about Baba, but should read *Shri Sai Satcharita* regularly and concentrate on the divine attributes (qualities) of Baba and meditate on His form. Only then can they become the worthy ambassadors of their Master and carry out His divine work.

– Guru Poornima, 2008

31

Writing on Spiritually Emotive Themes

On the Making of Shri Guru Bhagavat

When writing this New Year message, I suddenly remembered an important date, which I had been trying to recollect since long. During the years 2010 and 2011, my literary work captioned *Shri Guru Bhagavat* was published in Odia language, in four volumes. Readers often asked me as to when and why I started writing *Shri Guru Bhagavat*, which had culminated in the form of a voluminous treatise of about sixteen thousand lines. In my Preface to *Shri Guru Bhagavat* Volume I, I had stated that I started writing on some day in the latter half of the year 2001, at about 11 p.m. Now, I suddenly remembered that it was the day after Deepawali. In a flashback, I also recollected that I had started writing my other work, titled *Gopyaru Agopya*, also on the day after Deepawali or Kali Pooja as it is called in my native place, Odisha.

I have never consciously selected a date for writing on matters relating to spirituality or religion, but such coincidences sometimes make me wonder about their deeper significance, if any. Is it because my mother worshipped Shri Kali all her life? Is it because I have the highest regard for Shri Ramakrishna Paramhansa, who was the devotee *par excellence* of Shri Kali, besides being a Sadguru himself? Is it because I had burnt my right hand on the day of Kali Pooja?

When I came to study for my Post Graduate degree in Ramjas College, Delhi, I carried with me a metal statute of Shri Kali, given to me by my mother. Is it because I worshipped Shri Kali for decades that such events of importance had to happen around Deepawali, I wondered.

Be that as it may, let me now speak about how I proceeded to write *Shri Guru Bhagavat*. I continued to write for about eight years. At first, I used to write in a small diary, which had a photograph of Baba. Whenever I wrote, I used to put the date and time on top of the page. There was no fixed place, time or situation for writing. It could be in the drawing room, *pooja* room or under the open sky, in the lawn or even on the rooftop. It could be in the car during a journey. It could be in the hotel room where I was staying. I even wrote during my stay at a camp in Allahabad during Kumbha Mela. The flow of writing was so powerful and spontaneous that time and place made no difference to me. At times, I could write only twenty to thirty lines, but at times I could write 200 to 300 lines, or even more, at a stretch. One day someone gave me two voluminous notebooks. I filled them up with my writings quickly. By the time I completed the work, it was about ten to eleven volumes. Besides writing on Baba, at times I used to write on Cosmology and Cosmogeny, propounded by the ancient Hindu *seers*, in the same notebook. These writings later became a part of my other Odia treatise, titled *Gopyaru Agopya*.

Interestingly enough, I never preconceived the theme of my writings. I wrote as the thoughts came to me. Usually, I used to write at night from 11 p.m. onwards, till I felt that there was nothing more to write at that point of time. My nephew, Debabrata Satpathy, started helping me in typing the matter in Odia script, on a computer. It was a voluminous, arduous and meticulous task, which he undertook with utmost sincerity. At that time, there was no concept of chapters or sub-chapters. At the end of the writing session, I used to give a title of a generic or specific nature, keeping the basic theme in mind. The writings and typing work went on simultaneously for years. I must have written more than 1500–1600 pages in my own hand, as I am fond of writing. Sometimes, some pages used to get mixed up, creating a lot of confusion and then we had to sit down and serialize the pages, with an index.

A lot can be written on this subject, but keeping the limited space in mind, I am only narrating a bit of my experience. I am sure that other writers, writing on spiritually emotive themes, must have undergone similar experience in the past or may experience it in future.

What I have realized is that when faith and love towards the Master is intense, literature becomes a spontaneous mode of expression, rather than a literary exercise propelled by sheer intellectualism.

May Shri Sai Bless us all.

– New Year, 2012

Philanthropy and Sai

Before Maha Samadhi, Shri Sai Baba of Shirdi had spent several decades at Shirdi, serving His devotees in two ways. First, He tried to evolve them spiritually by putting them through a process of mental and physical control. This He did, first, by encouraging and emphasizing the reading of scriptures like *Bhagvad Gita*, *Ramayana*, *Jñaneshwari* and *Eknathi Bhagvat*, etc., and understanding their essence. He even prescribed specific books to specific devotees. He encouraged prayers, personally by devotees and also in groups, and also the continuous remembrance of God.

Second, He carried on with His humanitarian and philanthropic activities like providing food, clothes and, at times, shelter to the poor and destitute and healthcare to the sick. He used to help some people financially as well. Thus, the kind Master gave both spiritual and temporal benefits to a very large number of His devotees.

Presently, there are over a thousand temples dedicated to Baba in India and many in other countries as well. These temples are carrying on with ritual worship, feeding the poor and providing healthcare through dispensaries, etc.

It comes to my mind that Baba's temples can expand the scope of their philanthropic and charitable activities in the field of medicare and education, particularly to the physically challenged persons in the society. Each temple, within its capacity, can think of undertaking bigger and more expansive programmes pertaining to humanitarian activities. They can think of cutting down on avoidable and unnecessary rituals and concentrate on rendering help to the poor, needy and the sick. Opening educational institutions at various levels of education, setting up of dispensaries and hospitals for medicare, inclusive educational institutions for persons with disabilities, old age homes and good libraries are a few examples of such activities.

Shirdi Sai Baba, besides being the Spiritual Master, was a great philanthropist and humanitarian. He even took care of animals. Therefore, His devotees will do well to continue with such activities.

May Shri Sai bless us all.

– Maha Samadhi, 2012

Sai Path

We go to a temple, worship Baba, organize *jagran* of Maa, visit Ganesh temple, Hanuman temple, Shiv temple, offer *dakshina* to priests, employ remedies against the evil eye like keeping lime and green chilly, yet we do not find happiness. Happiness does not come from these activties. We get emotionally affected by the laughter, anger and talk of others. Until the time we can control our mind, none of the above would be of any use. Visiting temples, music, mantra, worship and so on may help only if we can keep our minds in check. Happiness depends not on external conditions, but on intrinsic, internal factors.

The external situation creates a reflection in the mind. Why look for weaknesses in others? Why not identify the weaknesses within ourselves? We will not be able to evolve if we keep pointing out the flaws in others and keep getting affected by their actions. Instead of reacting to what someone said and thinking negative thoughts, we should reflect on our own drawbacks and weaknesses. If we control our mind, we will gradually identify the weaknesses in ourselves. Till we do this, no saint, no God, no deity, nor any elder member of the family, can give us happiness.

A child born in a poor man's house starves for food. Throughout his life this child grows after suffering and enduring hardship. We have never faced the kind of disrespect that a poor man's child has to face, because we have food to eat, a car at our doorstep, a bank balance for our financial security. All these have been given to us by our father and forefathers. What is our contribution? If despite having received so much we still remain unhappy, then we are ungrateful to God.

Remember that we have not received so much because of our merit, but due to the merit and hard work of our parents. Each generation inherits the best from earlier generations. Be grateful to them and reflect on what you are contributing and how you can be sensitive to the needs of others.

Why do people worship Baba and all the other saints? Their human form has gone, but they are still remembered and worshipped. They are not worshipped because they had earned a lot of money. Not also because they belonged to the so called intellectual class or because they have performed miracles. They are worshipped because they were sensitive to the problems of others and felt compassion for them. Most people are extremely conscious of their own sentiments, their own sensitivities, but are often insensitive to the sensitivities of others. Let us try to be sensitive to the needs of others and behave accordingly. Let us stop unnecessary rituals and use our God given advantages to reach out to the poor, the needy and the weaker sections of society and try to relieve their suffering.

We might have read the *Shri Sai Satcharita* ten times, read other books, heard sermons from priests so many times, but what is the use? Read books, but not superficially. Do not pretend to imbibe *bhakti*. Going to the temple, all decked up, does not express devotion. Baba had advised Das Ganu not to do that. Be natural—the more natural you are, the better. Exhibition of religious fervour is just physical acrobatics. We don't need acrobatics. We need finer sense to prevail to understand the problems of others.

We should start from our own home because our home is our *peeth*. If we are not sensitive to the needs of those in our homes, for whatever reasons, then there will be no saviour for us.

Every man is humbled by old age and sees the world in a new way, the way in which he has not seen it during his youth. If this balance has to come—as time will surely make it happen—then why not accept it, to the extent possible, now itself and live our lives accordingly?

Guru *shakti* and Guru *sahitya* guide us so that we do not take the difficult path in our quest to evolve. The Guru teaches us, through his own experiences, so that we do not have to suffer in our path. Let us not condition our mind through whatever we read, see and hear superficially. Read the *Shri Sai Satcharita* regularly and concentrate on the divine attributes of Baba and meditate on His form. Let us pray to the Master to give us the correct emotional and mental capabilities to enable us to understand Him and walk on the path shown by Him.

May Shri Sai Bless us all.

—*New Year, 2013*

Pooja and Bhava

Chanting of *mantras*, recital of *shlokas* and individual or group singing of devotional songs (*aarti*) is considered to be an important component of worship, not only pertaining to the Deities, but also the Gurus in Hinduism. As has been found, devotees find it to be an easier task to sing devotional songs like *aartis* and *bhajans* in comparison to the chanting of *mantras* and *shlokas*. This is so because the bhajans and aartis are written in Hindi or local regional Indian languages but the mantras and shlokas are mostly in the Vedic style of Sanskrit, written thousands of years ago. Some of them were created even before the formulation of the Sanskrit language. The *Puranas* were written in a later period, somewhere between the Sixth Century AD and the Fourteenth Century AD.

Generally, this part of the *pooja* activity, that is, recital of *mantras* and Sanskrit *shlokas*, in temples and even homes is delegated to the priest and *pujari*. Many such pandits and *pujaris* are found to be ignorant about the real purport or the complete meaning of the *mantras* and *shlokas*. Some of them just go on reciting these as a matter of professional habit. At times, the pronunciation of Sanskrit words is highly defective and conveys different and awkward meanings. If the original authors of the *mantras* could listen to the present day archaic style of presentation, they would be shocked. Further, there are separate *mantras* for every occasion, be it a deity's birthday or death anniversary of some one's father. One comes across erudite pandits in some temples sometimes, but they are rare.

Thus, the ignorant but gullible devotee is waylaid on the devotional path by some of these so called panditjis at a huge cost of their time, money and energy. The unfortunate devotee has no choice but to agree to whatever the panditji says, does or prescribes to be done, under the fear of losing God's blessings or incurring a divine curse or losing the goodwill of the panditji, who often usurps the role of an intermediary between God and His devotees!

What the simple devotee does not understand is that the entire system of worship of God or Guru is meant to establish and sustain an emotional rapport between the God or Guru and the devotees. That is possible only when the devotee is truthful in his emotional beseeching or prayers. This part can't be delegated to the panditji, to be manipulated through the process of uttering of a few Sanskrit words (*mantras*), the meaning of which he may not be aware of.

That is why the enlightened souls like Guru Nanakji (*Guru Vani* written in Gurumukhi), Shri Tulsi Das (*Shri Rama Charitamanas* written in Hindi), Shri Sharala Das (*Mahabharata* written in Odia) and many others, tried to make it easy for the devotee to develop a direct emotional bond with God (or the Deity) by giving vent to his feelings through the medium of regional, local and understandable language.

In Maharashtra, saint Tukaram wrote *abhangs* in Marathi language and in Bengal, Shri Ramakrishna Paramhansa used to deliver his discourses in simple Bengali language and style. Such changes, brought about by these enlightened souls, were fully accepted by the common man of the society and they were highly beneficial in their spiritual progress. Shri Shirdi Sai Baba also prescribed His devotees to appeal to God in a faithful and truthful spirit, in whatever language the devotee found it easy to do so. Therefore, the devotees who recite *mantras* should try to understand the meaning of the *mantras* and *shlokas* and then recite them during worship and prayer, rather than doing everything mechanically. Worship (*pooja*) without *bhava* (devotional emotion) is an exercise in futility. *Bhava* is the pulsation of heart, uniting the human soul with God and there is no role of an intermediary character.

Shirdi Sai used to ask His devotees to just recite His name Sai-Sai lovingly. History has shown that numerous simple, uneducated (in the formal sense of the term), but faithful souls realized God in this manner.

– Ram Navami, 2013

Prophets of Doom

Human beings have an infinite capacity to adapt and cope with adverse and challenging conditions presented in everyday life and in their natural ecosystem. Whether by choice or compulsion, the human spirit has the tenacity and creativity to withstand and adjust in the most trying circumstances. Our forefathers, from the Stone Age and millenniums thereafter, survived natural hazards like floods, earthquakes, impact of asteroids, jungle fires and diseases, despite having limited intelligence. Their life, at that point of time, without any knowledge of science and technology, was fraught with immense and impending danger all the time. Dying of starvation was an ever-present danger. The fear of more powerful and deadly animals kept them on the run from place to place. Each day of being alive seemed to be like a gift from God. They did not have the concept of God, as we understand it, to give them a sense of protection. They acted instinctively and not intellectually like the evolved human races that came much later. Yet, the tiny human beings prevailed even when the huge and mighty Dinosaurs perished.

From Stone Age to the Modern Age of advanced science and technology, the human race has made a long and arduous journey to move forward in the path of evolution. In its never-ending sojourn into the unknown realms, the human society is making forays into the newer and more advanced vistas of perceptive realities of our existence. Space travel, genetic engineering, ocean explorations, communication through the internet, nuclear power, cloning of some species, are but a few examples of such advancement. Presently, the earth's environment is undergoing an ecological imbalance, evidence about which is available all over the media and internet.

Our science and technology is gearing up to these challenges. However, this is not for the first time that the earth is undergoing environmental and ecological changes. Over the last four billion years, the earth's climate has changed several times, such as from the Ice Age or Glacier Age. Similarly, global warming is not a new phenomenon on earth. If the human race, without any knowledge of science and technology, managed to survive these extreme changes, using their instinct and resourcefulness only, how can we imagine that the human society will be annihilated or destroyed when we have such continuously advancing scientific knowledge and technology?

On an astrological note, our ancient Indian civilization has schools of thought and doctrines making future predictions. However, it is important to note that the Indian Vedic *seers* were highly advanced in the astronomical system of time calculation. Indian astrology, based on Vedic astronomy, is more scientific and advanced than any other astrological system in the world. The Vedic astronomers have calculated time up to fifteen digits or more. Vedic astronomy proclaims the concepts of *Kalpa, Manwantara, Maha Yuga* and *Yuga*. According to *Surya Siddhanta* — the earliest tradition or doctrine of archeo-astronomy of the Hindus, the *Kali Yuga* started on 14th February, 3102 BCE. The total period of time of the *Kali Yuga* is 432,000 years and is running its 5115th year as on 2013 AD. Given this time scale, how can anyone accept the assertion that the *Kali Yuga* is getting over and *Satya Yuga* is coming soon?

One is surprised to read news items forecasting the end of the world on a specific date and time. Certain individuals and cults of India and other countries have recorded these claims hundreds of years ago, projecting themselves to be agents of God. Even though they can be excused for their utter ignorance, but how can the modern man, with all the benefits he is reaping from the use of science and technology, be excused for accepting such hilarious fantasies and, worse still, running to astrologers and temples for saving himself from such a catastrophe? Given the mighty dimension of the perceived problem, how can any person think that he alone will be saved by conducting such activities? It is interesting to note that, none of these Prophets of Doom had ever imagined and written anything about the great scientific and technological advancements the human society has undergone. Did anyone predict that human beings would land on the Moon?

From the age of ten, I have been hearing about such impending doomsday scenarios, intermittently. I have seen the panic reactions of people and the evil propitiation activities undertaken with frenzy — calling on the astrologers, running to the temples, conducting *Yagnas* and many such activities. Some people, it seems, are always prepared to listen to the preposterous predictions made by the Prophets of Doom, rather that listening to the teachings of the Divine Prophets. Such an attitude creates panic and confusion, rather than offering any solution. The true devotees of God or Sadguru should avoid reacting to such imprudent assertions made from time to time. After all, God and Perfect Masters are there to take care of our little existence. Whenever our mind gets afflicted by such thoughts, we should render prayers to God, the Sadguru, to reveal the truth to us. Believe me, it works.

May Shri Sai bless us all on this Guru Poornima Day.

— Guru Poornima, 2013

32

Global Sai Movement

During the last two decades, the Global Sai Movement, as it is called, has spread across the globe. I had the unique opportunity of joining this movement from the year 2000 onwards. It all started with Indians settling abroad during the last fifty years or so. The movement abroad of Indian IT workers, experts from various technical groups, doctors and academicians to different countries for medium or long periods of time has slowly introduced Baba to the western world. Starting from the early nineties of the last century, a few lakh Indian citizens migrated to the USA, Canada, Europe, Australia and the Middle East. It is in some of these countries that the maximum number of temples and organizations related to Shirdi Sai have come up.

A very large number of such Indians, visiting USA on various types of visas like Business, Visitor, student or temporary work permit, had been devotees of Shri Shirdi Sai Baba when they were in India. The families of some of them had been devotees of Baba for generations and had been worshipping Baba as their family deity. They used to read *Shri Sai Satcharita* and visit Shirdi along with their families. When these devotees started staying in USA for long periods of time, say three years or more, they felt they needed a temple to worship Baba. Even their parents and relatives, who used to visit them for a few months, started yearning for Baba's temple.

Towards the end of the last century, there were few Shirdi Sai temples in USA, although it is reported that the first Shirdi Sai Baba temple in the USA started in Monroeville, Pennsylvania, in the 1980s. However, the number of temples, organizations and activities pertaining to Baba had an exponential growth during the last fifteen years or so. Today, a large number of Shirdi Sai Baba temples have come up in different parts of USA. Further, Baba's statues have been installed in some of the already existing Hindu temples. Scores of temples are under various stages of construction. Some states have temples at different places in the same city. Such activities are going on in states like Georgia, Florida, New York, New Jersey, Ohio, California, Minnesota, Texas, Alabama, Illinois, Michigan, Washington and Massachusetts, to name a few.

Shirdi Sai devotees regularly visit these temples, particularly on Thursdays and weekends, in large numbers. They celebrate Ram Navami, Dussehra and other festivals and functions, following the tradition of Shirdi temples. Most of them undertake social and philanthropic activities to help the society in which they live.

Similarly, such activities are in progress in countries like Canada, Australia, New Zealand and in South East Asian countries like Singapore and Malaysia and even in distant countries like Fiji. In certain places in Africa like Nairobi, Johannesburg and elsewhere, Sai groups are quite active. A new temple is going to be inaugurated shortly at Auckland, New Zealand. There is a temple in Fiji Islands where a large number of Indians are settled. Temples are coming up in Sri Lanka, Mauritius and Nepal as well. Some devotees are associating privately and carrying on with Sai worship even in Middle Eastern countries like Abu Dhabi and Bahrain. Similar activities are going on in European countries like UK, France and Holland.

In the year 2000, *Sai Utsav* was celebrated at the temple in Chicago in which I participated. It was attended by about 2,500 devotees. From that time, I got associated with this global movement of Shri Sai and in activities such as installations and *pran pratishtha* of statues of Baba. I addressed devotees in Sydney (Australia), Kent (UK), Houston (Texas, USA) and in many other cities.

Presently, we have taken up the task of linking the activities going on in temples in India with Sai temples abroad and vice versa, mainly through internet. Events happening in any temple at any place in the world are communicated to temples at other places, directly through the internet, with live video streaming services, webcasting and through social media sites like Facebook and Twitter. Besides, we have evolved a system of communicating through email groups and magazines, both electronic and printed.

The web sites of the temples like saibaba.org are rendering yeoman service by covering events pertaining to Sai related activities. This goes a long way, not only in spreading the message of Baba to the remotest corners of the earth, but also creating a multi-dimensional, global interaction between all the devotees of Shirdi Sai Baba, wherever they might be. We should welcome, join and participate in this global movement of Shirdi Sai Baba.

May Shri Sai bless us all!

— Maha Samadhi, 2013

At the event 'Malik Ek Sur Anek' organized in 2011 by Star Plus TV Channel and Sai Prerna Trust, Mumbai, Mr Vivek Oberoi felicitating the Author for his selfless service in spreading the name of Shri Shirdi Sai Baba.

At a grand ceremony in Hyderabad in 2013, the Author dedicating his book 'Shri Guru Bhagabata Vol-I' in Telugu language to public.

At Shri Shirdi Sai Baba's Samadhi Mandir in Shirdi, Author, while releasing the book 'Shri Guru Bhagabata Eka Divya Anubhuti'.

Author being presented with the 'Building Bridges across Nations' award by Lieutenant Governor of the State of Washington, Mr Brad Owen, at the event organised by WASITRAC at Seattle, USA.

Author with Gnanapeeth Awardee Shri Sitakant Mohapatra and Shri A. R. Nanda, while inaugurating the Shirdi Sai Stall at Delhi Book Fair 2013, at Pragati Maidan, New Delhi.

Author's books 'Gopyaru Agopya' in Odia and 'Shrusti Tattwanuchintanam' in Sanskrit being released by His Excellency Shri Muralidhar Chandrakant Bhandare, Governor of Odisha, in 2010.

Author, at the International release of his music CD 'Vardaan Do Sai' at the event 'Shirdi Sai Sandhya' organised by the DFW Orissa Society of the Americas on 9th November, 2013 at Dallas Texas, USA.

Rashtriya Sanskrit Vidyapeetha University, Tirupati, India, conferred upon the Author the prestigious title 'Honoris Causa (D. Litt - Vacaspati)' on 25th February, 2012.

The Author felicitating noted classical and playback singer
Suresh Wadkar with the Title 'Pundit' on 30th August, 2009, at the
second Sai Utsav organised by Shirdi Sai Baba Temple, Chicago, USA.

33

The Sai Heritage

Shri Sai Baba of Shirdi left His mortal body on the 15th of October 1918, about eighty three years ago. Towards the last days of His mortal existence, a few thousand devotees, along with their families, used to visit Shirdi, some regularly and others occasionally. These devotees belonged mostly to Maharashtra and the neighbouring states. At that time there was no official or unofficial organization to look into Baba's affairs at Shirdi. Devotees, drawn by the majestic and compassionate personality of Baba, used to rush to Shirdi and get immense benefit, both temporal and spiritual, from Him. He was their God, their mentor, their father and their only anchor. Some of them affectionately called Him by different relationships and names. People of all ages, religions, castes and from different places came under the universal banner of Shri Sai. Devotees from various positions like Yogis, magistrates, judges, police and revenue officials, political activists, traders, businessmen, farmers, fakirs and the simple rural folk used to take shelter under Him. They were all treated alike and each was given material and spiritual help as per his requirement by the Master, who knew the ins and outs of their hearts and minds.

During the physical existence of Baba, beautiful and broad-based values and norms of human behaviour and ethical conduct were established through His exemplary conduct and precepts, for the later generations to follow.

At that time, no one had ever imagined or could have imagined about the shape of things to come at Shirdi, as it is today. The spread of Baba's name and institutions dedicated in His name, not only in India but throughout the world, was not predicted by anyone. However, it was predicted by a contemporary saint, Puntambe, who said, 'Shirdi is extremely fortunate to inhabit such a diamond (meaning a spiritual Master).' Similarly, Sant Anandswamy, during his Shirdi visit, saw Baba as a young boy and told the people of Shirdi, 'Even if He looks like an ordinary person from outside, but in reality He is an extraordinary person. All of you will realize it in future.' He had clearly seen the greatness of Baba and forecasted to the assembled villagers about it.

One day, sitting in Dwarakamai Masjid in one of His spiritually ecstatic moods (*zallali*), Baba indicated that, in future, Shirdi will become a famous holy place with huge buildings and visited by large number of devotees, who will make a beeline to visit the place.

What Baba had predicted about a century ago has become true, given the fact that an average of about sixty thousand people, from India and abroad, are visiting Shirdi every day and this number is ever on the increase. Devotees from the highest levels and also poorest strata of the society visit His Samadhi. This is the place of pilgrimage in India, visited by the largest number of devotees every day. Today, the sprouting-up of more than eighty hotels, restaurants and other facilities has made the innocuous Shirdi of yesterday an important holy place on the map of India.

Thousands of temples, where Baba's statue is worshipped, have been constructed throughout the country by self-motivated devotees. Hundreds of books, magazines and journals in different languages have been published by different trusts and individuals. The miraculous way in which *Sai-ism* is spreading all over the globe is an indication of the strength of the values and heritage on which it has been built.

When we go through *Shri Sai Satcharita,* an official publication of the Shirdi Sai Baba Sansthan at Shirdi, on the life history and deeds of Shri Sai Baba, as well as other books and journals, it becomes clear that Baba, as the highest spiritual power of the time, had brought into action the loftiest principles of humanism and spiritualism as has been enunciated in the *Gita* and other scriptures. His entire life at Shirdi was spent in inspiring and teaching these principles to the thousands that came to Him. It was on these principles that He wanted the future generations to build themselves.

The devotees looked upon Sai Baba of Shirdi as the *God Here And Now* and not the imaginary God residing with all His resplendence, somewhere in Heaven. Sai lived with them, ate and slept with them and played with them. He had no pretensions of a God, but they had no doubt that He was God in the human form — *Saguna Bramha.* He was Compassion Incarnate — every action, every thought, every minute was for His devotees and nothing for Himself. Just before His departure, Baba gave away the nine rupees He had with Him, to a devotee, for He had come to Shirdi as a penniless Fakir and also went away penniless. He did not set up any institutions or temples in His name, nor did He encourage people apotheosizing Him. For all the miracles attributed to Him by the devotees, He had only one thing to say, that is, 'Allah *Maalik',* that is, God is the Master.

Shri Sai left no property for His devotees, but He left a powerful and rich legacy of universalism as against individualism, humanism as against barbarism, religious tolerance in place of bigotry, mutual cooperation against antagonism, and spreading of love as a cementing force in the society in place of hatred, which had divided human beings into small groups. He even gave the highest consideration for species other than human beings. Thus when Shyam Karan, His horse at Shirdi, was whipped, He received the pain on His body, which had whip marks. He was the incarnation of the Supreme Reality and whatever the devotees suffered or enjoyed, He also suffered or enjoyed.

To follow what Shri Sai prescribed as the Path could not have been an easy task for any devotee, unless Shri Sai had, by His personal conduct spreading over sixty years in Shirdi, proven that even in the present day world, Divinity can be experienced directly. The methods He prescribed and practiced were—constant attempt to efface ego, follow the Master steadfastly, remember God always while carrying on the duties of the mundane life and be frugal in living but lofty in thinking. Those of His devotees who could follow Him in letter and in spirit turned into noble souls whom posterity holds with the highest adoration. Thus Das Ganu, the police Head Constable became Das Ganu Maharaj, Kaka Saheb Dixit the famous solicitor of Bombay relinquished his worldly ambitions and worked for Baba at Shirdi and was given spiritual evolution, Kashinath Pandit became Upasani Maharaj and a less educated man like Anna Saheb Dabholkar wrote Baba's life history called *Shri Sai Satcharita* in Marathi verse and became a name which every Sai devotee knows.

When we see the Sai movement all over the world today, there emerges a clear picture of a new pattern of ethical life in the Sai devotees, individually and also in groups. Having visited hundreds of temples of Baba in different parts of India and in other countries like USA, Canada, UK, Australia, etc., and having met a few lakhs of His devotees, I find that Sai's theme of brotherhood among the Sai devotees is a unique feature. Shri Sai used to address many devotees as *Bhau*, which in Marathi means brother. Thus He had given a clear indication about the emergence of a Sai Brotherhood. In the Dwarakamai Masjid, He encouraged group singing of *aarti* (devotional songs), group worship, group dinning and sharing of *chillum* (clay pipe) among different members of the group.

Today, the world is passing through a phase of transition. On the one hand, scientific and technological achievements of the human race are progressing at a rapid pace, but on the other hand, such a progress is not bringing about happiness and evolution of human values. As a result, racial, religious and national conflicts are raising their ugly heads.

Wars and battles have never solved human problems. What brings peace and continued prosperity is mutual tolerance, sacrifice and love. The universal brotherhood of man can only be achieved by understanding the spirit of God playing through the human beings. Shri Sai Baba of Shirdi was the embodiment of the Divine Spirit, which still continues in the subtle form. The only panacea to all the ills we face lies in ardently following the principles of the rich heritage He has left. Let us pray to Him.

Resolve

We pray to Shri Sai Baba of Shirdi, Our Master, to be with us and help us to carry on the rich legacy He had left for the generations to come. Love, tolerance, mutual cooperation and complete faith in the Master are the cardinal principles on which this heritage is built.

– New Year, 2002

34

Kaka Saheb Dixit—
The Devotee Par Excellence

The word *faith* is the most difficult word to explain but most easily used by people in the context of ethics or religion or spiritualism. If this word is to be understood as a state of mind, it would mean holding on to a concept or an individual embodying that concept, which one thinks is so true that one can unquestioningly rely on it, no matter what. Once such a conviction, usually built through a series of experiences, has set in, then there is no further questioning on it. The only thing is to be guided by it under all circumstances for the rest of one's life.

Let us think of a child, say a boy facing a mirror for the first time after birth. How would he react? He may be awed or surprised or happy to see his image in the mirror. He may try to touch the nose, eyes and face of the image. He may laugh at seeing his own image, which would seem funny to him without realizing that it is his own image. These initial reactions may continue for some days. But as he gets older and experienced with the mirror, he will not be awed, surprised or happy to see his image. He will only use it to clean his face or comb his hair, etc. Before picking up a mirror, no grown up person has the slightest thought or doubt that the mirror might or might not reflect his true image, because there is an intrinsic faith in the capacity of a mirror to reflect. In science, it is easy to have faith, say on the law of gravity, that is, if I release an object from my hand, it will fall on the ground due to gravity, as a natural course of action.

But this word *faith* cannot be used in the context of ethics, moral, a deity, God or Sadguru, in the same manner. It cannot be a mere intellectual exercise or an exercise of habit. It is much more than that. Lack of understanding of this basic concept leads to a lot of confusion in the minds of the devotees, who think that they have faith. This is the biggest problem facing the devotees.

Many devotees are heard saying that they have 'faith in Baba', 'full faith in Baba' or have 'surrendered to Baba' or God. Would one ask them as to why and how they got such a faith for Baba, the general reply would be that Baba had asked (often quoted from books like *Shri Sai Satcharita*) his devotees to surrender to Him or that Dixit, Megha, Mahalsapati, the famous devotees, did so, or that in their difficult times they prayed to Baba and got the required help and, therefore, think that Baba will help them whenever they desire to avoid painful situations or whenever they pray for desirable happenings. Some of them are even seen to criticize other devotees for not having as much faith as they have on Baba and thereby enjoy a sense of spiritual superiority, as if they and not Baba have the right and capacity to pass such value judgments on such matters about others devotees.

There is no doubt that in different stages of spiritual progress, faith has different or relative connotations, but at the highest stage of spirituality there can only be one truth, one definition and one experience about it. It is difficult or rather naive to believe that what Baba held to be faith is held differently by Shri Ramakrishna Paramhansa or Baba Tazzuddin of Nagpur. But many people, due to their ignorance, pride or a habit of using certain words, try to project as if they have realized 'the ultimate' meaning and experience of faith when it is merely the experience of a certain level of faith. Even Baba, when he was in his physical embodiment at Shirdi, was aware of such limitations on the part of His devotees. He used to test the faith of His most beloved and protected devotees from time to time.

Let us examine the example given under the caption 'Ordeal of Guru Bhakti' in *Shri Sai Satcharita* Chapter XXIII. Once, Baba asked Fakir Pir Mohammad of Malegaon, alias Bade Baba, whom Baba used to provide with shelter, food and also pay fifty rupees daily, to behead a goat. Bade Baba flatly refused to kill it and confronted Baba with the argument, 'Why should it be killed for nothing?' It definitely shows that a strong faith was lacking in Bade Baba. Baba then asked Shama, another close devotee receiving a lot of benefits, both material and temporal, out of Baba, to kill the goat. Shama went to the house of Radhakrishnamayi, another prominent devotee, got a knife and placed it before Baba but did not kill the goat. Now Radhakrishnamayi, in spite of all the devotion she had for Baba, quickly took back the knife when she knew of the purpose. It was not that she was being asked to kill the goat but that only her knife was to be used by someone else. Even that she would not agree to, knowing fully well that it was Baba's order. In the meantime, Shama took advantage of the situation and on the pretext of getting another knife, stayed back to avoid the problem and returned only after the problem was over.

Undoubtedly, both these good characters, in spite of reverence for Baba, had their own ideas about *paapa* and *punya*. They certainly had not developed full faith in Baba by then and had not surrendered to Him. At last, Baba asked Kaka Saheb Dixit, an educated Brahmin and famous solicitor of Bombay, to bring a knife and kill the goat. Given the prevalent social conditions in Maharashtra, it would have been impossible for a high caste Brahmin to even think of killing a goat by his own hands, not to speak of actually doing so. But Kaka Saheb Dixit responded quickly. He got a knife, positioned himself and raised it for hitting the blow on the goat, and looked at Baba for the final signal. Baba was testing him till the last moment and he said, 'What are you thinking, go on and strike.' When Kaka Saheb was about to strike, Baba stopped him and asked him as to how, being a Brahmin, he was trying to kill the goat. By this time, Kaka had already passed the test, having blindly followed the orders of the Guru, but Baba wanted others present there to know about the thought process in Kaka's mind, his level of faith in Him by asking such a question.

Kaka Saheb Dixit had revealed the quality of *bhakti* and faith in Him, as spelt out in the Gita and extolled by all saints. He told Shri Sai, 'Your word is law unto us, we do not know or consider whether it is right or wrong to kill, we do not want to reason or discuss things, but implicit and prompt compliance with Guru's order is our duty or *dharma*.' He did not try to bring his reason into play like Bade Baba, or think of right and wrong like Radhakrishnamayi or Shama. He was a renowned solicitor of Bombay who had become famous because he had represented Balgangadhar Tilak and had profound capacities of reasoning and language. He had also read many books dealing with religious and spiritual matters. But when the Sadguru ordered, he forgot all he knew and immediately got ready to obey the orders of the Sadguru, which was his only *dharma*. In agreeing to kill the goat, he was not playing the role of the good Brahmin, an intellectual or a solicitor. At that moment he was purely and simply playing the role of a most faithful disciple, carrying out the Guru's commands. It is because of this unshakable faith, under all conditions, that Baba promised to take him in a *vimana* (that is give him *sadgati*) at the time of death. The manner in which Kaka Saheb Dixit breathed his last, in a moving train in 1926, as mentioned in *Shri Sai Satcharita*, lends testimony to the strength of his devotion, unshakable faith and his closeness to the Sadguru.

Kaka Saheb Dixit was made an instrument by Baba to solve most of the important problems regarding His affairs and giving a lead to other devotees after Baba had left His mortal body. It is he whose intervention settled the quarrel between the Hindus and Muslims at Shirdi on the issue of entombment rituals concerning Baba's mortal body. It is he who was primarily responsible, along with others, in the creation of Shri Sai Baba Sansthan at Shirdi and also starting the publication of the *Shri Sai Leela* magazine. Further, for the convenience and lodging of devotees visiting Shirdi, he had built a big rest house called Dixit Wada under the orders of Baba. After Baba left his human embodiment, only a few devotees like Kaka Saheb looked after Baba's affairs at Shirdi.

Later, when the goat was taken away to another place, it died on the way. Not that Baba did not know that the goat would die under His care, but He was simply using the situation to test the faith of His devotees. Kaka Saheb Dixit, thus, was the *bhakta par excellence* of Baba and will always remain an example for the posterity in matters of faith on the Sadguru and the sacrifice and risks he was prepared to undergo unquestioningly and ungrudgingly.

When Kaka said, 'Your word is law unto us' or 'Prompt compliance with Guru's orders is our duty or *dharma*,' he was just stating, in different words, what Shri Krishna told Arjuna in Gita *'Sarva Dharma Parityajaya Mamekam Sharanam Braja'* (Leaving all religions, take shelter in Me, meaning thereby, following Me is the only *dharma*). Similarly, when he said, 'We do not know or consider if it is right or wrong to kill,' he was stating in different words what Shri Krishna had told Arjuna in Gita, *'Nimitta Bhabah Savyaschi,'* (that is, Oh Arjuna, be My instrument). Arjuna was not ready to kill his relatives in the war of Mahabharata, but Krishna told him that he (Arjuna) should kill in a *Dharma Yuddha* as an instrument of God and not suffer from the pangs of doership.

There are numerous examples which indicate the depth and expanse of Kaka Saheb's love for Baba and also the quality of his faith in Him. Just for example, once Kaka got a box full of rupees (maybe more than a thousand), which he had earned from a Native State. He placed it before Baba saying, 'Baba, all this is yours.' Baba at once distributed the entire amount to the crowd around and emptied the box, while Dixit watched quietly, without any reactions, while any other ordinary mortal would not have taken this with such equanimity.

Staying at Shirdi with Baba over long periods of time resulted in his neglecting his professional duties and other social obligations as a practicing solicitor. As a result, his income reduced to the barest minimum. Some of his well-wishers even came to Shirdi, met Baba and requested Him to spare Kaka Saheb, but Baba would not leave His dear child.

Whatever money Kaka had, had been spent in Shirdi. Only his house at Ville Parle and another one or two properties remained. Before coming to Shirdi, Kaka Saheb Dixit, with his fabulous earnings, used to live almost like a king and used to feed hundreds of people daily. But, there came a time, after Baba had left His body, that the same Kaka could not arrange thirty thousand rupees for paying off the debt of a Marwari who was pressing hard. But he had full faith in Baba's words, '*Kaka Tulakalji Kasli, Mala Sara Kalji Ahe,*' which means 'Kaka, why should you have any worry? All worries are mine.' Baba did arrange for the payment of the debt of Kaka by providing the amount in the most miraculous and dignified manner. This is Baba's *kripa.*

But the greatness of Kaka Saheb is that in spite of all the pressures from the Marwari, the fear of facing legal action and of losing social reputation, he waited for days for his Sadguru to help him, like an orphan, although he could have tried and succeeded in arranging that amount of money. No ordinary mortal, under these conditions, would have just waited for the Sadguru to provide the help in the manner Kaka did, because from the rationalistic and worldly point of view, such an action would have been considered utterly foolish.

The mettle of faith, therefore, can only be tested under adverse circumstances. Faith brings out the qualities of love, sacrifice and also agony, in their fullest form. Only the person who has the capacity and grit to go through these experiences should follow the path of Sadguru. The Sadgurus, by giving both temporal and spiritual support, try to improve upon the quality and magnitude of faith in the devotee. As the faith of the devotee increases and he starts taking bigger and bigger risks, the support of the Master increases and is given at critical moments.

Slowly, the devotee feels that neither his friends, family members nor the society around can permanently sustain him in this world and beyond. He believes that even if in this world some material or emotional dependence may be necessary from the family members, in the nether world after death only the Sadguru can help him. Therefore, like Kaka, he moves away slowly from the established norms of social or family relationships and enters into a more perfect, complete and eternal relationship with the Sadguru. The satisfaction of his needs gradually become minimal and he slowly starts depending on only the Sadguru. The society in which he was born, the immediate family members and the relatives, generally do not understand and appreciate such internal changes in the devotee due to their ignorance.

The way the Sadguru works on such a devotee is inspirational. Sometimes the devotee may even be seen acting like a possessed man while doing certain jobs pertaining to the Sadguru, which the closest of the relatives would not be able to understand at all. Even if they understand, their own insecurity prompts them to resist such changes. These relatives initially start opposing such changes in the true devotee. They reject his thoughts as impractical or as merely imagination and try to block his path through various methods. While doing so, the immediate family members who love him, generally think that they are trying to help the devotee to return to the reality of life, but they do not know that when the Sadguru is working on someone internally, no power on earth can stop his evolution.

Nevertheless, the devotee undergoes a lot of agony internally because of such misunderstandings, but is not able to explain in clear, logical terms as to why he is behaving like this – crying sometimes, singing at times, talking to himself or simply sitting for hours and only thinking. Slowly, he realizes that the *saathis* (friends) of life in different relationships like parents, spouse, children, friends, have a limited role for a limited period of time. But the *Saathi Aakhirkar,* the friend at the end, the friend forever, is the Sadguru. When such a faith is firmly established between the Sadguru and his devotee, then the worldly existence seems illusory to him. Kaka Saheb's own experience is depicted in one of his writings of 1922, which reads:

'Nanasaheb Chandorkar came to Bombay (now Mumbai) and he introduced Maharaj to people of Bombay through the *bhajans* and commentary of Das Ganu. Because of these *kirtans,* people from Bombay and surrounding areas became very attracted towards Maharaj and went for his blessings. The other person mentioned above is the writer himself. Since he was also very close to Maharaj during that time and came out of social activities of Bombay. Because of this, it seems, all the newspapers reported that this writer had turned *bairagi.* Many people even went to Shirdi to seek the blessings of Maharaj because of whom this writer had reportedly become a *bairagi.*

In spite of all the rumours and newspaper reports spreading different stories about him, Kaka Saheb Dixit, the child of Baba, relied on Him alone even when the society around was offering him many other options. During that time, he must have undergone tremendous agony, trying to explain to everyone his faith in Baba, and others not being able to understand. This is the quality of faith that is needed before anyone can talk about his own faith. In any case, a man having such faith in the Sadguru will be so egoless that he would not even talk about it. That is why I hold Kaka Saheb Dixit as the devotee *par excellence* of Baba and offer my respectful salutations.

– Guru Poornima, 2002

35

The First Magazine on Shirdi Sai Baba

Four years after Shri Sai Baba had left His human embodiment, the first issue of *Shri Sai Leela* magazine was published in 1923, in Marathi language, from Shirdi. Later, it was published in Hindi and English. Today, *Shri Sai Leela* is one of the most important publications of Shri Sai Baba Sansthan, Shirdi, and is subscribed by thousands of devotees all over the globe.

However, it is interesting to know that this was not the first magazine published from Shirdi on Baba. Very few people know that a printed magazine was being published from Shirdi as far back as in 1916, when Sai Baba was in His human embodiment. There is cryptic reference about this magazine in some books, but not in detail. The original copies of the publication are rarely to be found.

The aim of this article is to inform the Sai devotees about the devotional and literary work that was going on in Shirdi at that time. Even *Shri Sai Satcharita* was published years after Baba's departure. Hemadpant had, no doubt, collected a lot of information regarding Baba's personality, miracles, divine attributes, devotees and lifestyle at Shirdi before His Maha Samadhi. Similarly, Khaparde and Kaka Saheb Dixit used to maintain their diaries on the happenings at Shirdi and about Baba.

The name of the earliest publication from Shirdi was *Sainath Prabha* and it was published by an organization called

Dakshina Bhiksha Sansthan. It is interesting to note that like the usual practice of naming towns (for example, Allahabad, Faridabad, etc.), Shirdi has been aptly called Sai-abad or Saiabad in this magazine. This was a bilingual publication, with articles both in English and Marathi contained in the same volume. Basically, it is of the nature of a journal, but for convenience we shall call it a magazine.

The first issue of the publication was brought out in the month of April, 1916 and was priced at six annas per copy. The second issue of this magazine was published in September, 1916. The main body of the English portion of the journal consisted of 28 pages besides the front page, dedication page (an English poem), publisher's note, general information to the visiting tourists and devotees and the description of a vision by a devotee named Shri Ram Gir appended to the magazine separately. The Marathi portion of the journal is of 54 pages with some appendages.

Interestingly again, the name of the editor has not been mentioned in the publisher's note. Only 'The Dakshina Bhiksha Sansthan' finds a mention. Further, out of the eight articles contained in the English portion, six are written by Shri Ram Gir and two by Shri Sundar Rao Narayana. Similarly, the Marathi portion of the magazine contains four articles, two of which are written by a person named Kirat, and one each by Pandit Ram Lal and Shri Hari Ram. I intend to limit this article to the analysis of the English portion, as it has more features and English readers would be able to understand and appreciate them better. The Marathi portion can be dealt with separately.

This Dakshina Bhiksha Sansthan was set up by a prominent devotee of Baba named Rai Bahadur H. S. Sathe, who had built the first *wada* (dharmshala) at Shirdi, popularly known as Sathe Wada. He was a first class magistrate in the British Government and had the necessary influence and funds to bring out such a publication.

The quality of paper and printing is of high standard. Not many issues of *Sainath Prabha* were published beyond 1918. The reason was that Shri H. S. Sathe, unfortunately, got into a lot of controversy in the process of collection of funds for the organization he had set up. He also had a quarrel with Nanavali, another devotee of Baba at Shirdi, in 1916, who he (Sathe) thought would kill him and as a result Sathe left Shirdi and returned only after 1918, when Baba had left His body. Nonetheless, he was a great devotee, to whom goes the credit of building the first *wada* at Shirdi and publishing this first and exclusive magazine dedicated to Shirdi Sai Baba. He also tried, for the first time, to institutionalize certain activities around Baba at Shirdi, but the results were short lived.

Since this magazine was published when Baba was in His human body at Shirdi, most of the experiences mentioned can be taken to be based on first-hand information, more so when Shri Sathe had invoked the blessings of Sainath Maharaj in person in order to publish this magazine. To the best of my knowledge, some of the information pertaining to Baba's routine at Shirdi and His divine personality published in *Sainath Prabha* has not been published elsewhere. For limitations of space, I shall mention only a few:

- Shri Sai Baba has been addressed in this magazine with beautiful epithets as Sesha Sai, Renga Sai, Sai Prabhu, Muktidata and Shiladisha (Shirdi's original name is said to be Shiladhi).
- Shirdi has been mentioned as *Mukti Kshetra of the Yuga.*

Baba is quoted as saying that Shirdi, along with Nimgaon, Rahata, Rui, Pimpalgaon, Kopergaon, etc., have been given to Him by His *Maalik* (Allah). Baba used to call Shirdi the ancient residence of His people where His *sagai* (relatives) and *soirais* (marriage relations) used to live and further that Shirdi is His *sasurwadi* (father-in-law's home). Baba is said to have mentioned a number of times that He had visited Shirdi (Shiladhi) during His earlier lives. His latest appearance at Shirdi is said to be two hundred years after His last visit. Baba has assured many of his devotees at Shirdi that in future He would stay at Shirdi permanently. ''मी कुत्रे, मांजर, डुक्कर होऊन हिंडतो''

- This statement of Baba, when read along with His other statements, that His bones would speak from this tomb, from where He would help His distressed devotees, is the greatest assurance to all the Sai devotees of today and tomorrow.

- Baba had further revealed the past history of Shirdi, which He inhabited during His many incarnations. Shirdi, in ancient times, was a prosperous place with a large population. It was an affluent commercial centre. Later, Shirdi went into oblivion and by 1916 the population was about 1,500. Baba, the *Trikaladarshi*, knew about its past and also future. Thus, His utterances about the future, when in a state of Divine ecstasy, that Shirdi will again have a lot of buildings and a large number of people, big and small, from far and wide, will visit Shirdi, has proved to be absolutely correct, given the present situation at Shirdi. Baba has brought back, true to his words, the glory to His ancestral land, that is, Shirdi, which has become a place of international pilgrimage.

- Besides the above mentioned assurance and many other utterances Baba is quoted as saying,

  ''पन्नास हजार आले आणि, छप्पन हजार गेले त्यांच्याशीं आपल्याला काय करायचें? ज्यांची निष्ठा धड आहे आणि इमान शाबूत आहे त्यांला सात समुद्र न्याहाल करोन माइया माणसांना 72 पिढ्यांपर्यंत मीच संभालतों''

  This means, 'Fifty thousand come and fifty six thousand go. How does it matter to us? I will take care, up to 72 generations, of the devotees who have absolute faith and devotion towards me, beyond the seven seas.'

- Even today, many devotees are experiencing Shri Sainath Maharaj's divine existence through dreams, miracles, unusual connection with other people and happenings and also, at times, through visions. The main writer of six articles of this issue of *Sainath Prabha*, Shri Ram Gir, has narrated one of the visions of Baba, which is given below. He has written it in the most lucid and poignant language in the April, 1916 issue of *Sai Prabha*.

I was walking along a side foot-path, up a wealthy street, bedecked with huge and pretty sky-scrapers, during a summer afternoon. The extensive city, of which this street formed one of the busiest areas, looked more like a twentieth century one, as is often seen in the West. The twin white pavements of the neatly laid paths, garlanded, as it were, the pink metalled central cart-track, which wouldn't creak under the massive rollers of heavy buffalo-driven trucks exchanging the busy man's fortune, from godown to steamer-yard and vice versa. I couldn't find adequate words to describe the beautiful broad avenue, whose extremities could have measured a couple of miles, of palatial mansions, through so many attractive green squares between. I passed many such pretty centres, when my attention was suddenly twisted to a crowd of people attempting to cross my side, from the opposite foot-path, at a cutting of a lane adjoining a double row of parallel palaces. At this interesting corner, under the shade of a well-branched वटवृक्ष (Banyan tree), I observed the said group of people to proceed from. They had, evidently, refreshed themselves for a while on the square pavement around this green shade, and were crossing the road with leisured steps so gracefully to my side, that I cannot but note surprisingly, from their dress and it looked that they did not evidently belong to the city.

They spoke a language with many gutturals yet measured with musical gamkas (deep and majestic musical tone) that I believed they were uttering their hasty prayers to the Almighty Allah-Meah, for some miraculous success over human impediments. Their serious yet submissive features, with enquiring eyes, often centred towards their chief in their midst, exhibited a clear tone of their Sirdari relation to their adored Prince. Their uniforms, so spotlessly white, fell gracefully below their knees, sewing their sturdy Kadared (Indian shoes) feet, as used to brisk long walks. Of almost uniform height, they excelled each other in their noble countenance, as the loyal attaches of their princely lord in the centre. White-turbaned and white-robed, with not even a stick in their hands, their holiday attire, and yet, a serious religious tint to add to their noble manly faces. They had evidently followed their chief to the city, on important business of His, and they were probably to leave it soon. The brilliant group of His Sirdars were then seen to disperse in different directions, as per their master's bid, at the successive glances of the figuring Chief. There, he stood alone, in a moment, in my full view, with surprising rapidity, as he if descended from regions unseen. 'Was it a dream?' I said to myself, 'Where do I stand?' was the next flashing idea, and, it was, as quickly followed by a third query as to 'Where and how had they, those angelic Sirdars of His disappeared at such a wink of the eye?' As I wonderingly cast up an enquiring glance at His Lordly countenance, what did I see? Not the powerful Sirdar Prince, but my own Loving Father, with smiling lips, which consoled my surprised self, though He looked half as young as He now is. Though I had never seen him but at an advanced age, yet His prominent younger face had such striking similarities of His prominent features that, without erring, I recognized my own Guroo Maharaj Shree Sai Prabhu, in the middle aged princely chief of the loyal Sirdars that had so mystically disappeared. Thus confused, I mechanically fell at His feet and, as I rose, near Him, He lovingly passed His blessing hands on my head, and with one hand round my shoulders, ordered me to silently walk straight to the distant four-floored house at the corner of the street, and to get cash Rs. 135 in exchange for the piece of paper (a cheque which He handed to me from an inner pocket of His white angy) and hand over to Him soon, the

cash, while he would wait, at another corner, near where we
then stood. I ran to the window in the first floor of the Bank,
whose name I read in the cheque, cashed it, and returned as
quickly as I could to where my Lord was to be found, and paid
the amount into His hands. Receiving the cash, He handed
to me by the other hand, a copper sheet of about 2 ½" X 4",
with an order, as lovingly given, to keep the same with me
carefully, for future use. I prostrated once again, and before
I had time to ascertain what the copper sheet was for, He, my
Lord, blessed me once more, with His right hand on my head
first, and then all over my back, with His other, so closely
standing I was to Him. The next, I heard, was कालजीकरूनको
गरीबांन्चांअल्लामालिक My eyes were filled with drops आनन्दबाश्प
And, as further drops collected in increasing numbers,
the first collected ones were dropping down the cheeks,
challenging me, as it were, to aispise my past life. The hairs
on my body stood on their ends, and, as I, shivering, looked
up, found only the azure, spotted sky, ceiling irregularly the
rows of lofty terrace, on either side of the street, the beauty
of which I could never forget, as it spontaneously brought
to light a deep-laid secret. Oh! My Lord! My Guide! Where
have you gone to hide yourself? I cried; I wiped my watery
eyes, and cleaned my channelled cheeks with a hasty rub, yet,
my poor eyes had no sight to discern what I saw, in the blue
canopy over-head; fresher drops were collectively shedding the
older ones from below the over-full fountains to run over the
dry checks to disappear into my thick beard. My blinded seers
misinformed me. Many times I tried to see my Baba, in vain.
I ran here, and there, and nowhere did I find Him; without
whom, I thought I could not live. Then, mark, while I had
thus wonderingly crossed to the other side, a sweet call from
where the वटवृक्ष stood, drew me nearer to it, but to see none in
human form. A second voice, I heard, yet I could not discern
a body. When a third call rang in my ears, the sweet name
by which He usually calls me बुवा, suggested my master's
गुप्तवास्तव्य near the वटवृक्ष for reasons inexplicable to human

intelligence, but, by His supreme intelligence. I searched all around the mystic tree. I extended my wandering sight into all the shady branches of the huge trunk, but, no satisfaction was to my lot by such attempts. Yet, confusingly I closed my paining eyes and thought of Him who had thus shown me an ever-memorable scene, and questioned what I could gain therefrom. An anxious pause followed a sincere thought, when amidst a glorious sunny light, encircled by a crimson border; I discerned a miniature of my साईंप्रभू slowly developing into His usual life size. His lips seemed to move; words rang in my ears; eyes were getting filled, and the figure disappeared as quickly, after a pass of His blessing hand वरदहस्त on my head.

– Ram Gir

Written in 1916, this vision gives inkling into the past of Shirdi and depicts the future as well. Some portions of this mystique vision forecasted the present conditions of Shirdi. Ram Gir saw 'huge and pretty sky-scrapers', an 'extensive city', 'busiest city looking like a twentieth century one', 'beautiful broad avenue', 'palatial mansions', attractive green square', etc.

Today, when a person visits Shirdi, he will find to his surprise that within the last decade it has become an extremely busy place with a number of multi-storied buildings. Shirdi has been transformed in the pattern of a twenty first century township, with all the amenities. At this rate of growth, the future look of Shirdi would, predictably, be as envisioned by Ram Gir.

Baba's assurances to His devotees have come true, as also the vision given to Ram Gir. Is not this the greatest blessing of Shri Shirdi Sai to His devotees – past, present and future?

– Maha Samadhi, 2005

36

Relationship between Baba and His Devotees

Most of the devotees and disciples of a Sadguru or a Spiritual Master generally have certain fixed beliefs and ideas about the personality and working style of these magnificent beings. They not only conceive of them (the Masters) as Divine human embodiments with perfect qualities, but also expect them to function in accordance with certain standards conceptualized by them. The evolved devotees pray and worship them to make them (devotees) pure, take them out of the worldly entanglements and to lead them on the divine path. However, the number of such devotees is very small. On the other hand, the majority of devotees imagine a Guru as one who would forgive them always for their faults, satisfy even their most selfish needs, and perform miracles to protect them from all kinds of diseases and problems, save them from the consequences of their immoral and dangerous acts, etc.

With superficial knowledge gained through reading of a few books and listening to a few discourses, they are conveniently convinced that all the personal problems of the devotees, whether physical, financial, social or those relating to the family in case they are married and have a family, will get solved easily either through God's intervention or by the Master through the use of His miraculous powers. When they come to the Master with such preconceived notions, the very approach is distorted from the beginning. They are not ready to take into consideration the priorities and compulsions of the Masters—mundane and spiritual alike, when He is in a human embodiment.

No doubt a Sadguru is a Perfect Being with far superior qualities of head and heart than any human being on earth and is capable of existing in two states of consciousness simultaneously. By His sheer will, He can enter into the highest state of spiritual ecstasy or can come down to the ordinary worldly realities, with equal ease. Thus, when He in the state of spiritual ecstasy, which can be seen to be either peaceful or otherwise, that is, *jamali* or *alali* states, respectively, He can give revelations about future events, persons, places and can also create wondrous miracles like controlling the elements of nature like fire, rain, etc., curing diseases at once with touch or look and granting fulfilment of desires of the devotees. On the other hand, when He is in the state of ordinary human consciousness, He can be seen to cook food, purchase articles from the market, clean His own clothes, take care of His body, make jokes and even engage in arguments like any ordinary man. To maintain His body as a perfect machine for carrying on His divine role, He has to do certain mundane activities like cleaning His body, eating, sleeping, etc. In the case of Masters like Tukaram, Nanakdev and Kabir, besides themselves, they also had to take care of their family members and relatives. Once with a human body, the Masters will have to go through all the limitations and pains of the body they hold. Shri Shirdi Sai Baba had a daily routine of going to Lendi Bag for his daily ablutions and used to take a bath there at times.

Devotees who look up to the Master as a God more through their imagination than experience, think that the Master must be taking care of all His problems through the use of His miraculous powers and are sure that He would be having no problems whatsoever. However, the lives of some of the saints like Tukaram, who had a family, speak volumes about the amount of troubles they had to face because even their family members did not understand and appreciate their divine qualities. Many a times their divine benevolence and goodness were interpreted as weakness and exploited by the devotees and relatives alike.

Some of the devotees try to surround the Master always and never let Him have any privacy, even for prayers. 'After all,' the devotees hold, 'since He is in a God state, we are also His children as much as the ones born out of Him. Is not spending time with the family members and relatives, when there are so many people waiting to be helped, unbecoming of a real Guru?'

The situation is still worse when some people assume themselves to be perfect devotees and demand of the Guru to act in a certain manner towards them as per their desire. They are not aware that even in the spiritual world and hierarchy, there are perfect laws and conditions under which such mutual relationship between the Guru and disciple is established. Most of the so-called and self assumed disciples don't have any idea about these rules and conditions necessary for moving along the spiritual path with the Masters, leave alone speaking of following them. They seem to be more aware about their rights over the Master than about their duty towards Him. On the one hand, they want the Master to fully understand and appreciate their problems, but on the other hand, they don't even try to understand and appreciate the priorities and difficulties of the Master.

Even if there is a devotional aspect along with their self-interest, it is *sakama bhakti*. The Master rarely gets devotees with *nishkama bhakti*. But once such a disciple comes into contact with the Master, he or she is taken care of fully by the Him as His own child. Such a disciple is moulded and is slowly raised in the spiritual hierarchy by the Master.

There has been no focused research on this aspect covering the lives of the Perfect Masters. Would anyone care to find out the effects that such actions and thought processes of the devotees had on the daily life of some of the Sadgurus or Gurus, it would not only be revealing but shocking. To my mind, what makes the Sadgurus so perfect and magnificent is not their power of miracles or knowledge of God, but their infinite tolerance and compassion to satisfy even the smallest and undeserved demands of their devotees, at a total sacrifice of even their minimal comforts, out of their infinite kindness.

Let us take the example of Shirdi Sai Baba's daily life when He was at Shirdi. Baba's divine personality had influenced and advanced the lives and conduct towards righteousness of hundreds of families. Hundreds of people used to make a beeline to Shirdi daily. Both spiritual and material help was being given to all, whether at Shirdi or elsewhere, by Baba and that too, many a times, through miraculous methods. People who surrounded Him from early morning till late at night for the fulfilment of their multi-faceted desires, failed to realize (except a few like Kaka Saheb Dixit, Mhalsapati, Buti, Chandorkar, Shama, Tatya, Radhakrishnamayi, Baijabai, Laxmi Bai, Shelke, Megha, Bala Saheb Bhate and some others) the amount of suffering Baba had to undergo due to their indiscrete demands on Him.

Baba used to get a lot of offerings and *dakshina* daily from His devotees, who used to come to Him from different parts of Maharashtra and other places. The gifts were mostly in the nature of cash, food items, fruits, flowers, clothes, items for His personal use, items for pooja and other rituals, etc. He used to distribute most of them among the devotees, the destitutes and the poor. Money received as *dakshina* by Baba used to be given away not only to some of the daily receivers like Bade Baba, Tatya Kote Patil, etc., but also donated freely to some individuals and groups who used to approach Baba regularly. Such groups included *kirtan* groups, *majlis* groups, dance troupes, nomadic groups demonstrating rural sports, beggars, mendicants, Sadhus and Fakirs, needy devotees, destitute women and children, etc. Indeed, Baba's fame for charity had spread so far and wide that many families, along with their children, used to come and camp at Shirdi, only to live off Baba's charity. By 1915–16, this number had increased to hundreds and their daily demands on Baba were ever on the increase.

Some people would approach Baba on all sorts of pretexts to extract money and food. Knowing the attachment of Baba towards children, some of them would send their children to Baba on the sly, so that whenever any devotee presented food items and Baba was about to start His meal, these children would appear on the scene and start begging. The all compassionate Baba would distribute all the food items and many a times go without food Himself. Sometimes, the food items, clothes and also the utensils would be stolen. By 1915, there were more than thirty *kirtan* or singing parties, some of whom were extremely low in quality, who had mostly come from outside. They used to camp at Shirdi, only to get money by displaying their uninvited performance before Baba at Dwarakamai and also in the nearby areas. Some local touts busied themselves in managing these nefarious activities and used to take a cut from the profited parties.

Besides, there was another aspect which made Baba's stay at Shirdi most uncomfortable. Baba used to get periodic attacks of asthma. Even when He was under such an attack, some callous devotees would bathe Him with cold water, apply oil and *chandan* all over His body and make Him take milk, curd, rice and fruits, which an asthma patient should avoid strictly. All this they did just to satisfy their own sentiments. Baba continued to suffer physically from 1915 onwards due to such improper treatment at the hands of His ignorant devotees.

When Baba used to actually suffer physically, some ignorant devotees took it to be His *Leela* or Divine Sport. 'How can the Master physically suffer when He is in a God state? It must be one of His *Leelas*,' they would say. Their abysmal ignorance did not allow them to appreciate even the most fundamental question — Can a Perfect Master resort to lie or deception? And even if it seems to be so, can it be for His own worldly interest? Some of them brought down the concept of *leela* to its meanest interpretation, that is, that the Master is behaving in such a cunning manner for the early disposal of the devotees or because He has some other job to do. Some of these devotees even used to disturb Him during His prayer times, creating scenes near Dwarakamai Masjid on the distribution of *dakshina* or squabbling with one another. They would often complain to Baba about the greed and misconduct of other devotees, without looking into their own conduct. Each wanted more time from Baba even for his smallest needs, while pretending to be most considerate and blaming others for wasting His time.

Some of them tried to force certain material gifts on Baba, who hardly had any need of such gifts. Some of them thought that by giving such gifts, the adverse effect of their evil actions (*paapa*) would be mitigated. Some even used to derive a lot of ego satisfaction. They forgot that the only gift that Shri Sai desired from His devotees was devotional faith (*shraddha*) and patience (*saburi*). They expected the Guru to exhibit qualities of perfect calmness and not to hurt their sentiments and always serve them, even at odd hours and situations, forgetting His own interest and without demanding any thing in return.

In such circumstances, having done His best, Baba sometimes used to get vexed and about three of four times tried to walk out of Shirdi. But close devotees like Tatya and others used to prevail upon Him to return, promising that things would improve at Shirdi.

The available records indicate that things had reached such a crisis in November 1915, that Baba had to ask His most reliable devotees, Nanasaheb Chandorkar and H. V. Sathe, to make proper arrangements to feed and take care of the really poor at Shirdi. He said:

''माझे नाना आले नर गाय गरीबानां चांगले होईल आणि खावयाला मिलेल, आणि माझे सहेब आले म्हणजे सर्ब व्यवस्था होईल''

This means: 'If Nana comes here, then the condition of the poor people will be better and they will get food. If my Saheb comes, then proper arrangements can be done.'

Here *Saheb* refers to Shri Sathe, whom Baba used to address in that manner. Sathe, along with others, with the consent of Baba, created the Sainath Dakshina Bhiksha Sansthan at Shirdi in 1915 for better management of the affairs of Baba. The Sansthan formed a committee to manage the day to day affairs. The Sansthan decided to request all the devotees receiving money from Baba on a regular basis to donate a certain portion of it to the Sansthan, so that Baba's daily expenses could be met out of the collection. Except a few who can be named, most of those receiving regular donations from Baba refused to share even 10 per cent of what they used to get from Baba to meet His daily expenses. Further, the touts and the greedy devotees, whose interest got hampered, started condemning the Sansthan for such activities and created scandals. A worried and remorseful Baba told his close devotees at Masjid:

'' श्रीमंत आणि लाखपति असेल नर न्याला भेयें पेऊन बसून व्यवस्था करू दे, ह्या लोकानां पैसा द्रांद्र लागले म्हणजे समजेल! मी इथुन उटून बहिर जाऊन बसतो! पैसा कृद्न आर्णू आणि कुठपर्येंतदेऊं? पैसे देत नाहीं म्हणून भटार्थो काय मारामारी करायची कीं काय?''

This means: 'Shrimant, one who had lakhs of rupees can come and stay here and make arrangements for them. Here, when people start fighting over money, then only they will realize. I will leave this place and settle elsewhere. From where shall I get money and how long can I go on distributing?'

Figuratively, He used to refer to Telis and Banias breaking walls, that is, when He tried to bring unity among His devotees, they fought among themselves on the smallest of issues.

Nevertheless, some of the best of souls from Shirdi and Maharashtra flocked around Baba. Baba, like a real mother, took a lot of pain and taught them the spiritual practices, keeping a watch over them day and night during His sixty years of stay at Shirdi. He looked after the welfare of thousands of families and individuals, day and night. But the demands of some of the greedy ones, whom He tried to satisfy, remained till His last day. An examination of the daily happenings at Shirdi, after Baba's departure, reveals that except for a few ardent devotees, others, including those feigning devotion to Baba, had just vanished and had no contribution towards maintenance of the heritage of Baba.

Baba pardoned the biggest of weaknesses and imperfections in His devotees and always helped them. But some of His devotees did not tolerate the idiosyncrasies of the personality of this most Perfect Being, even when they depended on Him for all their wants. Some used to accuse Him of being partial to some devotees and used to create all sort of rumours. When Radhakrishnamayi, an ardent devotee of Baba expired, various types of rumours were spread all around. Baba, due to His spiritual approach to life, never took these into consideration. Baba only knew about the merits of each of His devotees and treated them accordingly, whereas each devotee wanted to be treated in a special manner as per his own opinion of himself.

This kind Baba never made His devotees feel that He was so sick as not to be able to help them. Similarly, Shri Ramakrishna Paramhansa, even when suffering from acute throat cancer, used to call and render spiritual discourses to his devotees, forgetting his physical pain. It is not that the saints don't suffer from physical pain when embodied in human form. They do suffer a lot. But their infinite kindness overrides all considerations of their personal pains and problems. Even when suffering, they take upon themselves the sufferings of others. The life of Christ clearly exemplifies this aspect. What makes Shri Sai a unique Saint is His infinite capacity to tolerate and absorb the imperfections of His devotees which, unfortunately, most of the devotees failed to appreciate. Those devotees, like Mhalsapati, Kaka Saheb Dixit, Tatya, Megha and others, who appreciated Baba as He was and not as they desired Him to be, advanced in the spiritual path. They were the perfect devotees of the Perfect Master.

Today, when Baba's invisible spirit is drawing lakhs and lakhs of human souls to Shirdi and protecting them, a question often arises in my mind — the most compassionate Sadguru Sainath Maharaj gives His best to each of His devotees, but do the devotees understand the pains He bears to make them happy?

— New Year, 2006

37

Sai Experience

In *Shri Sai Satcharita*, the experiences of a large number of devotees, with relation to Baba, have been incorporated. However, the experiences of a much larger number of devotees have been recorded in *Shri Sai Leela Patrika*, some other magazines, books (many of them are in Marathi) and correspondence between the devotees. There are a large number of books, written in different languages, but mostly in Marathi, in which the direct experiences of devotees, whose names don't find a mention in *Shri Sai Satcharita,* have been recorded. Baba used to meet numerous people and families every day. The details of all such meetings at Shirdi are not recorded.

Every devotee who came in contact with Baba, at some time or the other got some kind of a special experience. Most of the devotees feel that they were drawn to Baba under strange or unexpected circumstances. Some of these events can be interpreted as chance occurrences, but some of them are too direct to be interpreted as mere chances. Baba Himself had said that He draws his disciples from far and wide. He also said that even after His physical departure from this world, He would continue to take care of his devotees, old or new.

Today, thousands of people, from all over the world, are reporting about their experiences with Shri Sainath Maharaj. These are being regularly communicated by being published in books, magazines, electronic media, websites, emails, blogs, facebook posts, etc. No doubt, the devotees who had such experiences with Baba when He was in His physical embodiment were extremely lucky.

Most of the devotees wish that they had been with Baba or had seen Him or talked to Him. Given the Hindu theory of reincarnation, it is quite possible that some of them might have been with Baba in their former lives. Maybe, the memory of the past was built into their consciousness and is pulling them towards Baba, even if they are unaware of it. Similarly, at Baba's time also, Baba used to relate His connection with some of the devotees from earlier lives. It is well nigh impossible for an ordinary person to find out about this spiritual connection with Baba. This is better left to the saints like Him, who are spiritual personalities of the highest order. Yet, present day devotees emotionally speak of their possible relations with Baba in their earlier lives. They also have an eagerness to know more and more about the experience of others. I shall, therefore, strive to describe the experiences of some devotees. Some of the experiences of Shri B. V. N. Swami, Madras (now Chennai), published in Shaka 161, Chaitra Vaishakha Jeyeshta edition No. 1-2-3 of the *Shri Sai Leela* magazine are given below:

The experiences given here are just a few that are picked up from the surface, so to speak, with the least effort of memory. The number of actual experiences Baba had given me for so many years (at least since 1936) are so great that selection is difficult. Some are of a very private character. Some affect other persons and have consequently to be kept secret. Some experiences, though convincing in the midst of numerous other similar experiences, are not sufficiently strong when set forth separately. Several have been forgotten. Anyhow, the object of this article is not to give an exhaustive or fairly exhaustive account of all my experiences. I just refer to a few, to point out how Baba has favoured me with His help. Many readers will be content with that and regard them as a sufficient ground for their trying to get into contact with Sai Baba and obtaining similar or greater benefit.

In the first place, I must point out that I moved with many Saints and Sadhus, for years; and any statement of mine about any of them should not be construed as a reflection (implied or indirect) on any others. Comparisons are odious. To launch upon a comparison and pronounce on the comparative merits of saints, one must be above them all. No such claim is put forward here and I do not profess to sit in judgment over any. Hence this article (as also other expressions of mine elsewhere), must be generously construed and not taken as hits. Hits against anyone are improper and uncalled for – and are very far indeed from my intention.

There is one difficulty in doing justice to Sai Baba's influence on the devotee. Baba has identified himself with various saints and helpers. The help one has received long before one met the physical body of the Shirdi Baba has frequently been stated by Baba to have been rendered by Him. As Baba is God, this conclusion follows as a matter of course. Even if He were acting on the level of a Satathama or Sat Purusha, this would follow and can be easily understood. But in practice, such identification causes some confusion. Hence no mention is made to helps received by me from unseen sources before 1930 –1931. It is about 1931, that I have first heard mention of Sai Baba, saw his picture and resolved to visit Shirdi and Sakori.

At that time, a slight change was coming over my programme. I began to attach less importance to the study (as usually understood and conducted) of Vedanta and more to the sadhana or the practical steps that would destroy vasanas, especially egoism, develop the emotional side, chiefly love and would thus render Vedantic perfection possible and real. I was in quest of some institution where facilities could be found suitable to my condition and stage of development, to take me along the said course. I visited places noted either for the sanctity of their temples, or rivers and for their being resorts of saints, e.g., Pandharpur, Gangapur, Nasik, Brindavan, Kasi, Gaya, Prayag, Sakori, Hubli. In no place, however, did I get full satisfaction, i.e., the conditions exactly fitting my requirements. One saint pointed out to me that my failure was due to subjective causes, viz., the absence of total surrender to God or a Guru, viewed as God and felt to be God, i.e., surrender of Tan, Man, Dhan, i.e., of the body, the self and sense of possession or ownership. But to overcome this defect, some personality and suitable circumstances should bless me and arise, to disarm me of all vasanas, to subjugate the penchant for criticism and to develop docile submission to a superior power, superior purity, goodness and wisdom. It was my misfortune that I had not still come across such a dominating personality nor come under such overpowering circumstances.

With this mental dissatisfaction, I went to see a celebrated Datta Upasaka, Narayan Maharaj of Khedgaonbet (40 miles from Poona), who seems to have been favoured with the grace of Sri Dattatreya even from infancy – a grace evidenced by miracles wrought even at the age of 7 or 8. As I sat before the Datta temple there, (the power of the idol or Padukas there has been widely published), I entertained the idea of putting to the test both the Datta and Datta Upasaka of that place. As I sat in the hall along with many others, I saw sparrows chirping and flying about the place, and I said in my mind that if really the Datta installed there and the Datta Upasaka, Narayan Maharaj, were possessed of the spiritual and superhuman power attributed to them, one of the sparrows should sit upon my head. I at once closed my eyes in meditation or prayer. Lo! Behold! within five minutes of my prayer, my head was struck by something and as I opened my eyes, I saw a sparrow flying away from me before this. This sudden compliance with my request for proof filled me with the conviction that Datta installed at that place and Narayan Maharaj who installed it, are really possessed of superhuman and spiritual power.

As the only thing I wanted was a divine personality, a perfect saint should be contacted by me and control me in circumstances favouring a perfect surrender, I went to Narayan Maharaj and asked him for that as a favour. As I had to make my request in the presence of many people, I clothed my request in symbology and figurative speech. Said I, 'I am a merchant dealing in gems and a very unfortunate dealer. I have come across many gems but none hitherto has satisfied me. Each gem I get is very tiny, has dots, cracks or other blemishes. Will you please bless me so that I may get one pure big flawless diamond.' Narayan Maharaj after a moment's pause said 'Yes, You will have your desire,' or words to that effect. This was in the beginning of 1933. It took, however, some time for me to get the promised Kohinoor. I got possessed at last of that invaluable diamond, Sri Sai Baba, giving up everything else to buy it or get at it.

An attempt to get into close contact with Sai Baba through His devotees, that I made in 1934, was a failure. I was at Madras about April, 1936, still with the sense of an unfulfilled blessing when I received an invitation from a very uninfluential devotee there. Accepting it, I went to Poona and was just introduced to the Rasanes. As I was taking notes of their experience, Mr. P. R. Avasti's son came in and he drew me to his father, a retired Judge of Indore and a great devotee of Sai Baba. The moment Mr. P. R. Avasti learnt of my mission, his sincere soul was overpowered with joy and treating me as he would treat an old and dear friend, he placed himself and his influence entirely at my disposal. He introduced me to about 60 devotees of Baba who had personal experience of Baba's greatness, powers and goodness. Most of them were ignorant of English and could only speak in Marathi, which was unfamiliar to me at that time. Mr. Avasti's knowledge of the vernacular and English was of as great service to me as his influence and zeal to serve the cause of devotion to Baba by collecting, editing and publishing news about Baba.

From the very beginning, I was determined to collect, test and sift such materials, to arrange them and on their strength, to prepare a biography of Baba that would benefit earnest souls all over India, if not even beyond. For many months I was engaged in this work, with the invaluable help of Mr. P. R. Avasti, who sat up and interpreted to me Dabholkar's Sai Satcharita, Sai Lila Masik and other vernacular publications on Baba. He helped in this way for one year so vigorously that at the end of that period I could dispense with his help, as I could then read and translate Marathi books myself, with occasional reference to a dictionary. This itself was proof of Sri Sai Baba's favour to me.

But fresh evidence of it was forthcoming off and on in the course of that work. Experiences, especially experiences with one's Guru or God are very secret and are seldom communicated, especially to strangers. But except in a very few cases, every one that we approached was very soon inducted to unlock the portals of his heart and let us into his secret experiences. A Public Prosecutor who was an intimate friend of the Judge began, within a few minutes of his introduction to me, to unburden himself of his innermost experiences to me, disclosing facts which he had not till then revealed to his best friend Mr. P. R. Avasti. I typed these statements that I took and had left them all in one bundle with my friend Mr. G. B. Datar, Vakil at Thana.

When I was at Poona, Mr. Datar intimated to me that the entire bundle was lost and that in spite of his search for them, they could not be found. As I had no other copies, the loss would prove a very serious handicap to the progress of my work. Full of faith in Baba and praying to him for their recovery, I went to Thana. And at once I went to the table whereon he had placed his legal bundles. In one or two minutes I placed my hand on a bundle and picked it out. Lo! that was the typed set of statements relating to Baba.

More than one devotee warned me against being too credulous and against accepting bogus devotees and faked experiences and asked me how I, a stranger to the men, manners and languages of Maharashtra, was hoping to ensure the purity and reliability of the information I received. I, however, knew one and only device. Sai Baba was my filter. He would not pass humbug into my sacred collection, I said. At least in two cases, I received strange and unexpected warnings and revelations showing what I should reject. Some statements were thus wholly rejected and some in part. It was quite obvious to me, as also to my Bombay friends, that Baba was favouring the publication by me of his biography and removing the hindrances thereto, step by step.

After collecting about 150 statements, I began publishing part of them in English in the columns of the Sunday Times for some 30 to 40 issues in 1936–37. As that journal has or had a circulation exceeding 20,000, the initial work of interesting the devout public, all over India, in Sai Baba was well started. It had a further good result. A highly respected friend remarked to me that these experiences, standing by themselves, produce a very unfavourable impression. Baba there resembles a juggler with rare powers rather than a great soul, he said. 'What of the miracles of Sri Krishna?' was the reply given by me, 'Oh they are part of the Sri Krishna's nature,' my friend retorted. 'Exactly, so are the miracles of Sai part of Sai's nature,' I submitted. 'That is just what is left out of your articles,' my friend pointed out.

My friend was right. He is a pure and holy person, not afflicted with jealousy or hatred of other saints than one's own Guru. He represents a group that, in its desire to stress metaphysical and ultimate truths, is apt to underrate the importance of miracles to those who are just beginning their spiritual life. So, I felt that the entire defect was that I was producing the separate bricks lent to me by each devotee in the shape of his experience. Hardly any of these devotees had a conception of what the building was into which his brick had to be fitted, i.e., Baba's real nature. So, I appealed to Sai Baba himself – much as Sri Ramakrishna complained to Kali Mata that she should be represented as a Tamasic deity by a learned pandit.

I felt an inner warning that I should abandon thinking in English and in terms of newspaper articles and that I should try to write out a reliable but orthodox biography of the saint in my own mother tongue. As I began that task, even in the earliest chapters, Baba's nature, His powers, their nature, His Guru and what the Guru did for Him, came up for consideration. And I discovered passages in what Baba had spoken which, with passages from Scriptures, showed how Baba's Guru was saturated with Divinity, i.e., was God, and how that Guru God's self was poured upon Baba, resulting in the latter's merger in the Divine and consequent manifestation of wonderful powers.

What Baba was taught and what Baba taught or conveyed by radiation or unseen influence came in to fill up the picture. For the first time, so far as I knew, a clearly intelligible picture of Baba's nature, powers and course, materialized and was presented by me in the book Introduction to Sai Baba. The first edition of that was published in November 1938 and now within 11 months, a third edition is having a rapid circulation. The statements of Devotee's experiences have also been published as Part I and Part II in support of much that is contained in the introduction. This introduction has been done into all the Madras vernaculars, Tamil, Malayam, Kanarese and Telugu. The total number of books on Sai Baba published on this side is about 16,000. These facts are clear evidence that Sai Baba has favoured the spread of His Bhakti — especially in this Presidency.

One striking fact supporting the above conclusion is that thousands have become devotees of Sai Baba here within the space of the last 15 months. Over 100 meetings have been held. Aratis of Baba have been conducted and a few words about Baba have been uttered to the audiences. Baba's support of the movement is further evidenced by the fact that over 30 devotees in this Presidency have had several experiences of their own which they have communicated to me and which are now being published as 'Madras Devotees' Experiences'. It is needless for me to quote my own numerous experiences. But I shall single out two of them, a very striking character before closing this account, as they reveal the greatest of the blessings Baba has conferred on me. He has granted the prayer of my life for an increased and still increasing measures of self surrender, by promoting in me vuU; fpark. Ananya Chinta, i.e., intense and all-time concentration on Himself, based on the realization that He is looking after all that may still remain (after my passing into the Vanaprastha Ashram) as my needs and responsibilities, thus assuring deep mental peace.

In November 1937, I was at Tiruvannamalai and was intending to start for Madras, by train. Then, a friend, Sri Tulsidas P. Sahani, offered to take me to Madras in his car, wherein he pointed out that he, Miss Uma and I could be singing Bhajana songs or Namavalis all along the 140 miles of the journey. The weather was rainy and I consulted Baba, by prayerfully casting chits before Him and picking a chit at random. Baba's direction was that I should go by train. I went to apologise for my not being of the Bhajana party, but was induced to change my mind. I returned to my quarters and pleaded with Baba. The rule with Baba was and is that once a decision is given, a second consultation on the same matter should not be sought because साईरामोद्विनात्रिभाशते. I however pleaded with Baba that He should permit me to transgress His orders for that once, as the object of the transgression was pious and I prayed that the penalty that was bound to follow a transgression may be lenient for the same reason.

Then I started with the two pious friends in Sri Tulsidas's car. There was rain off and on all the day and all the way. But we, with singing, cheered the way and the journey started very pleasantly. After the fifth mile, the car was proceeding slowly; and suddenly the sound of some thing snapping was heard. The owner alighted, examined the car and found that the back axle had broken in two. The journey thus came to an abrupt end. It was still raining. And at the place where the car stopped, there was no shelter. Help for repairing the car was out of the question. Then, for the first time, I revealed to my two companions that I had joined them in their motor trip against the express direction of Sai Baba. I at once submitted myself to Sri Sai Baba, thanked him for the lightness of the penalty and prayed for direction whether I should, at that stage, try to go by train or by car alone. Baba directed me to 'go by car alone'. That was all very good. But where was the car that I could take to Madras? Mr. Tulsidas's car would take a whole day at least to repair and meanwhile what were we to do in the wet weather on the road?

While I was waiting thus for 45 minutes, not knowing what was to happen to us, a car from Tiruvannamalai drew up. It was the car of P. Krishnamachari, salesman of Volkhart Bros., Madras, and he was the only occupant of it. He enquired about our condition. By his kindness, Miss Uma and myself got into his car, leaving Mr. Tulsidas to attend to his own car. As soon as we got in, Mr P. Krishnamachari remarked that he was wondering at what happened. That very morning he had written home to Madras that he intended to stay four more days at Tiruvannamalai and that they need not expect him for that period. But at 11 A.M., he suddenly changed his mind and wished to start back to Madras in his car, without any clear reason for such a wish. He went to Ramana Maharshi, at whose Ashram he stayed and asked for leave. The leave was granted at once. And at once he got into his car and was driving towards Madras when he came and saw our plight. He said that his sudden change of mind and the hurry he was in to get back to Madras was puzzling him till he saw our helpless position. It is because we were in a forlorn condition that God must have sent him so suddenly to our rescue, he said. I at once confirmed his statement and informed him that God Sai had done so. Sai had asked me go to Madras by car alone at 11 A.M. He alone could *find a car to take us to Madras and he did. He could and did change Mr. P. K's mind to suit his high and benign purposes.*

Another piece of help from Baba is more remarkable still. He had told H. S. Dixit that he was taking all care and responsibility for Dixit's welfare upon himself and that Dixit need not worry himself. The latter put him to a severe test when a debt of 30,000 rupees had to be paid to a Marwadi within four days. H. S. Dixit put the entire burden on Baba and sat quiet, trusting to Baba for the clearance of the debt. The third day the son of a recently departed friend of Dixit walked into his office, to consult him about the investment of a fund of Rs.30,000 and lent him that money to clear the debt.

Somewhat similar to the above, there was a young man of good position, whom I was bound to help, two or three years ago, who badly needed starting in life and who applied to me to get him decent employment. When I asked him to appeal to God or Sai Baba, he wrote back that he had no sufficient faith in either. Then I prayed hard to Sai Baba as His Devotee that the young man should be given faith and some decent appointment on Rs. 300. Within a few months of the prayer, an appointment was conferred on the youth without settling the pay. Nine months later, the employers, of their own accord and without being asked to give the above rate, fixed the above rate as his salary from the time of his joining their office. This was convincing proof to all concerned of Sai Baba's kind intervention; and that youth became a staunch devotee of Baba.

Another series of memorable helps derived from Baba is to be found in the case of Rao Sahib B. Papaiya Chetty of Madras. For years, he was almost bed ridden and the symptoms of his troubles were so complicated that doctors could neither be positive as to diagnosis or render any appreciable help. As no hope appeared to come from doctors, his mind turned to saints. And the most remarkable of the saints he had read of was Sri Sai Baba, whose kind achievements for His devotees filled the columns of the Sunday Times just then (1937). Learning that I was the writer of those articles, he invited me to go to see him.

In three days I explained to him all about Sai Baba. He got great faith in Sai Baba and started praying to Baba for guidance. He had a box full of Homeopathic medicines. Selecting at a time a few that were described as good for each ailment, be sought Baba's guidance by prayerfully casting chits before His picture and choosing one chit. He found that each time Baba chose a medicine that was effective in dealing with the particular symptom. Thus he went on with a dozen or more of medicines. In the course of two or three months, there was remarkable improvement in his condition. He was strong and healthy enough then to leave his bed and he climbed upstairs and went downstairs to the ground floor. He then tried a motor drive to Royapettah from town. By reason of those efforts, his health did not suffer. Though he did not succeed in effecting a complete cure, the partial cure effected was itself wonderful and totally unexpected.

He then began to take more interest in life and tried to write books. Though he was not even a graduate and had no literary distinction, he started rendering Bhagavad Gita into Telugu. He was surprised at the free flow of language and wondered how he could ever have produced such a work. Then he translated the Upanishad into Telugu prose. He further rendered the gist of all the statements I had taken in Bombay, into Telugu, and published the first big work on Shri Sai Baba in Madras,viz., his Sai Leela. These translations, which he attributes to the power derived from Baba, were so greatly appreciated that the Arya Vysia Conference held at Masulipatam this year awarded him the title 'Anuvadha Kalanidhi'.

His business also, which he could attend better with his improved health, was and is prospering. But above all these benefits, there is one for which he feels very greatly indebted to Sai Baba. Formerly he had no powerful sheet anchor in life, no personality in whose shelter he could feel that he was safely resting. Now, come gain, come loss, come joy, come sorrow, he has the feeling that Sri Sai Baba is at his back and will safely see him through all turns and vicissitudes. These ups and downs of life do not agitate or affect him now as they once did. This, the assured peace of mind that he has secured, he counts as the greatest gain in going to Baba.

The first few of the series of over hundred meetings regarding Baba that I have addressed till now were held at his house in George Town and then The Sai Mandali, Madras, was started, of which he is the active Secretary.

— Ram Navami, 2006

38

Good and Evil Syndrome

God is generally perceived by people as the most benevolent, powerful, permanent and an all pervading consciousness who controls everything and everyone in the universe, past, present and future. All philosophies and religions have theorized that God is the greatest, kindest and perennial giver of all sorts of happiness to His creation. He is *Ananda Murti* or the repository of all and eternal happiness.

God is called the Omniscient, Omnipresent and Omnipotent Almighty and is highly apotheosized in all religions, with oriental or occidental hyperboles. Leaving aside the spiritually evolved persons or the genuine seekers, most of the devotees, when praying to God, nurture a secret expectation in their conscious or subconscious minds that their prayers will somehow draw kindness, help, benefit and happiness from God. Happiness here means a solution to those material or psychological aspects of life that are problematic to the person.

One who in his prayers seeks a solution to his personal problems alone cannot be called a true seeker on the spiritual path. A genuine seeker on the path towards God cannot expect only pleasurable or desirable events to happen. He has to experience and bear both pleasurable (so called good) and painful (so called evil) experiences with equanimity, visualizing God's divine role in both. It is not in the scheme of things of God the Almighty, or the law of nature through which God operates, only to give pleasurable experiences to all life forms including human beings. If God is only 'good' then where does the so called 'evil' emanate from? If good is opposed to evil, then there has to exist some other powerful entity who must be equal and opposite to the benevolent God in its evil capabilities. But if God alone is the giver of both the good and evil experiences, then there cannot be a separate entity called 'Satan' or 'evil' beyond His overall scheme in the management of the universe.

In Hinduism there is a concept of *devatas* (Positive forces of nature) and *Rakshasas* (negative forces of nature). Hindu mythology also explains that these powerful negative forces called *Rakshasas* or *Asuras* used to draw their power only from God. There are numerous instances of Lord Bramha, Vishnu or Shiva empowering these *Rakshasas* through their blessings. Therefore, these *Rakshasas* or negative forces of nature have a specific and important role in the overall scheme of God. Hence, in the scheme of God, good and evil forces and experiences are necessary concomitants to each other, just like light and darkness. Neither can exist alone. Every good event or good action contains an aspect of evil in it and every evil contains an aspect of good, howsoever small it may be. Thus there cannot be something called pure good or pure evil.

These qualities of good and evil, as symbolized as *Devatas* and *Rakshasas* respectively, are inbuilt into the very fabric of human nature. These two attributes of a human being, when in interaction with the same or similar attributes of another human being and of the overall nature around, create a conflict between the two opposing forces. To the ordinary mind, such conflicts are perceived as human problems. Given the Dialectic Theory of nature, without such an interaction of two opposing forces, nothing can be created. If water and fire elements were not predominantly existent on earth, no life form would have been possible. An understanding and acceptance of the play of two such equally opposite forces in one's material, mental or spiritual life is a *sine qua non* to spiritual evolution. Both are necessary correlates in the divine matrix. Without such an understanding, it is difficult, nay impossible, to progress in the path of spiritual evolution.

Through religious and spiritual practices, one can reinforce and enhance the positive qualities in oneself. Such practices, however, do not immediately destroy the evil qualities but keep them in a dormant state. Hence, one cannot reject the evil qualities in oneself or in others but accept them as an aspect of nature or God. A worldly man cannot either run away from the world or from the evil, but can try to contain or minimize the negative compulsions it creates in the mind. Through religious or spiritual practices, so long as the divine qualities are kept at a higher level, the evil qualities remain subdued and silent. But when a person strays away from religious and ethical conduct, some of the evil qualities do raise their head, even if he has some very good qualities.

Therefore, to expect that through prayers or other religious practices one would get only material or mental pleasures by divine intervention is a fallacy. Since the very foundation of acceptance of God only as a pleasure giving entity is defective, most people suffer more due to such misconceptions than due to the evil qualities of others. The nature, intensity and possibilities of the negative or positive thoughts of a person can only be understood by conscious observation and analysis of his own thoughts. However, most of the people do not find this necessary or possible due to their total involvement in the day to day affairs of the world.

Those seekers, who achieve God realization, were the ones who had gone beyond the conflict of good-evil and pleasure-pain through strenuous and long drawn mental practices, as prescribed by their Spiritual Master. They were the real spiritual seekers.

Jai Shri Sai.

– Maha Samadhi, 2006

Epilogue

"He followed God and history followed Him"

In 2018, four years from now, the centennial celebrations of Baba's Maha Samadhi will take place. We don't know if there lives a soul that remembers having seen the great saint. The unique history of His divine majesty can be experienced even today on the streets of Shirdi, where He once roamed, begging for alms, from door to door. Shirdi Sai Baba never looked back at His own history as He had no time for it. The spiritual evolution of His devotees was His prime concern. Myths surrounding Baba could not conceal His historic contribution in bringing the devotees under the single banner of *Sabka Maalik Ek*, which means God is the Lord of all. This theme has continued for more than a century and shall continue for ever. The Age of Shri Sai has already made its advent, carrying with it the revelation of the future.

C.B. Satpathy
1st January, 2014

Our Books on SHIRDI SAI BABA

Shirdi Sai Baba is a household name in India as well as in many parts of the World today. These books offer fascinating glimpses into the life and miracles of Shirdi Sai Baba and other Perfect Masters. These books will provide you with an experience that is bound to transform one's sense of perspective and bring about perceptible and meaningful spiritual growth.

SHIRDI within & beyond
A collection of unseen & rare photographs
Dr. Rabinder Nath Kakarya
ISBN 978 81 207 7806 1
₹ 750

Baba's Divine Symphony
Vinny Chitluri
ISBN 978 81 207 8485 7
₹ 250

The Loving God:
Story of Shirdi Sai Baba
Dr. G. R. Vijayakumar
ISBN 978 81 207 8079 8
₹ 200

The Age of Shirdi Sai Baba
Dr. C. B. Satpathy
ISBN 978 81 207 8700 1
₹ 225

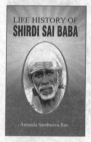

Life History of Shirdi Sai Baba
Ammula Sambasiva Rao
ISBN 978 81 207 7722 4
₹ 150

The Eternal Sai Phenomenon
A R Nanda
ISBN 978 81 207 6086 8
₹ 200

Ek An English Musical on the Life of Shirdi Sai Baba
Usha Akella
ISBN 978 81 207 6842 0
₹ 75

SHRI SAI SATCHARITA
The Life and Teachings of Shirdi Sai Baba
Translated by Indira Kher
ISBN 978 81 207 2811 8 ₹ 500(HB)
ISBN 978 81 207 2153 1 ₹ 300(PB)

A Diamond Necklace To: Shirdi Sai BabaSai
Giridhar Ari
ISBN 978 81 207 5868 1
₹ 200

Shri Sai Baba's Teachings & Philosophy
Lt Col M B Nimbalkar
ISBN 978 81 207 2364 1
₹ 100

BABA- May I Answer
C.B. Satpathy
ISBN 978 81 207 4594 0
₹ 150

God Who Walked on Earth:
The Life & Times of Shirdi Sai Baba
Rangaswami Parthasarathy
ISBN 978 81 207 1809 8
₹ 150

STERLING

Baba's Vaani: His Sayings and Teachings
Compiled by Vinny Chitluri
ISBN 978 81 207 3589 1
₹ 200

Baba's Gurukul SHIRDI
Vinny Chitluri
ISBN-978-81-207-4770-8
₹ 200

Baba's Anurag Love for His Devotees
Compiled by Vinny Chitluri
ISBN 978 81 207 5447 8
₹ 125

Baba's Rinanubandh Leelas during His Sojoum in Shird
Compiled by Vinny Chitluri
ISBN 978 81 207 3403 6
₹ 200

The Gospel of Shri Shirdi Sai Baba: A Holy Spiritual Path
Dr Durai Arulneyam
ISBN 978 81 207 3997 0
₹ 150

Sai Baba's 261 Leelas
Balkrishna Panday
ISBN 978 81 207 2727 4
₹ 125

Spotlight on the Sai Story
Chakor Ajgaonker
ISBN 978 81 207 4399 1
₹ 125

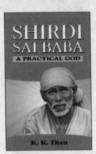

Shirdi Sai Baba A Practical God
K. K. Dixit
ISBN 978 81 207 5918 3
₹ 75

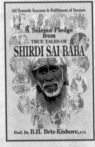

A Solemn Pledge from True Tales of Shirdi Sai Baba
Dr B H Briz-Kishore
ISBN 978 81 207 2240 8
₹ 95

I am always with you
Lorraine Walshe-Ryan
ISBN 978 81 207 3192 9
₹ 150

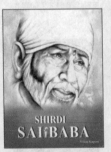

Shirdi Sai Baba
Vikas Kapoor
ISBN 987 81 207 59701
₹ 30

Unravelling the Enigma: Shirdi Sai Baba in the light of Sufism
Marianne Warren
ISBN 978 81 207 2147 0
₹ 400

STERLING

Sab Ka Malik Ek

Shirdi Sai Baba
The Divine Healer
Raj Chopra
ISBN 978 81 207 4766 1
₹ 100

Shirdi Sai Baba and
other Perfect Masters
C B Satpathy
ISBN 978 2384 15081 207 9
₹ 150

The Miracles of Sai Baba
ISBN 978 81 207 5433 1 (HB)
₹ 250

Sai Hari Katha
Dasganu Maharaj Translated by
Dr. Rabinder Nath Kakarya
ISBN 978 81 207 3324 4
₹ 100

Shri Sai Baba- The Saviour
Dr. Rabinder Nath Kakarya
ISBN 978 81 207 4701 2
₹ 100

The Thousand Names of
Shirdi Sai Baba
Sri B.V. Narasimha Swami Ji
Hindi translation by
Dr. Rabinder Nath Kakarya
ISBN 978 81 207 3738 9
₹ 75

Sri Sai Baba
Swami Sai Sharan Anand
Translated by V.B Kher
ISBN 978 81 207 1950 7
₹ 200

Sai Baba: His Divine
Glimpses
V B Kher
ISBN 978 81 207 2291 0
₹ 95

Shri Shirdi Sai Baba: His
Life and Miracles
ISBN 978 81 207 2877 6
₹ 25

108 Names of
Shirdi Sai Baba
ISBN 978 81 207 3074 8
₹ 50

Shirdi Sai Baba Aratis
(English)   ₹ 10

Shirdi Sai Speaks...
Sab Ka Malik Ek
Quotes for the Day
ISBN 81 207 3101   200978 1
₹ 200

STERLING

Divine Gurus

Hazrat Babajan:
A Pathan Sufi of Poona
Kevin R. D. Shepherd
ISBN 978 81 207 8698 1
₹ 200

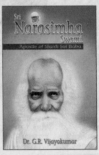

Sri Narasimha Swami
Apostle of Shirdi Sai Baba
Dr. G.R. Vijayakumar
ISBN 978 81 207 4432 5
₹ 90

Lord Sri Dattatreya
The Trinity
Dwarika Mohan Mishra
ISBN 978 81 207 5417 1
₹ 200

Sri Swami Samarth
Maharaj of Akkalkot
N.S. Karandikar
ISBN 978 81 207 3445 6
₹ 200

Guru Charitra
Shree Swami Samarth
ISBN 978 81 207 3348 0
₹ 200

Shirdi Sai Baba Box

Shri Sai Baba
978 81 207 6920 5
Box size: 23.5 x 16.5 cm
₹900

Shri Sai Satcharitra

Sai Baba Mandiramdhil
Arataya & Mantrochar - Mp3

Vibhuti

Dateless
Calendar

Sai Baba Photo Frame

श्री शिरडी साई बाबा

शिरडी अंत: से अनंत
डॉ. रबिन्द्रनाथ ककरिया
978 81 207 8191 7
₹ 750

श्री साई सच्चरित्र
श्री शिरडी साई बाबा की अद्भुत
जीवनी तथा उनके अमूल्य उपदेश
गोविंद रघुनाथ दाभोलकर (हेमाडपंत)
978 81 207 2501 0   ₹ 250 (PB)
978 81 207 2500 3   ₹ 300 (HB)

साई सुमिरन
अंजु टंडन
978 81 207 8706 3
₹ 90

**बाबा की वाणी-उनके वचन
तथा उपदेश**
बेला शर्मा
978 81 207 4745 6
₹ 100

बाबा का अनुराग
विनी चितलुरी
978 81 207 6699 0
₹ 100

बाबा का ऋणानुबंध
विनी चितलुरी
978 81 207 5998 5
₹ 125

बाबा का गुरूकुल-शिरडी
विनी चितलुरी
978 81 207 6698 3
₹ 125

साई की आत्मकथा
विकास कपूर
978 81 207 7719 4
₹ 200

साई संवाद
उर्मिल सत्य भूषण
978 81 207 7777 4
₹ 200

बाबा-आध्यात्मिक विचार
चन्द्र भानुसतपथी
978 81 207 4627 5
₹ 150

साई शरण में
चन्द्रभानु सतपथी
978 81 207 2802 8
₹ 150

श्री शिरडी साई बाबा

श्री शिरडी साई बाबा एवं अन्य सद्गुरु
चन्द्रभानु सतपथी
978 81 207 4401 1
₹ 90

पृथ्वी पर अवतरित भगवान शिरडी के साई बाबा
रंगास्वामी पार्थसारथी
978 81 207 2101 2
₹ 150

साई - सबका मालिक
कल्पना भाकुनी
978 81 207 3320 6
₹ 125

साई बाबा एक अवतार
बेला शर्मा
978 81 207 6706 5
₹ 100

साई सत् चरित का प्रकाश
बेल शर्मा
978 81 207 7804 7
₹ 200

श्री साई बाबा के परम भक्त
डॉ. रबिन्द्रनाथ ककरिया
978 81 207 2779 3
₹ 75

श्री साई बाबा के उपदेश व तत्त्वज्ञान
लेफ्टिनेन्ट कर्नल
एम. बी. निंबालकर
978 81 207 5971 8   ₹ 100

साई भक्तानुभव
डॉ. रबिन्द्रनाथ ककरिया
978 81 207 3052 6
₹ 90

श्री साई बाबा के अनन्य भक्त
डॉ. रबिन्द्र नाथ ककरिया
978 81 207 2705 2
₹ 75

साई का संदेश
डॉ. रबिन्द्र नाथ ककरिया
978 81 207 2879 0
₹ 125

शिरडी संपूर्ण दर्शन
डॉ. रबिन्द्रनाथ ककरिया
978 81 207 2312 2
₹ 50

मुक्ति दाता - श्री साई बाबा
डॉ. रबिन्द्रनाथ ककरिया
978 81 207 2778 6
₹ 65

स्टर्लिंग

सबका मालिक एक

श्री नरसिम्हा स्वामी
शिरडी साई बाबा के
दिव्य प्रचारक
डॉ. रबिन्द्र नाथ ककरिया
978 81 207 4437 0   ₹ 75

साई दत्तावधूता
राजेन्द्र भण्डारी
978 81 207 4400 4
₹ 75

साई हरि कथा
दासगणु महाराज
978 81 207 3323 7
₹ 65

**शिरडी साई बाबा - की सत्य
कथाओं से प्राप्त - एक पावन
प्रतिज्ञा**
प्रो. डॉ. बी.एच. ब्रिज-किशोर
978 81 207 2346 7   ₹ 80

**शिरडी साई बाबा की दिव्य
लीलाएँ**
डॉ. रबिन्द्र नाथ ककरिया
978 81 207 6376 0   ₹ 150

श्री साई चालीसा
ISBN 978 81 207 4773 9
₹ 50

शिरडी साई बाबा
विकास कपूर
978 81 207 5969 5
₹ 30

Shirdi Sai Baba Aratis
(Hindi)   ₹10

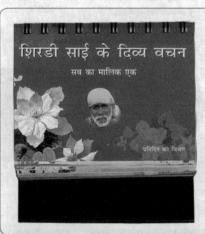

शिरडी साई के दिव्य वचन-सब का मालिक एक
प्रतिदिन का विचार
978 81 207 3533 0
₹ 180

स्टर्लिंग